the whole language evaluation book

the whole language evaluation book

Edited by

KENNETH S. GOODMAN

YETTA M. GOODMAN

WENDY J. HOOD

HEINEMANN
Portsmouth
New Hampshire

IRWIN PUBLISHING
Toronto
Canada

Heinemann Educational Books, Inc.
70 Court Street   Portsmouth, NH 03801
Offices and agents throughout the world

Published simultaneously in Canada by
Irwin Publishing
1800 Steeles Avenue West   Concord, Ontario, Canada L4K 2P3

We are grateful to the following for permission to reprint previously published material:

Chapter 2: The quotations from Leslie Mangiola's journal and Lynne Griffiths' guide are reprinted by permission of the authors.
Chapter 15: From *The Hungry Giant* by Joy Cowley in the series entitled THE STORY BOX®. Used by permission of The Wright Group Publishers, 10949 Technology Place, San Diego, CA 92127.
Figure 16–2: Rudy's New Red Wagon, from SCOTT, FORESMAN READING SYSTEMS, Level 2, Book E, by Aaron et al. Copyright © 1971 by Scott, Foresman and Company. Reprinted by permission.
Chapter 21: The quotes from the WRAT (Wide Range Achievements Test), 1984 version, are reprinted by permission of Jastak Associates.
Afterword: Carol Avery, "Laura's Legacy," originally appeared in *Language Arts* 65:2 (February 1988). Copyright © 1988 by the National Council of Teachers of English. Reprinted with permission.

LIBRARY OF CONGRESS
Library of Congress Cataloging-in-Publication Data

The Whole language evaluation book / edited by Kenneth S. Goodman,
Yetta M. Goodman, Wendy J. Hood.
    p.   cm.
  Bibliography: p.
  ISBN 0-435-08484-4
  1. Language experience approach in education—United States.
  2. Students—United States—Rating of.   3. Teaching—Evaluation.
  I. Goodman, Kenneth S.   II. Goodman, Yetta M., 1931–   .   III. Hood,
  Wendy J.
  LB1576.W4868   1989
  407—dc19   88-16593
                                                             CIP

CANADIAN CATALOGUING IN PUBLICATION
DATA

Main entry under title:

The Whole language evaluation book

Bibliography: p.
ISBN 0-7725-1711-8

1. Language experience approach in education.
2. Students—Rating of.   3. Teaching—Evaluation.
I. Goodman, Kenneth S.   II. Goodman, Yetta M.,
1931–   .   III. Hood, Wendy J.

LB1576.W48   1988   407   C88-094994-5

Designed by Wladislaw Finne.
Printed in the United States of America.

10   9   8   7   6   5   4   3   2   1

CONTENTS

WHOLE LANGUAGE IN SECONDARY AND ADULT EDUCATION

REVALUING POTENTIAL LOSERS

REFLECTIONS

ABOUT THE AUTHORS

Carol Avery teaches first grade at Nathan C. Schaeffer Elementary School in Manheim Township School District, Lancaster, Pennsylvania. She also has been an elementary school librarian and a high school English teacher. She was a member of the 1987 English Coalition and serves as a consultant for teaching writing at the elementary level. Her previous publications include contributions in *Breaking Ground*, edited by Hansen, Newkirk, and Graves (Heinemann, 1985); *Seeing for Ourselves*, edited by Bissex and Bullock (Heinemann, 1987); and articles in several professional journals.

Lois Bridges Bird is a whole language consultant in the San Francisco Bay Area. She teaches graduate reading courses at San Francisco State University and a whole language course at the University of California, Berkeley. She serves on the Council of Teachers for the National Center for the Study of Writing.

Phyllis Brazee is Assistant Professor of Reading/Language Arts at the University of Maine, Orono, Maine. She teaches undergraduate and graduate courses in reading and language arts from a whole language perspective and directs a whole language summer reading/writing program for graduate students and children every summer.

Richard Coles is a Grade 8 teacher in an inner-city area of Toronto. He is interested in the literacy development of middle school, or junior high, students. Rich is currently researching adolescent reading habits in a non-school setting.

Paul Crowley, currently an Assistant Professor of Reading at Sonoma State University, Rohnert Park, California, most enjoys working with junior high school students. His teaching experience includes work with children labeled behaviorally disordered and learning disabled from all grade levels in St. Louis county and Columbia, Missouri.

Toby Kahn Curry is a seventh-grade teacher at Burton International School in Detroit, Michigan. She has presented at the National Council of Teachers of English conferences and is a pioneer member of Detroit's Teachers Applying Whole Language. Toby is actively pursuing the formation of a Pre-K to eighth-grade whole language magnet school within the Detroit public schools.

Karen Sabers Dalrymple is a teacher in the Integrated Curriculum Program at the middle level in Eagle County School District, Colorado. The National Council of Teachers of English (NCTE) selected the program, designed and implemented by classroom teachers, as a Center of Excellence in 1985. Karen has taught grades one through eight. Karen, a teacher of teachers, networks with teachers and is a member of ASCD, IRA, and NCTE. She serves on the Board of Advisors for the ASCD Teaching Thinking Network and is assistant editor of *Cogitare*, the network's newsletter.

David E. Freeman directs the Secondary Education Program and co-directs the Language Development Program at Fresno Pacific College in Fresno, California. In both programs he prepares teachers to apply whole language in classes for limited or non-English-speaking students. He recently coauthored an article that appeared in the *TESOL Quarterly* on his research using sheltered English for second language high school students. His work with composition for secondary second language learners will be reported in *Richness in Writing: Empowering ESL Students*, published by Longman.

Yvonne S. (Bonnie) Freeman directs the Bilingual Education Program and co-directs the Language Development Program at Fresno Pacific College in Fresno, California. She works with students in her courses to help them understand and apply whole language in the classroom. Her work on Spanish language reading materials and whole language for bilingual students has been reported in *The Reading Teacher* (March 1988). She also worked with Ken Goodman, Patrick Shannon, and Sharon Murphy in preparing the *Report Card on Basal Readers*, published by Richard C. Owen.

René Galindo spent four years as a bilingual teacher and consultant in the Tucson Public Schools in Arizona. René is now a doctoral student at Ohio State University.

Debra Goodman is a fifth-grade teacher at Burton International School in Detroit. She has been a reading specialist and a writing teacher and is a consummate reader of chldren's books. While Debi is working toward the establishment of a whole language magnet school in Detroit, she also pursues her interest in writing children's books (as yet unpublished).

Kenneth S. Goodman is Professor of Education at the University of Arizona in the Division of Language, Reading, and Culture. He continues to research and write about the reading process. He has recently completed a study of the basal reader with Pat Shannon, Yvonne Freeman, and Sharon Murphy, which has been published by Richard C. Owen. He has written a popular book about whole language, called *What's Whole in Whole Language?*, published by Scholastic Canada and distributed in the United States by Heinemann.

Yetta M. Goodman, Professor of Education at the University of Arizona in the Division of Language, Reading, and Culture, not only teaches courses in oral and written language development, reading miscue analysis, and children's literature, but also spends time working with whole language teachers in classrooms and in organizational settings. Yetta's latest publication is with Dorothy Watson and Carolyn Burke: *Reading Miscue Inventory: Alternative Procedures*, published by Richard C. Owen.

Geane R. Hanson is working on a doctorate in language, reading, and culture at the University of Arizona. She has taught kindergarten through middle school in urban Pennsylvania and Arizona as well as in the Navajo Nation. Geane is a contributor to *Just Beyond Your Fingertips: American Indian Children Participating in Language Development* (ERIC, 1987).

Myna Matlin Haussler designed and participated in a two-year teacher-resercher project in Bob Wortman's classroom. She is a whole language advocate who has consulted and worked with teachers and administrators from schools and districts in the western United States and in the South Pacific. At present she is in professional development in the Tucson Unified School District, Arizona.

Susan W. Haynes is a special education teacher at Mount Desert Island High School in Bar Harbor, Maine. She has acted as a consultant to other English teachers who are concerned about their students' reading and writing abilities. She has a master's degree in special education and is currently working on a master's in reading/language arts at the University of Maine.

Wendy J. Hood is in her sixth year as a Chapter I bilingual kindergarten teacher in Tucson, Arizona. She has also taught fifth grade and at the preschool level. She has been involved in curriculum development and adoption committees in her school district. Wendy is a past chair of the Tucson Teachers Applying Whole Language and has authored a position paper on academic freedom, articles for *Learning Magazine*, and curriculum materials.

Susan Howe-Tompkins, an Arizona native from Tucson, currently teaches Navajo children in Chinle, Arizona. She has taught third grade, kindergarten, and Chapter 1 ESL. Susan has been a member of the district Writing Sample Committee and Curriculum Committee. She is working on an MA in ESL at Northern Arizona University.

Orysia Hull is an early childhood consultant for St. Vital School Division in Winnipeg, Manitoba. She has been a classroom teacher, a resource teacher, and a special education (resource) consultant for the Manitoba Department of Education. For the last ten years, she has been a member of a whole language support group known as CEL, Inc. (Child-centred, Experience-based Learning). She has published articles in the CEL newsletter, *Connections*, and has contributed to the NCTE publication *Ideas and Insights*. Orysia has directed the preparation of a developmental kidwatching guide for K–2 teachers in her school district. In her spare time, she is working on her master's degree in educational administration and developing her thesis on the resource teacher as a professional development agent in a whole language school.

Debra Jacobson has worked in education for the past fourteen years with junior high students in Spanish Harlem, with third graders on the Navajo Reservation, in an alternative school, and in many other settings. In her current position as reading specialist in a Tucson elementary school, Debra started a "publishing company" for students' writing. She is the founding editor of the newsletter *Teachers Networking* (Richard C. Owen), secretary of the Tucson TAWL, and Communications chair of the North American Confederation of Whole Language Support Groups.

Mary M. Kitagawa is a fifth- and sixth-grade teacher at an urban Tucson, Arizona, school with a 97 percent minority population, primarily Yaqui Indian and Mexican American. Although her desire is to write fiction, Mary has published articles in *Language Arts* and *The Reading Teacher*. Her latest publication is a book coauthored with Chisato Kitagawa, *Making Connections with Writing: An Expressive Writing Model in Japanese Schools*, published in 1987 by Heinemann.

Ann M. Marek works in the Nevada Departments of Education and Human Resources as a research and evaluation consultant to programs in early childhood special education. Ann is a past chair of the Tucson Teachers Applying Whole Language, and she worked with other whole language teachers in writing *A Kid-Watching Guide: Evaluation for Whole Language Classrooms*.

Maureen Morrissey is a bilingual teacher in Tucson, Arizona. She recently completed her master's and gave birth to twins in the same semester. Undaunted, Maureen will soon be switching from third to first grades and is looking into doctoral programs.

Sandra Wilde is Assistant Professor of Education at the University of Nevada at Reno. On the basis of her dissertation on spelling and punctuation, she was chosen as one of four promising researchers by the National Council of Teachers of English in 1987.

Carol E. Woodley has taught in many grades and settings in the Southwest. Currently she is a primary teacher in Denton, Texas.

John W. Woodley is Professor of Education at the University of North Texas. In his studies he has created software for computerizing reading miscue inventories.

Robert Wortman, after thirteen years as a kindergarten teacher, has just become a whole language principal. Bob is a past chair of the Tucson Teachers Applying Whole Language, author of curriculum materials, and a whole language consultant.

PREFACE
Kenneth S. Goodman

The whole language movement is a grass-roots movement among teachers. It has been motivated in part by a positive view of teaching and learning and an attempt by informed teachers to use new knowledge about language development and learning to build better, more effective, and more satisfying experiences for their pupils and themselves. In that sense it is the successor to a long line of child-centered positive movements in education, going back to the "New Education" of the early part of the century. It also represents a rejection, sometimes quite courageous, by teachers of imposed methods, narrow curricula, and mandated materials. Whole language teachers use a range of authentic, natural, functional materials to build literacy. They integrate oral and written language development with conceptual learning. That is, they believe you learn to read and write while you read and write to learn.

Whole language teachers have rebelled against behavioral objectives, textbooks, mastery learning, and narrow curricula. And they have rebelled against traditional evaluation, particularly standardized tests, because they find them synthetic, contrived, confining, and controlling, out of touch with modern theory and research. The tests reduce reading and writing to trivial, decontextualized, abstract skills to be tested with multiple-choice questions.

In their curriculum planning whole language teachers create opportunities for pupils to use language in authentic, richly contextualized, functional ways. The language is kept whole so that all the necessary data for language learning will be present. Whole language teachers believe that evaluation can be useful only if it takes place in these whole and richly contextualized learning experiences. Traditional evaluation is inappropriate and tends strongly to underestimate growth in functional use of language.

An increasing number of middle-level administrators (principals, central curriculum supervisors, and state department of education personnel) are supporting and actively encouraging whole language teachers to move away from textbook and test-dominated teaching and to make their evaluation fit the principles and requirements of whole language.

Evaluation that is acceptable to whole language teachers promotes whole language classrooms.

All forms of evaluation are consistent with principles of whole language if:

1. They are holistic and do not fragment language.
   They employ natural language in authentic contexts.

They are meaningful and relevant to learners.

They are interesting and functional.

They treat language difference with accuracy and respect.

They integrate oral and written language development with development of thinking and knowledge.

2. They treat both teachers and learners with respect.

They do not control teachers.

They draw on what pupils can do and reveal their competence.

They allow for variations in background and development among both teachers and learners.

They are designed to encourage independence among both teachers and learners.

3. They are consistent with the best scholarship on language, learning, teaching, and curriculum.

4. They are innovative, creative, and dynamic.

Whole language evaluation plumbs the limits of the potential of both teachers and learners.

They reflect or are ahead of the best practice in the field.

5. They are open-ended.

They allow for modification and change.

They are never permitted to be closed and completely self-contained.

allows for creativity

Whole language teachers have chosen to take back their classrooms; they work very hard. One of the most exciting aspects of the whole language movement today is the creativity it is unleashing. In this book we share some of the creative ways that whole language teachers build evaluation into their teaching.

The book is intended to be a coherent set of articles by whole language teachers on how they evaluate in their classrooms. We've tried to achieve this coherence by ensuring that the articles have some common threads and at least a minimum of parallel structure. But we have urged the contributors to keep their own voices and root their accounts in their own classroom realities. We've included a small number of articles that provide the research and theory base for whole language evaluation. These offer some of the theoretical themes that unite the classroom practices.

Our intent has been to ensure that each article:

1. Is rich in vignettes—illustrative episodes involving evaluation of one pupil, a group, a whole class.
2. Deals with incidental, informal, and formal evaluation.
3. Represents each teacher and each classroom. We have attempted to provide coherence, but we have no intention of eliminating each teacher's voice, style, or personal code of good teaching.
4. Deals with self-evaluation by teachers and pupils, evaluation of pupils by teachers, of teachers by pupils.
5. Deals with ongoing uses of evaluation in planning and improving teaching and learning.
6. Deals with reporting to parents, other teachers, and administrators.

WHAT WHOLE LANGUAGE TEACHERS DO AND WHY

We've tried to make clear why whole language teachers do what they do. We've done this in many ways, most particularly with the vignettes and descriptions of what happens in our classrooms. In showing how we use evaluative insights, we've tried to make clear why we do what we do.

It has been hard sometimes to avoid overlooking what to us is commonplace or obvious. Our most successful practices have probably become so intrinsic to our teaching that we think everybody knows about them and uses them. We've found it helpful to ask for suggestions from a colleague, aide, or the pupils—or one another—about what happens in our classrooms that is really worth telling others about.

As you read, keep these points in mind about whole language evaluation:

1. In whole language, evaluation is mostly ongoing; it happens in the course of the teaching/learning. It is therefore an integral part of the curriculum and not something separate.

2. Self-evaluation is the most significant kind of evaluation; pupils and teachers need to have a sense of why they are doing what they are doing so that they may have some sense of their own success and growth. Reporting progress to parents is an important but secondary purpose of evaluation. It is most successful when it makes it possible for parents to evaluate growth themselves. Evaluating to provide marks or grades on report cards is, at best, the outgrowth of evaluation for improving teaching and learning. Pupils should know why they get the grades they do. Grades should represent growth, not external absolutes or points on bell-shaped curves.

3. Whole language is not simply concerned with measuring changes in behavior. It uses behaviors as indications of developing knowledge and underlying competence.

4. Informal—and even formal—evaluation measures may be used in whole language classrooms. But when they are used it is because they add to the information available. There is always a learning function as well as an evaluative function: readers may discuss their own miscues; peer-editing conferences may offer constructive criticism; a test stemming from unit-based concepts may refocus discussion and stimulate reflective thinking; a group project may distill knowledge gained from reading and discussion.

5. In evaluation, whole language teachers use interaction, observation, and analysis. These relate to incidental, informal, and formal procedures, with interaction tending to be more incidental and analysis more formal. But there can be formal observation, informal analysis, and so on.

6. When whole language teachers reject traditional evaluating techniques such as standardized or multiple-choice tests on lectures and textbooks, it is because the content, nature, and uses of such devices are in direct conflict with the whole language teacher's view of teaching, learning, and curriculum. That's why we can't provide one-to-

one substitutes that meet behavioristic criteria. It's also why whole language evaluation can't be reduced to precise right or wrong scores.

7. The contrast between objective and subjective evaluation is inappropriate for whole language classrooms. Whole language teachers are professionals who accept all pupils, their language, and their culture. They are careful not to let personal feelings or prejudice get in the way of their judgment, but they are not detached or impersonal when they teach and when they evaluate. They view all evaluative information, whether incidental, informal, or formal, in the context of the personal and social goals of the learners and the school. Whole language teachers trust their professional judgment, but they're constantly open to new insights.

8. The curriculum in a whole language classroom is an integrated dual curriculum. Language and thought are developed through being used to build knowledge, so whole language teachers are always evaluating linguistic and cognitive growth in knowledge and ideas.

COPING WITH PRESSURES

We must be aware that one reason behind this book is the concern for how whole language teachers cope with the standardized tests and pressures from administrators and local and state authorities to evaluate by gains in scores on these tests. We've shared with our readers the ways in which we cope with, resist, ignore, or get around these pressures and help our pupils do the same.

We've tried to keep the focus positive: How do we, as whole language teachers, judge how well we're doing, and even more important, how do we help our kids to do so?

SUPERTEACHERS?

Every diligent teacher spends a professional lifetime learning how to teach. We all learn from our errors just as our pupils do, so we haven't been reluctant to share our failures and mistakes as well as our successes. It is terribly important that readers of this book see what we are doing as possible for them. Ironically, one attack on whole language is that it requires superteachers to do it. Whole language teachers are caring, informed professionals. What we do is hard work, but any competent teacher who wants to do so can become a whole language teacher.

Self-evaluation is an important part of becoming a whole language teacher. Whole language teachers evaluate themselves as they evaluate their pupils. Because whole language teachers have liberated themselves from the constraints of textbooks and mandated programs, they are free to grow. We may not all become superteachers, but through self-evaluation we will become better teachers.

It should be obvious to readers of this book that there are great differences among whole language teachers. None of the writers in this book is saying, "My way is the only right way." We are not offering ourselves as paragons to be cloned. Rather, we are saying, "This is how I do whole language. This is how I evaluate in my teaching." We are all saying, "It works for us and our kids. Join us in doing whole language your own way."

theory
and
general
principles

EVALUATION OF STUDENTS:
EVALUATION OF TEACHERS

Yetta M. Goodman

The power of evaluation in whole language classrooms lies in the process of becoming—the changes or moves that people make from what they are to what they come to be. These moves are important not just for students but equally for the professional development of teachers and the dynamic nature of the ongoing curriculum. As we begin this book —a dialogue on evaluation among teachers, administrators, and teacher educators—it may be helpful to consider the concept of reflection and the mirror image as a metaphor. In our classrooms, as we critically examine what students do in order to help them grow as educated human beings, we become consciously aware that at the same time we are seeing a reflection of ourselves. We keep in mind that teachers are prime movers in organizing the environments in which learning takes place. Our planning and organization influences the classroom environment in so many ways that the evaluation of the students becomes an evaluation of ourselves and of the curriculum. Seeing ourselves reflected in our classrooms and in the responses of our students helps us to understand the nature of language learning and at the same time helps us become aware of our influences on that learning and on the relationships between teaching and learning. The dynamic transaction between teachers and students results in change in all the actors and actions involved in the teaching/learning experience. Evaluation—the exami- *Ø* nation of that change—reveals the development of the learning, the teacher, and the curriculum. At the same time that we look into the mirror to see the reflection of our teaching in the students and their learning, we also take advantage of what we see to reflect on our own professional development as teachers.

EVALUATION: AN INTEGRAL PART OF CURRICULUM

Evaluation is part of curriculum: it cannot be divorced from classroom organization, from the relationship between teachers and students, from continuous learning experiences and activities. To think about and plan for evaluation, it is necessary to keep in mind the classroom community and its organization. There is no way to separate the role of evaluation from the dynamic teaching/learning transaction.

Whole language teachers value the social community of the classroom. Respect for all the members of the learning community suggests that each plays a role in teaching, each is involved in continuous learning, and therefore each has a role in the evaluation process. The classroom belongs to the community that lives there, with the teacher providing the major leadership role but respecting the students' ideas about how the classroom can be organized to be an effective place in which to live and to learn. In planning for evaluation, we must understand and utilize the power of the social group. The classroom community is part of the larger community in which teachers and students live and communicate daily. It is, therefore, also important to involve other teachers, administrators, and parents in the evaluation process.

Whole language classrooms are rich in resources and opportunities. Students are enabled to use language in all its forms. Students are trusted to care for a variety of resources, which are available and accessible. The social community in the classroom is organized so that every member knows the responsibilities and privileges of access to the tools of learning. In whole language programs students learn in an environment that invites them to participate in all the activities in the classroom and to make choices about the kinds of experiences in which they participate.

Functional and authentic experiences are planned by both teachers and students. That means that students see the potential in their experiences to solve their problems and to gain the knowledge they need as citizens in a democracy. As members of the learning community plan together, they include opportunities for the evaluation of their own experiences.

BUILDING A PROFESSIONAL SENSE

Teachers continuously monitor the development of their students during their daily contacts. Thinking as parents about our own kids at home will help us explore this idea. How do we know when our kids have grown physically, intellectually, and emotionally? I remember having to buy them larger-sized clothes, spending more money on food. The doctor would measure and weigh my kids, but the figures simply confirmed what I already knew as an observant and caring parent and what the children knew about themselves. The measurements were only additional bits of statistical information. All the other important information had already let me know that my kids were growing up, how they were changing, what they knew, and how much they cared.

I remember sitting at the dinner table and looking across at my eldest daughter and suddenly realizing that I was looking straight into her eyes; I was not looking down at her anymore. I was evaluating her growth with a practiced eye. When your son or daughter walks into the house from school, you can often tell whether something terrible or wonderful happened that day. And then you confirm your initial judgment by gathering new information. First you sense the change, then you find ways to confirm what you sense.

When children begin to ask questions about people's health or their economic condition, we begin to see growth in their empathy for others. When they join in conversations about current events, we realize that their interests and knowledge base have changed. As parents we use all of our developing senses to make decisions about the growth of our children. Those senses often called common sense aren't common to all. They are common to parents who build their parental sense over a period of time.

Teachers build similar senses, but I prefer to identify these as professional senses. Teachers not only build these senses through their interactions with and reflections about students but also professionalize their senses by confirming their judgments through their reading and continued scholarship in areas such as human development, language learning, and practices in effective schooling.

Initially, professional senses are intuitive. Beginning teachers are often unaware that they are thinking intuitively, using their background knowledge whenever they have to make decisions such as whether a student is a good reader, which are the appropriate ways to make presentations to the class, and what their students understand about scientific or mathematical concepts. Once teachers begin to take account of what they know about learning, language, and conceptual development, however, they then build confidence in their ability to make judgments about students' growth. Their reflective thinking grows and takes on new dimensions.

One of the objectives of this book is to help legitimize the power of the professional intuition of teachers, which has largely been ignored for at least two reasons. The first reason, I believe, is related to a lack of respect for teachers as thinkers and decision makers. Therefore as a profession we avoid giving voice to this power. It is not discussed much in the educational literature or in pre-service or in-service teacher programs. Although scholars such as John Dewey (Archambault, 1964) and Eliot Eisner (1976) have explored the significance of reflective thinking, educational connoisseurship, and criticism for teachers, the educational establishment does not seem to respect the thinking abilities of teachers enough to give the concept of a developing professional sense legitimacy. Eisner states:

> What I belive we need to do with respect to educational
> evaluation is not to seek recipes to control and measure practice
> but rather to enhance whatever artistry the teacher can
> achieve. . . . Good theory in education . . . helps us to see more;

. . . theory provides some of the windows through which
intelligence can look out into the world.   (p. 140)

The second reason why the professional sense of teachers has not
been adequately explored may be the unexamined belief in statistical
information. Because numbers take on an aura of objectivity, *which
they do not intrinsically deserve*, statistical test data are equated with
the development of knowledge and are valued more highly than the
sense of an informed, committed professional who uses knowledge
about the students, the community, and the context to make judgments.

Of course educators need to know the limitations of their professional
sense and discover a variety of ways to confirm their intuitions. But
when the power of professional intuitions is denigrated with comments
such as "It's just subjective" or "Test scores are better than nothing,"
we cannot develop the forum in which to discuss both the power and
the limitations of professional judgments and explore the legitimate uses
of the professional sense of teachers. Whole language teachers who
know they are competent are willing to assume responsibility for their
judgments and have no difficulty being accountable to their students,
the parents, and the other professionals in their schools and districts.

Professional sense comes from the interplay of what teachers know
about language and learning, what they observe in their relationships
with students, and the knowledge that is built on those relationships.
The professional sense becomes more focused as teachers seek opportunities to raise their intuitions to a conscious level.

BUILDING A KNOWLEDGE BASE

In order to evaluate language and conceptual development as well as
the physical and emotional growth of students, it is necessary for teachers to be lifelong learners. As a result, the professional sense of whole
language teachers develops continuously. Whole language teachers learn
from their students through the evaluation process; they learn from their
interactions with other practitioners as they share ideas and problems;
and they learn from child-study groups organized within the school by
resource teachers or principals. They attend classes and become active
in professional organizations. They attend workshops and conferences
not only to hear from other knowledgeable professionals but also to
present their ideas in order to think them through and get responses
from others. They read the latest scholarship in professional journals
and books about their subject-matter specialties, about the kinds of kids
they work with, and about language and learning. They critique research
about language and cognitive development and relate it to their classroom setting, and they participate in action research in their own classes
to learn more and to see if research they think has merit rings true for
their own kids. Building a knowledge base becomes the foundation on
which professional sense grows. John Dewey suggested that genuine
freedom comes from reflective thinking that interacts with an ever-
developing knowledge base:

the power of thought, an ability to turn things over, to look at
matters deliberately, to judge whether the amount and kind of
evidence requisite for decision is at hand, and if not, to tell where
and how to seek such evidence. If . . . actions are not guided by
thoughtful conclusions, then they are guided by inconsiderate
impulse, unbalanced appetite, caprice of the circumstances of the
moment.   (Archambault, 1964, pp. 258–59)

Thinking reflectively about a knowledge base in order to build a professional sense cannot be accomplished quickly. The process is cumulative
over a professional lifetime. We can't hurry learning in kids, and we
can't hurry learning in ourselves as teachers. Whole language teachers
have to be as patient with themselves as learners as they are with their
own students.

THE DOUBLE AGENDA OF EVALUATION

Evaluation is part of the double agenda in the whole language classroom. As shown in Figure 1–1, the right side of the agenda, *Students
Are Learning*, indicates where the students and teacher are busily and
actively involved: in reading to solve problems, to add to their scientific
knowlege and their aesthetic pleasure; in writing to express their meanings, to discover what they know, to create artistically, and to take care
of everyday business; and in using oral and written language to learn
about the world. The left side of the agenda shows that while the classroom
community is engaged in learning, the *Teacher's Evaluation* is monitoring
the goals of language learning and conceptual development.

Evaluation doesn't get in the way of the kids' learning. At the same
time that the students are involved in the plans for the day as one
part of the double agenda, evaluation is a constant part of the other

---

Figure 1–1   *The Double Agenda*

TEACHER'S EVALUATION	STUDENTS ARE LEARNING
TEACHERS	KIDS AND TEACHERS ARE
INVOLVED	INVOLVED
EVALUATION	LEARNING ABOUT THEIR WORLD
	ANSWERING THEIR QUESTIONS
OF	SOLVING THEIR PROBLEMS
	EVALUATING THEIR OWN LEARNING
LANGUAGE DEVELOPMENT	THROUGH
COGNITIVE DEVELOPMENT	LANGUAGE USE
CURRICULUM	
A	
CONTINUOUS	READING
ONGOING	WRITING
INTEGRAL	SPEAKING
PROCESS	LISTENING

aspect of the agenda. Teachers are involved in evaluation during all aspects of the curriculum. It is a continuous, ongoing, integral process.

Whole language teachers don't decide to think about evaluation in June; they don't start to focus on evaluation in order to get ready for report card time or for parent conferencing. Whole language teachers know that evaluation is going on all the time; it is built into the plans every day. It is integral to the process of teaching and learning, not a separate, discrete activity. As the kids and the teacher are involved in learning about their world, answering their questions, and solving their problems, another part of that learning is to answer other kinds of questions: What am I learning? How are things going? Who is getting things done? How are students' concepts and hypotheses changing? Who seems confused? How did things go in our discussion group? Did we do an adequate job of cleaning up after our art activity today? Did I organize the writing area so those who wanted to continue to write could do so?

OBSERVING, INTERACTING, AND ANALYZING

A few years ago a group of whole language teachers in Tucson, Arizona, began to explore the issues of evaluation in their classrooms. They were involved in a variety of kidwatching activities and wanted to share what they were doing with other teachers, especially those new to whole language. They realized that kidwatching activities usually occur in three different ways. They became aware that they were evaluating whenever they were observing, interacting with, and analyzing students (Marek, Howard, et al., 1984). These became categories that proved useful in thinking about whole language evaluation.

Observation includes examining what students are doing as the teacher stands on the sidelines. The teacher may choose to observe one student working alone, a student as a member of a group, all the members of a small group, or the class as a whole to make judgments about language use, problem solving, leadership, and collaborative capabilities.

Interaction includes ways in which a teacher converses or conferences, participates in discussions, interacts in journals, and raises questions with students in order to discover what students know and to encourage or challenge students to explore beyond what they are thinking at the moment.

Analysis includes eliciting information in ways such as the reading of a story, the written response to a book, a composition, or an oral conversation on tape and then using psycholinguistic and sociolinguistic knowlege to analyze in depth what the students know about language and how they show development in their language use.

Like so many other aspects of whole language, these three types of evaluation are separated for purposes of spotlighting the importance of each, but in most cases when these are in practice they are overlapping and integrated. They are strong evaluation tools, especially when they are used in concert. Each can help confirm the information gained from the use of the others.

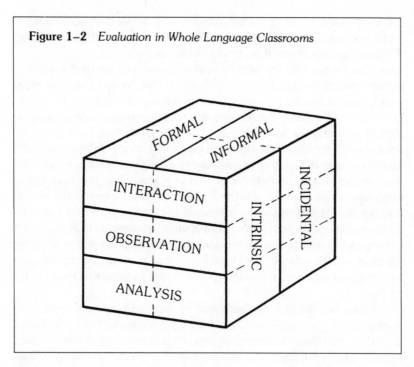

Figure 1–2 *Evaluation in Whole Language Classrooms*

Figure 1–2 shows the relationships of observation, interaction, and analysis within the classroom setting. Each may be done formally: for example, records kept of an activity following a particular procedure at regular intervals. Or each may be informal and occur at any time the teacher and the student or students come in contact. Observation, interaction, and analysis may occur incidentally whenever the teacher perceives that the students are engaged in an activity that will reveal important understandings about a student's learning or development. Or it may be part of a planned activity with a variety of forms and materials at hand to assist in the collection and analysis of the information. I will discuss each with relevant examples. In addition, the chapters that follow are filled with specific and dynamic examples of how teachers are constantly involved in evaluation through observation, interaction, and analysis.

OBSERVATION

Confident and knowledgeable teachers are often able to sense when a student's staring into space means that he or she is deep in concentration, involved in some painful thoughts, or daydreaming about some activity not directly related to the work at hand. Of course the professional verifies such observational judgments through interacting by engaging the student in conversation or asking a question, or through more formal evaluation if warranted. The use of such professional hunches followed by appropriate confirmations is a legitimate part of evaluation. Initial judgments based on observation are helpful in gaining insight into the learning processes of particular students.

Informal observations, which most often take place as the teacher moves around the classroom, build an intuitive sense of an individual or a group of students. Teachers are watching and listening to discussions of small groups; they're noticing students engaged in reading or writing, working on scientific experiments, researching for reports, or solving math problems; teachers are becoming aware of the interactions taking place and how the interactions relate to the tasks at hand. The teacher may keep a notebook or two in a few strategic places in the classroom to jot down general impressions by noting key words, dates, and names. At a critical moment, when something important happens that provides signficiant evidence about development, it may not be convenient to write a complete anecdotal record, but a few notes in an "Impressions Notebook" can be used later at a more convenient time to stimulate the memory in order to record more formal and long-lasting records.

Formal observations can be made by keeping anecdotal records of a very specific nature. These are dated, the names of the students are recorded, and these records are kept in a student's portfolio or permanent file. Some teachers are careful to observe every student at least once every two weeks. Other teachers find it best to do such recordings once a month or twice a semester. Teachers who find formal anecdotal entries useful are careful to rotate around the room at different times of the day or week, making sure to record appropriate information about each student working in different subject-matter areas and different settings in the classroom and participating in different activities such as silent reading, journal writing, collaborations, small-group discussion, and so on. These formal entries, of course, are supplemented by less formal observations.

Teachers who use formal observations may do so for the first few months of the year only. Then the teacher may add informal observations to the anecdotal records file on a less regular basis as important new information arises. As the teacher comes to know the students better as the semester goes on, less formal observations are made when the teacher recognizes information that may add to the profile of the student's development and evaluation. At the end of the semester or year or near the time for reporting to parents, the teacher finds it helpful to reread earlier entries, discuss them with the student, and then observe more intently for a period of time in order to illuminate a student's development and add a few more formal entries on each student.

Anytime any of these recording devices seems not to be working for the teacher, it is helpful to experiment with new ways of observing. A system that has outgrown its usefulness simply becomes a chore and loses its power as an evaluation tool. Formal methods of observation may include check sheets for different subject-matter areas as well as written narratives about a student's development. Perhaps someday teachers will have machines on which to record oral information on students regularly. The tapes will then be given to the school secretary, who will type up the transcripts and add them to the students' files.

INTERACTION

Interaction with students may be the most powerful aspect of the process of evaluation in whole language classrooms because of its immediate relationship to instruction. As teachers interact with students, they are not just discovering what students know about any particular learning but are also using the moments of interaction to question the student, to encourage, to stimulate, and to challenge.

The power of the interacting aspects of evaluation and their relationship to curriculum are supported by the work of many scholars in education, ethnography, psycholinguistics, and sociolinguistics. Vygotsky explores the "Zone of Proximal Development" (1987), Bruner (1978) discusses the importance of "scaffolding," and Halliday (1988) talks about the role of "tracking." Piagetians have built into their research design the method of clinicial exploration (Ferreiro and Teberosky, 1982).

These scholars have theoretical differences concerning language and learning, but they have important thoughts in common in relation to the notion of interaction that informs whole language evaluation. They all suggest that two heads are better than one, that students learn more and can do more with the support of others, especially a knowledgeable teacher, than they are often capable of doing by themselves. These interactions lead to the critical teaching moments when the teacher learns that the student knows more than the teacher expected or shows creative thinking that is not along the lines of conventional adult forms. The teacher not only evaluates at these moments but uses them to plan immediate or future lessons or experiences to capitalize on the intellectual functioning of the student.

Carefully considered and appropriate questions at such moments gently push kids to consider greater, conflicting, or different information and become powerful in moving students toward moments of disequilibrium so they have to reorganize their concepts and rethink their ideas. Such questions can be specific to a particular task. For example, Ferreiro and Teberosky explored with children why Spanish speakers say the word for *chicken* in different ways. (The *ll* in the word *pollo* can be pronounced three different ways in the area in Argentina where this study took place.) The researchers questioned the children in such a provocative way that they were able to come up with some profound conclusions about dialect variations (1982, p. 254). One child concluded her discussion by saying, "Yes, but there are other countries where they speak different and they have to say it how they say it. They're not going to start to talk . . . as if it was wrong. We're not going to have to teach them, no. They teach them like they know."

In more general ways teachers can encourage kids to examine their statements and their knowledge base critically with open-ended questions such as: Why do you think so? Is it possible? What if we tried this instead? What if I said . . . ? I wonder if. . . . If teachers help students believe that they really expect explorations in their interactions with the objects of learning, then the evalutation of the students takes on new and exciting dimensions. Students become aware that a focus on single correct answers is not what is valued, and their learning changes qualitatively to a more critical analysis of whatever they are studying. Students begin to reflect on their own learning, which results in self-evaluation on the part of the learner.

Interaction has its informal moments through daily conversations and discussions, the teacher's movements in and out of small groups of students working together, and the times when the teacher's authentic questions and wonderments are shared with students.

Interactions can be formally planned to be intrinsic to curriculum activities as part of reading and writing strategy lessons. A well-designed selected slotting or cloze passage is an example of such a strategy. Two students work together. The teacher participates, especially the first time the students work at this kind of lesson. For the most part, however, the students take the lead. As they discuss which linguistic units belong in particular blank spaces, the students often comment on what kinds of language are appropriate for particular slots. The teacher listens and discovers what students know about language as well as about the content of the material. The teacher evaluates what the students know and also helps students become more consciously aware of what they know about language. This aids in building confidence and provides opportunities for student self-evaluation. Notes may be kept of such interactions to show how students' problem-solving strategies change over time. In addition to strategy lessons, regularly planned individual or small-group reading and/or writing conferences also provide opportunities for formal evaluation through interactions. Teachers keep formal records of their reading and writing conferences with their students. Formal interactions can also take place in written form through dialogue journals or learning logs kept between students and the teacher.

ANALYSIS

Teachers use many analytical tools that have been developed over years of reasearch as formal devices for evaluating the reading and writing processes. As teachers become competent in the use of such formal tools, they can eventually be used informally. Teachers who have done a great deal of formal miscue analysis (Goodman, Watson, Burke, 1987) build a strong understanding of the principles underlying miscues in reading and are always in a position to evaluate miscues as they listen informally to kids reading during an individual conference. Those who have carefully analyzed the spelling or punctuation development of their students using linguistic insights (Read, 1971; Wilde, 1986) understand the developmental moments in the spelling and punctuation of their students and can eventually point out a student's development by informally examining the student's composition.

There are many teachers, schools, and school districts that have developed writing and reading portfolios to keep files of students' work so as to allow for formal analysis of that work at any time. Students can be involved in such record-keeping procedures. They can help select the pieces of writing that will be collected weekly or monthly for the portfolio. They can record the names of the books they have read. If teachers have the children read from a selected text and then retell onto an audio tape at intervals during the year, this account can also be kept in a student's evaluation or reading portfolio. These materials can be evaluated using many different kinds of analytical procedures, depending on the knowledge of the teacher and the particular focus a teacher wants to take at different times during the school year.

If the school faculty has worked together to develop a language policy, then a committee of teachers may decide what aspects of analysis to focus on for a particular year, depending on the teachers' concerns, their knowlege about language, and the concerns of the parents, the community, and the students. Holistic scoring procedures, analysis of story grammar, variation and flexibility in styles of writing and genres of reading, interests, spelling and punctuation development, and qualitative miscue changes all lend themselves to in-depth analysis.

SELF-EVALUATION

The ultimate goal of the evaluation process in whole language classrooms is self-evaluation for both the teacher and the student. Professional development is continuous when teachers assume responsibility for decision making in the classroom. Whole language teachers do so confidently. At the same time the teachers are in the position to help students assume responsibility for understanding, capitalizing on their strengths, and finding ways to diminish and overcome their areas of weakness.

Through self-evaluation the teacher involves the kids in serious examination of such questions as: How am I doing? Are things going as I planned? What can I do to see that things go better next time? Students help by keeping records about their own learning experiences and meet with the teacher in conferences to evaluate what they have accomplished and what goals they hope to achieve, planning with the teacher how these are to be met. In this manner the teacher helps the kids learn about themselves and their capabilities. Simultaneously teachers reflect on their own development as they see their practices and plans reflected in their students' responses to learning. If individual learners are confident and knowledgeable enough, they will know how their own learning is working for them. Reflecting on their own learning is enpowering. John Dewey says:

> By putting the consequences of different ways and lines of action before the mind, it enables us to know what we are about when we act. It converts action that is merely appetitive, blind, and impulsive into intelligent action. . . . Only when things about us have meaning for us, only when they signify consequences that

can be reached by using them in certain ways, is any such thing as intentional, deliberate control of them possible. (Archambault, 1964, pp. 212–13)

While the teacher is evaluating students and involving them in their own self-evaluation, there is constant opportunity for self-reflection on the part of the teacher. How students do is strongly influenced by the kinds of interactions the teacher has with the students. Opportunities kids have to learn, their access to resources, the support and encouragement they have from teachers will determine how students see themselves as invited into or excluded from the literacy club or the learning club (Smith, 1986).

As teachers examine the ways in which they invite their students to learn, they are reflecting on their own teaching—self-evaluating—and informing their own teaching practices.

Working with colleagues in study or support groups also provides teachers opportunities for critical self-evaluation. As teachers talk about the forms they want to develop, the portfolios they plan to keep, and their plans to change and improve what they are doing in the classroom, the opportunities for self-reflection are heightened. Social interaction with other teachers allows for critiquing, team learning, sharing, and many other means of examining one's teaching.

In the following chapters you can judge for yourself the kinds of professional development that occur as teachers are involved in evaluating their own students. Most of the authors are active teachers in elementary and secondary classrooms. Their articles confirm the reciprocal relationship between the evaluation of students and the self-evaluation of teachers.

THE ART OF TEACHING:
EVALUATION AND REVISION
Lois Bridges Bird

Good teaching, like good writing, is created and crafted through a continual process of revision. The teacher, like the writer, asks, "What is working? What isn't working? What do I have to rework, and how should I go about it?" Such questions lead to changes, to appraisal of the results, and to further revision.

When you teach in this manner, you free yourself of the traditional perception of the profession as a precisely patterned, scientifically methodical activity. As a student teacher in the mid-seventies, I spent hours writing and rewriting my behavioral objectives for each lesson. Like the stage directions for a school play, every instructional move was carefully planned and orchestrated. I had my script; the goal was to get the students to follow theirs.

Whole language teachers work without a script, without long lists of short-term objectives, without the questions at the back of the teachers' manual. This doesn't mean they are teaching without a plan or tolerating a free-for-all in which children do exactly as they choose when they choose. On the contrary, whole language teachers, like good teachers everywhere, give students guidelines and a clear sense of direction. But they go one all-important step further; they include students in the curricular planning. What happens in the whole language classroom is the result of an interaction between the students' developing needs and interests and the teacher's developing expertise as a professional educator. This is responsive teaching. Margaret Donaldson (1978) describes it this way: "The essence of the teacher's art lies in deciding what help is needed in any given instance and how this help may best be offered" (p. 104). Frank Smith instructs us, simply, "Respond to what the child is trying to do" (1983, p. 24).

Third-grade teacher Diane Lohman responded in this manner, and later, in a written self-evaluation, described the results:

> The kids were my greatest teachers. They taught me to catch the moment. Whenever I responded to their genuine interest, it worked. If I tried to insert something that was artificial, it died. Example: new guinea pigs. We put them on the floor along with a long roll of butcher paper. There is a flurry of pictures, poems, songs and stories.

This is the power and the joy and the challenge of real teaching. It is not accidental. It happens because of four essentials that characterize whole language teachers:

1. Whole language teachers understand how children learn and how language develops.
2. Whole language teachers are skilled observers of children. They are kidwatchers.
3. Whole language teachers have a clear, long-range vision of their instructional purpose and goals.
4. Whole language teachers engage in continual evaluation of and reflection upon their students and themselves.

THEORY AND OBSERVATION

Although I have listed them separately, theory and observation go hand in hand in creating a classroom where learning flourishes. Whole language teachers must have a theoretical understanding of how children learn, of what language is and how it develops. Theory and research form the knowledge base, which provides teachers with a framework to use as a guide in observing, interpreting, and assessing children. Observation plays a critical role in teaching. It is the link between theory and practice. As Angela Jaggar (1985) reminds us:

> In education we often mistakenly assume that good teaching is a matter of "knowing the research" and "putting theory into practice." But for research and theory to be meaningful, teachers must be able to relate the findings and ideas to their own models of language and to what they know about their students' language and ways of learning. (p. 4)

With a sound knowledge base, then, coupled with careful observation of their students, teachers are in a position to develop their educational philosophy and practices. In whole language the child is at the center of the curriculum. Teachers begin with what the child knows and gradually help the child move into new realms of knowing.

This process of theoretically guided observation as the basis for instructional decision making is exemplified in the words of Leslie Mangiola, a fifth-grade teacher at Fair Oaks School, a whole language bilingual school in Redwood City, California. In a journal she keeps to record significant events in her classroom Leslie writes:

> Irena is one of the most literate students in class. Her insights into literature are sophisticated. She listens to others' writings and sees what needs to be done. She questions gently—probing the child-author for his/her meaning. She might suggest alternatives, but generally she asks very open-ended questions. She is likely to say, "What can you do about it?" She's a powerful person.
>
> She's a sensitive reader, also. Her comments on *Bridge to Terabithia* [Paterson, 1977] indicated her ability to put herself inside the book and appreciate Katherine Paterson's craft. She was so taken by the book that she decided to make her next book, *The Great Gilly Hopkins* [1979], a Paterson book. I'm looking forward to our literature studies on the book—largely because Irena always has something penetrating to say.
>
> . . . But her writing is stuck in a third grade time warp. It doesn't reflect the knowledge and sensitivity I know she has. After reading Nancy Atwell's article "[Writing and] Reading [from] the Inside Out [1985], I think I know what I need to do: I'll talk to her about the connection between literature (reading) and writing. . . . I might use examples from the Atwell article. Then I will initiate the written conversation about books with her. She is such a reluctant writer.
>
> It's like beginning again—reading, generating a plan of action and carrying it out.

VISION

Taking her instructional cues from her students, Leslie "begins again." She knows that there are no absolutes. Teaching is an art, a creative process of continual revision. We step back to let students take the lead when they are able, and we step in when, like Irena, they need some instruction and support. This ebb and flow of teaching and learning is governed by the teacher's overarching vision, by his or her long-term goals for the students. Arising from the teacher's theoretical understanding, coupled with skilled observations of the students, this vision sets the instructional course.

The interior dialogue begins again:

- What do I know about language and learning?
- What do I know about my students as socially and culturally based but unique language learners?
- What can I do as a professional educator to best support the process of learning?

These are questions that must be asked the first day of school. Chris Boyd, an experienced whole language teacher at Roadrunner School in Phoenix, Arizona, speaking at an in-service for teachers at the Fair Oaks School, suggested that sometimes teachers act like the pussycat in the Mother Goose nursery rhyme, who traveled to London to visit the queen and spent all her time chasing mice around the queen's chambers. In much the same helter-skelter fashion, if we are not careful, we may find ourselves and our students pursuing bits of knowledge around our curriculum.

Specific facts and details are the nuts and bolts of the instructional framework. Without the framework, however, they become little more than a pile of loose screws of the sort one is likely to find at the bottom of a junk drawer—all shapes and sizes but of little utility.

Following the lead of James Britton, many whole language teachers have developed a language policy. Not unlike a philosophy of education, a language policy outlines the teachers' or school's understandings about language and learning and describes the classroom environment that would best support the process of learning.

At the Fair Oaks School, where I serve as a language and literacy consultant, teachers have written "Visitor Guides" to their classrooms. These guides provide a succinct statement of each teacher's educational philosophy as well as a description of the activities a visitor to the classroom can expect to see and why. These guidelines are kept in an envelope next to the door so that every visitor who steps inside the classroom can, at a glance, share in the teacher's instructional vision and understanding and interpret the wide range of teaching and learning events and interactions taking place in the room.

There is a joke among whole language educators that when you open the door of a whole language classroom, you can't find the teacher. That's because the teacher is likely to be sitting on the floor, conferencing with a student about his twelve-page novella, or crouched behind a puppet theater helping the puppeteers rehearse their lines before their show for the kindergarten class down the hall. Momentarily invisible or not, the whole language teacher is a real and powerful presence in the classroom. Students are independent learners who work alone and with peers on projects of their own choosing, but they are not without teacher direction and guidance. Teachers and children meet in formal and informal conferences and negotiate and collaborate on each piece of writing, each science experiment, each dramatization of a favorite author's story. Students and teachers work together to plan and define what is to be done and how best to go about making sure it is completed in a satisfactory way within a reasonable time.

Little is left to chance. Although good whole language teachers are delighted daily, they are seldom surprised. They have carefully created and crafted an environment that allows and supports optimal learning.

Lynne Griffiths is a whole language resource teacher for learning-disabled children at Fair Oaks. But her instructional vision is in no way limited by lowering expectations for her special education students. In her "Guide" she explicitly warns visitors to her classroom not to expect less:

Don't be fooled by the children of room 16! These youngsters are true students continually concentrating on the serious business of learning. Whether it's creating their special books, assisting other writers, listening to a taped story or just enjoying the company of a good book, these kids are learners. They know what it means to be a student.

They learn by doing, not watching. They read to learn, not learn to read. A book is chosen for what it has to offer or because the author is a familiar friend. In literature studies they talk about "whys" not "what." Since comprehension is assumed, elements of literature are discussed at a new level. These kids know about voice, similes and metaphors. Not bad for an elementary "learning disabled" resource room. They read because they want to, not because they have to. They choose their own books.

Sometimes they select student work to read. These kids write their own books! They go through a five step process to achieve this and the results speak for themselves. Check the back shelf for the latest in student authors. They conference with the teacher or each other to work on content, style and grammar. Spelling and punctuation are not issues until the author is satisfied with the content.

Journal writing is another element of their experience. This is written conversation where meaning is the driving force. Students strive to be heard, share their experiences. No corrections are made because communication is the key, not correctness.

Students learn to be readers and writers by following the natural progression of oral language. They learn to read and write the same way they learned to speak, by experimenting and making mistakes. They are encouraged to take chances with learning and by risking, internalize their insights. These kids not only accept this challenge—they surpass it. They are supportive of each other and share their expertise. Together they are a force to be reckoned with.

The students of room 16 are also learning about themselves as they explore the world. They are beginning to see that while education is enjoyable, it requires work and effort on their part. They are striving for self-discipline, a force far more effective than external constraints. They are thoughtful of each other and are encouraged to be supportive of the group. In short, students are learning skills that will help them become successful and integral members of society. They are students of life. Watch them in action.

REFLECTION

Whole language teaching evolves from a coupling of theory and observation. It is shaped by the teacher's instructional vision and refined through reflection. What to do on Monday morning won't be found on the next page of the teachers' manual. Where do the answers lie? In Gutherie's sudden flash of insight as he mumbles under his breath, "I don't like the sound of this" and, grabbing a pencil, deftly draws a line through an unnecessary sentence in his piece on his new bicycle. In Charlene's musings during literature study that Sarah, the main character in *Sarah, Plain and Tall* (MacLachlan, 1986) is not unlike Laura in the Laura Ingalls Wilder books. "They are both strong women who know what they want."

Theory enables the teacher to understand the significance of these events; vision sets the instructional course. It is reflection that informs the teacher whether or not the course taken is the best one. Mike Torbe explains:

> There will be a constant reflection on what has been going on, an interrogation of both the process and the product of teaching and learning. Teachers who have grasped the significant connections between thought, language and learning [know] the importance of "debriefing," of standing back from their learning and interpreting it. (1986, p. 161)

This "standing back" to examine and evaluate is reflected in third-grade teacher Diane Lohman's classroom journal:

> I have found that it takes time to implement the ideas. I am impatient. If something doesn't work right away, I tend to think my kids aren't ready or I'm not ready. Actually it usually just means I need to take more time. For example, peer conferencing didn't seem to be that successful. The children were doing a real quick reading of their story. Their partner would say, "It sounds OK to me," and that was it. I was about to wait until later in the year to try again. Then a fellow teacher encouraged me to give it another chance. I again modeled for them how a good conference would go. We talked about why this step was important. They conferenced again. I definitely saw progress.

A teacher in my graduate course at San Francisco State University confessed recently, "I spent my first three years in the classroom teaching behind closed doors. It was really a grand experiment!" She was speaking ruefully, but she was right in this respect: all teaching is experimental in the same sense that writing is experimental. Donald Murray says of writing, "You will use writing as a way of learning, a way of discovering and exploring, of finding what you may have to say and finding ways in which you may say it" (1983, pp. 5–6). We can say the same of teaching. When we shift our focus from ourselves as teachers to our students as learners (and likewise appreciate ourselves as learners), then we can understand the experimental quality, the revisionary nature of teaching. The only constant, in fact, is change. Our teaching will change as we grow as learners through our interactions with our students, our colleagues, the books we read, the courses we take. It will change as we interact with new groups of students. It will change as we reflect on and evaluate our art.

A WHOLE LANGUAGE PROGRAM

For three years we at the Fair Oaks School have been working to implement a whole language program. Self-evaluation and revision have been an integral part of the process. These are some tactics we have used to assist us in our learning process:

ANECDOTAL RECORDS

Like the ethnographer with a notepad, whole language teachers capture the events and interactions of their classroom in their anecdotal records. Written on a notepad, loose leaf binder, or index cards, these records serve as a daily journal of classroom happenings that relate to student and teacher learning. The teachers record significant events (observation), and as time allows and reflection reveals, they interpret them as well (analysis).

Chris Castro, one of two teachers in a Fair Oaks K–3 classroom, noted that her young student Carlos was resisting journal writing. Later she interpreted this observation:

> Sometimes I think kids feel that they are not in control of their own writing and that they are writing for the teachers not for themselves. For Carlos, it seems that it was important for him to realize that he could write *for* himself and that it didn't always have to be shared and hopefully this helps him to *process* some of the stuff that's going on with him.

These records not only guide Chris in her instructional decision making but also provide her with a frequent opportunity for self-evaluation, enabling her to assess her role as a teacher. Through her notes on Carlos she was able to determine that she needed to help him discover and value the personal nature of writing. In her next entry Chris wrote that Carlos had returned to his journal and was writing about issues he was grappling with at home. In this way Chris was able to evaluate her role as a teacher. Her conference (interaction) with Carlos had worked; her professional judgment had been right. She had learned with Carlos.

Anecdotal records are the mainstay of a whole language classroom. They support the teachers in their dual roles as educators and learners.

VISITOR GUIDES

Since the Fair Oaks School is one of the few bilingual whole language schools in the United States, it receives visitors weekly. It is not possible or desirable to talk with visitors during class time, and therefore, as I have previously mentioned, teachers have developed guides to their classrooms, which provide visitors with a class schedule and a statement of the teacher's educational philosophy.

Our visitors often comment on how helpful they find these guides. They, however, are not the only beneficiaries. Fair Oaks teachers themselves have found the process of writing a philosophy of education invaluable.

Indeed, any teacher in any school can profit from asking and answering the question "What are my basic assumptions about teaching?" The resultant self-examination is often truly revealing. It can also be extremely helpful; for trying to teach without a philosophy of education is like trying to sail without a compass. You will inevitably sail somewhere, but you may not reach your destination.

The process of self-evaluation, then, begins before one enters the classroom. It continues as one interacts with class after class. And it invariably leads to changes.

In the final chapter of her remarkable book *In the Middle: Writing, Reading, and Learning with Adolescents* (1987) Nancie Atwell explains the process of change, self-evaluation, and revision that guides her as a teacher and learner. "New observations and insights will amend theory," she writes. "The process by which I translate theory into action will change. The agents for change are my students. The classroom itself becomes an evolving text—a communal scribble we revise together" (p. 254).

VIDEO AND AUDIO TAPING

"The camera never lies," as the saying goes, and accordingly we have put it to work in our classrooms at Fair Oaks, filming ourselves teaching.

After viewing a videotape of herself conducting a literature study with a small group of students, fifth-grade teacher Pat Yencho remarked to me, "I learned more from that video, Lois, than anything you could have tactfully tried to tell me."

These videotapes can also be shared with colleagues at staff meetings, as we have done at Fair Oaks, and in this way serve as the starting point for an analytical discussion about a particular lesson or a specific instructional strategy.

We found such sessions especially helpful when we were attempting to implement a new model for literature studies that Carole Edelsky (1988) and Karen Smith had shared with us. With Carole as our guide, we viewed tapes of Karen conducting literature studies with her students. Next we taped our own study sessions and then analyzed these as we had done with Karen's. Pat Yencho's comment testifies to the effectiveness of this evaluation tactic.

Those who do not have access to a video camera will find audiotaping nearly as effective. Both will give the gift of time, enabling a teacher to escape the rush of classroom activity and go back later to review his or her teaching.

Pat Yencho audio-taped her literature study sessions with her fifth graders last spring and is spending time over the summer reviewing them in preparation for teaching next fall. Focusing on the students as she listened to the tapes, she discovered that she could categorize the wide range of student response. As she listened a second time to the tapes, she clearly perceived her role as both listener (observer) and group participant (interactor). Pat has become aware of how she can either enhance or hinder the group response in a literature study. As she reviews the tapes, she revises her teaching, thus attaining an ever-higher professional standard.

Webster's defines the professional as a "person who does something with much skill." Self-evaluation may well be the most valuable tool of the teacher who aims at becoming a true professional.

OBSERVATION IN COLLEAGUES' CLASSROOMS

At Fair Oaks, with the help of a grant we received from Raychem, a neighborhood corporation, we have been able to hire substitutes, freeing teachers on a rotating basis to spend time in one another's classrooms.

We have found that watching a colleague in action invites self-analysis. Introspection is inevitable.

Those observed benefit as well, provided there is time to share and discuss and an open atmosphere that supports collegial relationships. Teaching can be a lonely profession. We need to find ways to overcome the physical barriers of separate classrooms and to work toward developing a system of peer review based on caring and mutual support. We have not yet reached this level of peer review at Fair Oaks; nonetheless, observation in one another's classrooms is an important first step.

GRADE-LEVEL MEETINGS

Fair Oaks principal Norman Smith sets aside time every other week for grade-level meetings. He considers them an invaluable component of staff development. Much like a peer conference in a writer's workshop, these meetings provide a forum for reflection, evaluation, and revision. Teachers take turns describing both their difficulties and their triumphs. Avoiding the labels "good" and "bad," we focus instead on the questions "What works?" and "What doesn't?"

Teachers listen to one another, share their impressions, relate their own experiences, ask questions, and suggest alternative strategies. Together we probe the problems and search for solutions as individuals within a community of professional educators. Each teacher rethinks and revises his or her teaching.

Fair Oaks faculty members bring to this workshoplike meeting not only their personal experiences in the classroom but knowledge learned from outside reading and course work. Our resource teacher, Gloria Norton, keeps us well supplied with articles from *Language Arts, The*

Reading Teacher, and other educational journals. As professionals, Fair Oaks teachers have a vested interest in keeping abreast of the pertinent research and literature.

Guided by their theoretical understanding of language and learning, whole language teachers are skilled observers of their students. Instructional decisions evolve naturally from this melding of theory and observation. But it is self-evaluation that tempers the teaching-learning process. Whole language teachers learn to use self-evaluation as the editor does a blue pencil, the sculptor a chisel. Through self-evaluation, whole language teachers revise and refine their teaching art.

Diane Lohman admits that at one time she equated self-evaluation with negative self-criticism. Her year at Fair Oaks as a whole language teacher has changed that. "Now I welcome it as an opportunity to stop and reflect, to renew my vision and honestly assess where I am and how effectively I am moving toward my goal."

CONCLUSION

In all these ways, then, you can evaluate, revise, and improve your teaching. It has been done at Fair Oaks; you can do it in your own classroom. Together you and your students will grow in understanding, and you will realize anew what you as a good teacher must already know—that while your art demands hard work, it also gives much joy.

school
beginnings

"IF THE TEACHER
COMES OVER, PRETEND IT'S
A TELESCOPE!"

Wendy J. Hood

Outside the kindergarten classroom stands a large painting easel covered with butcher paper. It greets the kindergartners on their first day. "Sign in, Please. Firmen Aquí," it reads at the top. I hold a fresh box of crayons out to the children as they approach. "Hi, my name is Wendy," I say to each. "Which crayon would you like to use to write your name here?" One by one the kids sign in, some easily, some with only a little encouragement, and some very reluctantly.

As the wide-eyed kindergartners move away from the easel, my instructional aide, Terry, greets them: "Can I help you find your name tag?" She watches or helps them as needed and then directs them to tables set with paper, pencils, and crayons. "Draw a picture of anything you like," she says as they choose their seats.

Outside two children still stand, crayon in hand, facing the easel, looking almost as anxious as the two mothers standing close behind them. One mom leans close to her little boy. Softly, patiently, she whispers as he writes, "*D . . . a . . . n . . . i . . . e . . . l.*" I greet Daniel, who smiles and rushes into the room to pick out his own name tag.

Tears begin to come to the lone little girl's eyes as her mother says to her in Spanish, "You remember how. Come on now. *V. . . .*" The girl stands, sadly frozen. Mom wraps her hand around the little girl's and moves her hand to shape a *V.* Now the tears are flowing. "That's a fine *V,*" I say to them both. Veronica sniffles as I slip my arm around her and we walk away from her mother, away from the easel, and into the room. Although there is only one name tag left, Veronica does not choose it for herself.

As the kids finish their drawings, Terry and I wander about the room looking at the pictures, talking to the children, and asking them to "write that that's a truck" or whatever. Most of them do write, or pretend to write. "Read it to me," I say. And most of them do. I respond in writing: "Where is the truck going?" This is the beginning of our journal writing.

After writing my responses I ask the children if I may keep their papers. I invite them to choose a book to read on the rug. One by one they complete their journal pages and meander, sometimes by way of the toy areas, to the rug area and the bookshelf. When all the children are there, we put away our books and begin our group time.

So the day goes. After group time we move to directed activities, followed by choices time, followed by supervised clean-up, followed by a final group time. When the bell rings to go home, moms, dads, and various other relatives greet their excited children. "Did you like your first day of school?" they all ask in their own way. "Yes," the kids reply. "What did you do today?" the proud families ask. "Play!"

Terry gives me a knowing look as we say good-bye. We have seen the children for one half day and we know so much about each one already. We are kidwatchers.

We have name-writing samples. We know which children can write their first names, which can approximate their names, which write letters for their names, which write letterlike characters for their names, which can probably write their names but are already afraid to be wrong at school (like Daniel), which make writinglike strokes for their names, and which seem not to know what name writing is all about.

We know the primary language of most of the kids. Did they follow what we said in English? What language did they respond to? What language did they use to say good-bye to their families? What language did they use to "read" us their journal writing? What language did they speak at group time? Did they sing along with the English or Spanish songs? And so on.

We know if they can recognize their name. Did they choose their own name tag? In some cases we know if they read their name or if they recognized it logographically. Did they choose a name that looked like theirs? Martin reached for Maria's tag, but she was not fooled by his tag or by Mario's.

We know to some extent their previous experience with writing implements. How did they use the pencil or crayon? Did they concentrate intently on the process of making marks, or were they enough at ease to enjoy an artistic endeavor? Did they pick up the pencil in a knowing way and hold it with an experienced grasp, or did it appear clumsy in their hands?

We know something about their understanding of writing. Did they write words we could read? Did they approximate the conventional spelling of a word or two? Did they write a small group of letters preceded by a consonant that is often associated with the initial sound of the word they intended? Did they write groups of letters or a string of letters? Did their writing have linear directionality? Did they use letters or letterlike figures? Did they selectively use the letters of their name? Did they use geometric shapes to represent letters? Did they write a connected series of hills and valleys? Did they duplicate the original picture when asked to "write" it?

We know more about their understanding of writing and reading processes when we watch how readily the children write or pretend to write, read or pretend to read back what they have written. Do they eagerly write in their chosen style and then insist they can't read? Do they say they've forgotten what they wrote? Do they read and giggle as if they are pulling a fast one on us, seeming to say, "Imagine, the teacher actually believes that this says something!" When they say, "I can't," does it mean that they do not know what writing is, that they are aware that there are conventions to writing that they do not know, or that they do not know how to spell what they want to say? Do they write in their best five-year-old invented spelling and read back what they intended to say?

We know something about the children's book-handling experience. We have yet to meet a new kindergartner who does not know what a book is. They all find the bookshelf, select books, open them, and turn pages. Some leaf through before settling on one book. Some curl into cozy spots hugging their selections. Some go through many books quickly; others seem to savor each page. Some read stories out loud to themselves or a friend. Some find a special picture to share with someone. Most find the front cover before opening the book. The few who don't still hold the books right side up or turn them around within a page or two. There are one or two who plead with the nearest adult, "Read to me?"

We know, from our group-time activities, some of the kids' math abilities. Who predicts what number will come next when we sing "This Old Man?" Who can maintain the proper number of fingers held aloft on the same song? When we sing "One little, two little, three little brown bears" (we choose not to sing about Indians in this song—we don't want to be offensive), who is able to sing and count right along with us? Who can read the date on the calendar? As we moved about the room earlier in the day, we learned more about their math abilities. Who was heard counting the kids at the table or the number of bears in the room? Who was observed comparing the length of his or her name with a new friend's name?

From the rest of the group-time (adult-directed) activities and free-choice time (child-directed) activities we know much more about the kids in our room. We have a good sense of the children's prior school experiences and their understanding of the pragmatics of school: the ability to share, take turns, participate in discussions, operate in small and large groups, and make decisions when presented with many choices. We know who are the risk takers. We know who is not self-confident and needs our encouragement and who is shy and needs our reassurance.

We even know many of the small things often considered significant in kindergarten development. By offering the children crayons and listening to their responses, I learned about their knowledge of colors. Did they point and say, "That one?" Did they say, "I want red?" Did they ramble, "Don't you have any pink? I like pink, you know. I guess

I'll use blue. No. Can I use a different color for each letter? First blue, then red, then . . . ?" Did they quietly take a crayon and say nothing?

By watching them write and cut (the cutting is part of the adult-directed activity) we have learned who is right- and who is left-handed, who uses a conventional pencil grasp, who can cut well, and who has never used scissors before. Our informal classroom research reveals a correlation between unskilled scissors use and jaw movement. Children new to the use of scissors open and close their jaws with great intensity as they open and close the scissors. Somewhat more skilled cutters move their jaws with their mouths slightly open, while fairly skilled ones move their jaws with their mouths closed. Highly skilled scissors users show no jaw or mouth movement related to cutting. No significance is assigned to this; it is simply another thing kidwatchers notice.

As the children leave, we invite them to return tomorrow to play some more. We smile at the parents' puzzled looks and invite them to come and play with us sometime too.

EVALUATING/VALUING READING AND WRITING

When the room is quiet, Terry and I begin systematically to go through the journal samples, adding the students' names before we forget which piece is whose, sharing our insights and excitement about each child, pointing out things to each other that one of us may have missed. Occasionally we make a few notes on the back of a journal page if there is something puzzling or inconsistent that we want to follow up on. Alberto's journal said "ABLTRBARTSE," or as he read in English to me, "The airplane is flying into the tank. Is going to crash him." I had responded to Alberto, "I hope nobody gets hurt." Terry's eyes showed great surprise as we shared this page. "His father told me that Alberto speaks no English." This we noted on the back of the page. Usually we make mental notes about our discoveries and proceed about our business of designing a program based on what we have learned about where the children are from what the children have shown us, creating activity and play situations that encourage the students to blossom and grow. And, like the father in *Leo, The Late Bloomer* (Krauss, 1971), we watch them for signs of blooming.

We put the journal samples into their files. Later in the week, and throughout the year, we will collect name-writing samples for the files as well.

Many of the children we work with are not "average" kindergartners. They come to school from low socioeconomic backgrounds, often from single-parent or large extended families in small, densely populated housing units. Often their parents have had little or no successful school experience. For most of them English is a second language.

The statistics on these children make for discouraging reading. We are a "target" school. Our schoolwide scores on standardized tests are well below national and city averages. Better than 90 percent of our kindergartners qualify for Chapter I services based on test scores. The drop-out rate at our neighborhood high school is well above both national and city averages.

These children are considered to be at risk, potential losers. They are frequently assessed in terms of the "can't"s—all the things they can't do that somebody somewhere thinks they ought to be able to do. It is my responsibility, then, as a whole language teacher and advocate, to look at each child in terms of the "can"s.

At the outset of the school year I begin to document where the children are when they enter the classroom. I start, as I have described, the first day of school and continue as the school year progresses and the children grow.

For the children of greatest concern, careful and deliberate documentation is essential. When Geraldo approached the sign-in easel, he had a blank look on his face. His sixth-grade brother had brought him to the door and left. I held out a selection of crayons. He took one, saying nothing. He stood and watched a few other children make their autographs. He made a nondescript squiggle on the paper and entered the room. He did not find his name tag but nodded when it was chosen for him. Later in the day I asked the children to draw a person and write their name on the paper. (See Figure 3–1.) Geraldo's name consisted of four large circles. They were made in a random way indicating no control over directionality. When the children wrote journals, Geraldo always made a "*monstro*." The "*monstro*" he drew was not

Figure 3–1   *Geraldo's Name, September 1986*

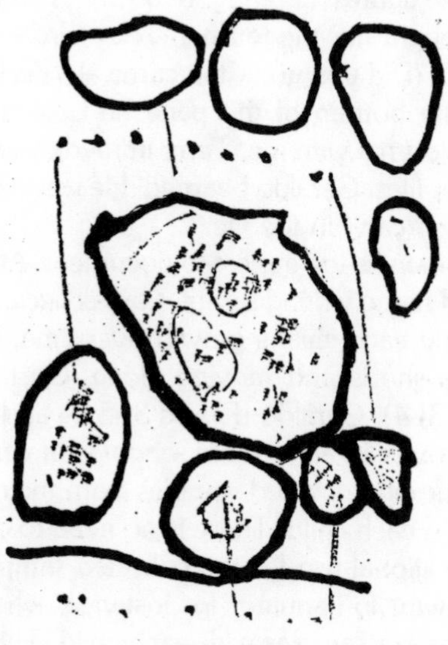

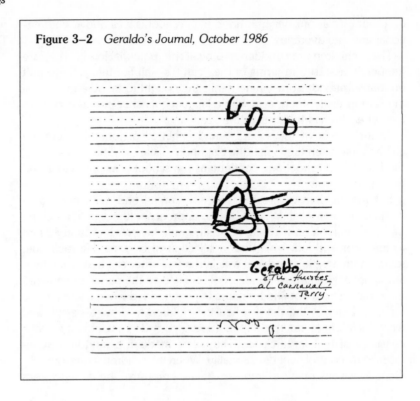

Figure 3–2 *Geraldo's Journal, October 1986*

a recognizable form. He responded to the request in Spanish to write about the "monstro" by duplicating the form. In late October a carnival came to town. One day, October 28, there on his paper, near the picture, were a few letterlike figures. (See Figure 3–2.) "You wrote!" Terry said when Geraldo brought her the journal. Terry wrote back to him, "Tu fuistes al carnival?" (Did you go to the carnival?) As Geraldo wrote the squiggle toward the bottom of the page he quietly said, "Sí." After sharing Geraldo's journal with me, Terry immediately photocopied that special page for our files. Geraldo beamed. He was beginning to bloom. And there was one "can" in the file.

Writing development is the easiest to document. At monthly intervals journal entries and name writing samples are collected. This enables us to document clearly each child's growth over time, starting with each child where he or she is and moving along. Gustavo (Figure 3–3), Fernando (Figure 3–4), Geraldo (Figure 3–5, A and B), and Veronica (Figure 3–6, A through F) all came to school with very different name-writing abilities. The photocopied samples from their files clearly show significant growth in each child. There is no need to compare one child to another. An additional use for the collected samples is to help kids see their own growth. In January, for instance, when filing the latest copies, we share earlier samples with each child. The children can see their own growth and, with the teacher, set some new goals, such as writing their last name or remembering to start from the left.

Figure 3–3 *Gustavo*

Figure 3–4 *Fernando*

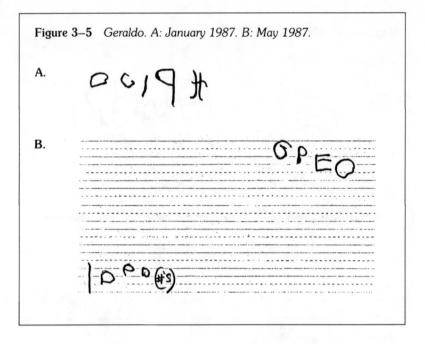

Figure 3–5   *Geraldo. A: January 1987. B: May 1987.*

Examples of significant jumps in growth, such as Geraldo's beginning (*see* Figure 3–2) and the day Spanish-speaking Gustavo wrote "I love you" (Figure 3–7), are copied and placed into the file as well.

On March 5 Veronica, the same child who wept on the first day, selected a book in the school library. She walked over to the check-out counter, picked up a fat red pencil roped to the counter, and slowly wrote her name in the tiny space on the book card. She glanced at a friend next to her and then wrote her room number, 10. This was the first time she had ever written her name on her own! She knew it was different from her prior approximations. The look on her face as she handed me the book displayed her pride. Our understanding librarian allowed me to borrow the card long enough to make three copies; one for my files (Figure 3–8), one for the librarian to share with other librarians, and one for Veronica to give to her mother—the mother who had patiently and supportively been waiting for Veronica to bloom.

Reading is easily observable but harder to document. I use a check-off system that I mark when I note changes. To save time and be more efficient, I combine all my lists into one list. After experimenting with various types, I have settled on two forms. Form A (Figure 3–9) documents how one child grows in a variety of areas over the school year. Form B (Figure 3–10) is used to document on a single date what all the children are currently doing in a variety of areas. Form B is more practical when I am actively kidwatching. Information from that form is easily transferred to form A, which stays in the children's files.

Rene did not recognize his name when school began. He soon was able to find his cubby and his own toothbrush but could not select his

Figure 3–6 *Veronica. A: Early September 1986. B: Mid-September 1986. C: October 1986. D: November 1986. E: January 1987. F: May 1987.*

A.

B.

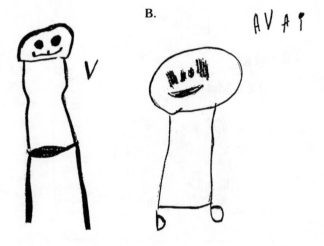

C.

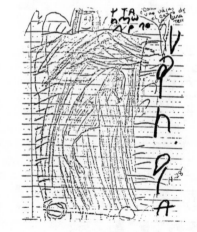

D. ViRALƷ

E. ʯ9bEVCᴙ

F. VEROniRA
ROniC

Figure 3–7 *Gustavo: "I Love You"*

I LAVBJLL   GUS tavo

JASLELEh

Figure 3–8 *Veronica's Book Card*

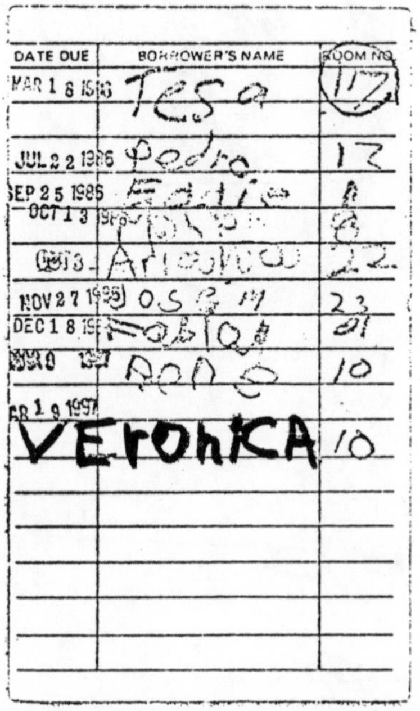

DATE DUE	BORROWER'S NAME	ROOM NO
MAR 1 8 1986	Tesa	17
JUL 2 2 1986	Pedro	17
SEP 2 5 1986	Fatin	A
OCT 1 3 1986		8
	Arleohoo	22
NOV 2 7 1986	OS g M	23
DEC 1 8 19	obiQ#	21
	AoA o	10
FR 1 9 1997	VEFOhKA	10

Figure 3–9 *Sample Kindergarten Growth Documentation Form A*

Name _____   Language _____

　　　　✓ = does this   B = beginning to   E = English
　　　　　　　　　　　　　　　　　　　　　　　　　　　　　　　　S = Spanish

	Date	Date	Date	Date
Recognizes name in limited contexts				
Recognizes name in many contexts				
Writes first/last name (indicate F/L)				
Approximates print in writing				
Relates print to pictures				
Uses invented spelling				
Selects writing as a choice				
Uses writing spontaneously				
Reads pattern books				
Knows print carries meaning				
Reads some environmental print				
Reads back own writing				
Selects reading as a choice				
Uses written resources				
Uses second language				
Counts to (#)				
1:1 correspondence to (#)				
Numberness to (#)				
Writes numbers to (#)				
Reads numbers to (#)				
Maths in play settings				
Solves problems				
Predicts outcomes				

name card among the other children's. One day in late October Rene came running up with a bag full of candy. There were nineteen identical bags on the counter. Rene had chosen only the one with his name on it. That day was carefully noted with the date written into the box under the column "Recognizes name in many contexts" on the check-off list.

It was November before Geraldo began to select his name even in familiar places. We wrote that date on his check-off list. One December day Geraldo had not chosen to move his name card from the "Not

Here" to the "Here" side of the pocket chart. Rene wanted to help, so he moved Gabriel's card. Geraldo sat looking for a minute and said to Rene, "No es mío." (That's not mine.) Rene took a second look and then returned Gabriel's name and after some searching replaced it with Geraldo's. Geraldo smiled. That activity was noted in both of their files. I was smiling too. A few more "cans" added to their growth record.

Many children enter school with a great deal of reading ability. They are highly aware of environmental print and can recite many pattern language books as they turn the pages. For these children we look for movement from approximations toward the expected form. When a child becomes irritated with a classmate for turning the page of *Brown Bear, Brown Bear* before completing "What do you see?" we know that he or she is cueing more closely to the print. We watch our kids

---

Figure 3–10 *Sample Kindergarten Growth Documentation Form B*

Date_____   ✓ = does this   B = beginning to   E = English
                                                              S = Spanish

Student's Name	Reads name F/L	Writes name F/L	Reads signs, logos (other?)	Writes (how?)	Counts to	1:1 to	Number-ness to

as they interact with print. The reading checklist contains some items found in the "Bookhandling Task" (Marek, Howard et al., 1984). At regular intervals, about four times a year, we note where the kids are on the checklist. We use the actual Bookhandling Task selectively with kids, like Geraldo and all the little "Leo's" for whom we want to document as much growth as possible.

EVALUATING SECOND-LANGUAGE GROWTH

When "monolingual" Spanish-speaking Alberto read his journal page to me in English, I learned a great deal about what he knows about language use. His father was unaware that he spoke English because Alberto has always spoken Spanish to his father. While attending pre-school Alberto had learned quite a bit of English, particularly the English of school settings. Alberto has assigned roles for his languages—Spanish at home and English at school. What incredible decisions he has made for a five-year-old!

Although Geraldo tended to keep quietly to himself, he used only Spanish when he spoke—except when counting or naming colors. He counted only in English and only to ten. When he spoke of colors, his language would mix: "Quiero el troque green" (I want the green truck). Spanish rules, however, always governed his syntax. By November Geraldo could often be heard in play settings conversing in English where needed. Expressions like "Gimme" and "Stop it" were appropriately used. Late in the school year, while they were working together at an art center, Rene commented to Geraldo, "You don't speak any English." Geraldo without hesitation replied (in English!), "Yes, but you don't speak any Spanish."

Henry seldom paid attention when I spoke Spanish but would become fascinated by the names of animals or other things in games, books, and songs in Spanish. During a bingo game he generalized the Spanish possessive *mío* (mine) while pointing to another child who had the matching item and called out, "Him-o."

Jesse complained each time a story or film was in Spanish. He always asked for his notes for home, books, dictation, and so on to be in English. When carefully watched, Jesse could be seen enjoying a Spanish story at the listening center, answering in English questions that were asked in Spanish about a lesson presented in Spanish, acting as an interpreter among children in small-group settings, and following all directions regardless of language.

Sometime during the school year an official school district diagnostician will test each child, one by one, for language dominance. Alberto will test dominant and proficient in Spanish and functional in English. Henry will test proficient in English and nonfunctional in Spanish. Jesse will show proficiency in both languages. Geraldo will probably be diagnosed as Spanish-dominant but nonfunctional in either language.

In the whole language bilingual classroom, however, kidwatching can, in most cases, reveal more than a standardized language-proficiency measure. From the first day of school, through the school year, we interact with each child daily. First- and second-language proficiency is informally assessed on a daily basis through each interaction. While the tests report the kids' language deficiencies, assessing childrens' language through observation focuses on what children do and know. The kid-watching that occurs in the classroom reveals the knowledge the children have about language and the decisions each one makes about language use. Kidwatching revealed Geraldo's developing oral language, his abil-ity to express himself as needed and to adapt his language to his en-vironment, Henry's interest in and development of his second-language use and his understanding of morphology, Alberto's self-developed rules for school and home language, and Jesse's reluctant bilingualism.

In the whole language classroom language dominance is not really what we want to identify. The whole language teacher assesses language proficiency through children's sensitivity to the pragmatics of language use. When Henry thanks a visiting African artist by saying, "Gracias!" we know that he is beginning to understand the appropriate uses of a second language. Kidwatching can document things tests can never measure.

EVALUATING MATHING

Just as children may be observed interacting with print and playing with oral language in a language-rich environment, they may be observed mathing in any whole language setting that is rich in the elements of life. Mathing, like reading and writing, is a language process (or perhaps part of the language process). Many whole language teachers limit their view of whole language to what has traditionally been called the lan-guage arts. Just as whole language evaluation of written language aware-ness looks beyond each child's ability to recite the alphabet or call the names of printed words or letters, our mathing evaluation looks beyond each child's ability to recite numbers sequentially or draw numerals. Part of what we look for, then, as an integral part of whole language evaluation is the language of mathing and mathematical thinking. (The major source for the math evaluation here is *Mathematics Their Way*, Baratta-Lorton, 1976.)

The arithmetic strand, consisting of basic number concepts, is eval-uated in formal and informal ways. Formal procedures are used when spontaneous occasions for such evaluations don't occur. The formal evaluation is done a few times a year, one on one, and recorded on my checklist. The kids are asked to count out loud. When they stop, I ask, "And then?" Next, blocks are placed in front of them. "How many blocks are there?" I note the child's one-to-one correspondence on the checklist. Does the child touch each block and say one number? Does the child arrive at the correct answer without touching the blocks? Does the child have an organized way of counting the blocks? Additional blocks are placed or blocks are taken away as needed to get a true sense of the child's ability. Some children cannot organize a group of piled blocks but have no problem counting them if they are placed in a line. Some children can count to a higher number when manipulating objects.

Numberness is the most important of the number concepts that is assessed. Sometimes called conservation of number, numberness is rooted in mathematical thinking and visualization. When Pedro looked into his cubby and saw three cars rather than the five he had placed there, he ran to Terry saying, "Someone took two of my cars." Pedro has numberness for five.

Unfortunately (or fortunately for Pedro) this doesn't happen very often, so numberness is often formally assessed (although with Pedro I'd begin assessing with six). Together the child and I count three blocks. I hide one while the child watches. "How many do you see?" "Two." "How many are hiding?" "One." We look to see that this is correct. After the first demonstration, the correct answer is not revealed. We do the three blocks, hiding either one or two, a few times. If the child grasps that, *using a different color block*, we count out four blocks and repeat the procedure. If the child is correct for each of the combinations, we count out five of a different color and proceed. The final number at which the child is successful is recorded.

In September some children who can count very high do not have numberness, while others who have one-to-one correspondence only to six may have numberness to six as well. A few do not have numberness with three objects, but I've never met any children who didn't have it with two, even if they couldn't count beginning with one.

There are many classroom opportunities to observe the children using the other areas of mathematics at play and as a part of directed activities. Children compare things as they work and play. While in the process of rolling out the dough for some gingerbread people, Erika said, "I'm going to make a very fat one." Debby got down on her knees to look at the dough from eye level and said, "Mine is fatter." She turned to Fernando and said, "Yours is so skinny it will burn." Then the children began to compare things around the room to the thicknesses of their dough. "If it [the dough] were as thin as the writing paper, it would burn," said Fernando. "Yes, if it were as thick as a journal it would be just right," Erika replied.

They discuss shapes as they build with blocks, as they create artistically, as they read and write. They measure as they cook. They measure as they build. They measure as they play with dress-up shoes. They use logical thinking as they predict the outcome of stories, as they manipulate a prized toy away from another classmate, as they wait until the teacher is not looking to be just a little naughty.

Weapons are not allowed in my classroom, not even ones kids create with building toys. David loves giant Tinkertoys. He spoke to Antonio as he built: "I'm making a machine gun." Antonio recited our class rule to him, to which David responded, "If the teacher comes over, I will pretend that it's a telescope. Then she will like it!"

Kids talk about time in terms of lunchtime, after-school time, journal time, choices time, summertime, yesterday, tomorrow, and birthday time. They work with money in real and play situations: bus money, lunch money, book money, fund-raiser money, tooth fairy money, money for the classroom post office, store, or restaurant, and the odd pennies and dimes that roll through their fingers in their pockets. They write numbers on calendars, on paper left near telephones, on scrap paper that resembles forms, on price tags for items in stores, and on restaurant order forms.

When Monica returned her midyear report card, she had marked in *every* unmarked box. Upon further inspection it could be seen that Monica had marked letters next to the letters I had marked and numbers next to other numbers. She obviously knew the difference between letters and numbers although she still called them all numbers.

Each child is observed involved in many of these mathing events. Through these observations we are able to see the children using mathematical language and demonstrating mathematical thinking. We are also able to note which children do not seem to follow the mathing going on around them. When we observe children who do not seem to understand or who are seldom observed mathing, we design activities to promote mathing.

Even when we sang counting songs, Beth would appear lost. Formal evaluation revealed that she did not begin counting with the number one. When asked to count, she would hold up one hand, fingers spread, and proudly say, "I am five." She did not know how many fingers were on her hand. Beth liked to play in the playhouse. She'd place one doll in each of four chairs and proceed to set the table for four. When another child wanted to bring a high chair up to the table, Beth informed her that there were not enough plates. Through kidwatching we knew that Beth did have one-to-one correspondence and some numberness. What she lacked were the labels, the language to describe what she already knew.

VALUING KIDS

Eventually each teacher is faced with the promotion of students to the next grade. The first decision that is faced is the basis for promotion. Are children promoted because they perform a given number of tasks with a given proficiency? Or is learning defined as growth, and promotion based on real learning? For decades educators have been asserting that teachers should begin with each child where that child is. From there the child grows. The evaluation that takes place in my classroom documents that growth. It starts with each child where that child begins and documents real and important growth. Children are evaluated and promoted based on their growth and compared only to themselves.

Occasionally someone questions the reasons for promotion of an individual. They want an explanation why a child so far behind the average has been allowed to continue when that child "can't" do so much compared to others. For each child in our kindergarten we have documented the "can"s—what each one can do and how each one has shown growth. Growth has been documented through anecdotal records, journal and name-writing samples, mathing evaluations, book-handling tasks, and a warm, caring relationship developed and cultivated between the instructional aide, the children, and the teacher. Not all of the information has been documented in written form. Some of it is in that knowledge we develop about children when we get to know them well; like Leo's father from the book, we watch for signs of blooming, and like Leo's mother from the book, we know they will bloom.

Patiently we explain where the children started. Using the documented data, adding anecdotes and further explanation that draw on the mental notes made on each child that come to mind when the samples are reviewed, we show how much that child grew, how far that child came, all the things that child *can* do, and all the things that the child knows about school and about doing.

All children grow. That growth is documentable. And in their own good time they all bloom. They are neither losers nor potential losers. They are learners.

EVALUATION IN A CLASSROOM ENVIRONMENT DESIGNED FOR WHOLE LANGUAGE

Robert Wortman / Myna Matlin Haussler

In a kindergarten–first-grade classroom six-year-old Allen approaches the teacher to share his journal entry. He voluntarily reads his entry, and the teacher writes a response. Allen reads the response and writes, "I like it two." Then he asks, "Is that the right *too*?" The teacher spends several minutes pointing out the differences among *to, too,* and *two*, after which Allen changes his entry to read "*too*." Within five minutes three other journals are shared with the teacher that have incorporated *to, too,* and *two* with some very creative spellings ("toow," "tow," and "twoo"). Over the next few days the spellings of *to, too,* and *two* are experimented with a great deal by a number of children who are operating at varying levels of literacy development and who have received no direct instruction.

Bob Wortman is the whole language teacher in this class. Throughout the entire event Bob is evaluating. He is making decisions that teachers are faced with every school day. He evaluates Allen's question and knowledge and makes the deliberate choice to take advantage of a teachable moment. Bob decides to offer this child a rather lengthy response to his question even though he rarely "corrects" a child's personal writing in a dialogue journal.

Bob has chosen to use dialogue journals as an instructional strategy in place of language workbooks. His was a conscious decision based on an evaluation of how young children learn. The acceptance of students' approximations and collaborations and the trying out of new information is important for learning. Bob realizes the ramifications of his interaction with Allen as he observes and evaluates other students' use of homophones (words that sound alike but look different) over a span of time. This ongoing evaluation is planned, supported, and im-

45

plemented through the deliberate decisions Bob makes in setting up his classroom.

What is the nature of Bob's classroom that it supports and encourages this type of evaluation? What does it look like? How are the children grouped? How is the classroom managed? The vignette described took place in a primary self-contained classroom in many ways similar to other primary classrooms across the United States. There are tables and chairs, chalkboards and bulletin boards, a designated language arts curriculum, and available texts. The students represent a mixture of races, socioeconomic groups, family backgrounds, cultures, and abilities. The differences between the rich literacy exchanges in this classroom and the literacy experiences afforded many other kindergarten and first-grade children in American schools lie in the philosophical stance and knowledge of the teacher.

The literate environment of this classroom is based on sound principles of child development and language learning. In this environment whole language and a variety of learning experiences, oral and written, provide the functional context for reading and writing development. This necessarily requires that language not be segmented into abstract skills nor separated from sociolinguistic context. Evaluation is formative, descriptive, qualitative, and longitudinal, and involves samples of students' work.

This chapter addresses the question of how evaluation is managed in a whole language environment. We describe the literate environment in which evaluation, especially kidwatching, is best constructed by examining the physical arrangement of the classroom and the emotional and social context within which activities takes place.

THE PHYSICAL ARRANGEMENT OF THE LANGUAGE-LEARNING CLASSROOM

The physical arrangement of a classroom is a basic aspect of whole language and assessment. Certain settings are more likely than others to encourage collaboration and peer-group support. If indeed the teacher is interested in encouraging children to utilize resources of materials and peers, and in evaluating their progress, then the room is set up in such a manner as to make these resources readily available. In any classroom teachers have options about how to arrange and rearrange the physical setting, based on the careful observations and assessment of their students' learning in the classroom. In Bob's classroom, formative evaluation is used to create the naturalistic learning environment and in turn evaluate:

- The use of alternative grouping strategies.
- Optimal use of available space.
- Facilitation of children's access to a wide range of literacy materials.
- The use of existing facilities.
- Teacher selection of literacy materials.

ALTERNATIVE GROUPING STRATEGIES

Alternative grouping strategies are the various options available to teachers for grouping children in classrooms for specific purposes: large groups, small groups, pairs, or individuals. A naturalistic literate environment is organized so that space is available for children to work in a variety of social groupings. Evaluation must occur in a variety of contexts in order to obtain a complete picture of children's abilities and strengths.

In large groups children have the benefit of using individual peers as resources as well as drawing on the group for support. In this setting teachers are able to assess which children stay on task, which children are confident enough to risk speaking out or leading a group, and which use group support to learn from others. Teachers can make special use of large-group interactions to evaluate their own lessons and teaching strategies by observing how different students respond, how interested and involved the students remain, and what needs to be followed up in small-group or individual contexts.

More intensive kidwatching takes place when teachers observe students in smaller groups or pairs. This yields information for evaluating development and planning future instruction. For some children it is easier to take risks with a special friend than in front of an entire class. In the whole language classroom there is more time for each child to participate in a variety of social contexts. The teacher is able to observe which children the others seek out for assistance, which children act as learners, and which take on the role of teachers in varying social, topical, and situational contexts.

The classroom setting must also provide opportunities for children to work alone and to become self-sufficient and self-evaluating. On their own, children may think through and extend knowledge learned in group settings. These thoughtful and reflective periods require a specific space relatively well sequestered from the distractions of a busy classroom. Observing students working by themselves helps teachers to see how each learner develops and uses strategies for writing, reading, and thinking.

OPTIMAL USE OF SPACE

The layout of the classroom and the amount of space available in it are fixed factors that often limit the ways in which the class can be organized. But the allocation of the space is critical to whole language evaluation. If space is allocated to a large-group meeting area, that limits the amount of space that may be allocated for small-group and individual work. Whole language teachers extend the concept of floor space in their classrooms to include other areas. Figure 4–1 shows Bob's classroom. A high platform area such as a reading loft can help extend space to provide quiet reading areas. Hanging charts and art from ceilings also extends space for environmental print and conserves scarce bulletin board and wall space. Areas that allow movement, activity, and noise are best kept away and sectioned off from areas reserved for quieter activities. Often it is possible to extend space by moving noisy or messy

Figure 4–1 *Physical Environment for K–1 Whole Language Classroom*

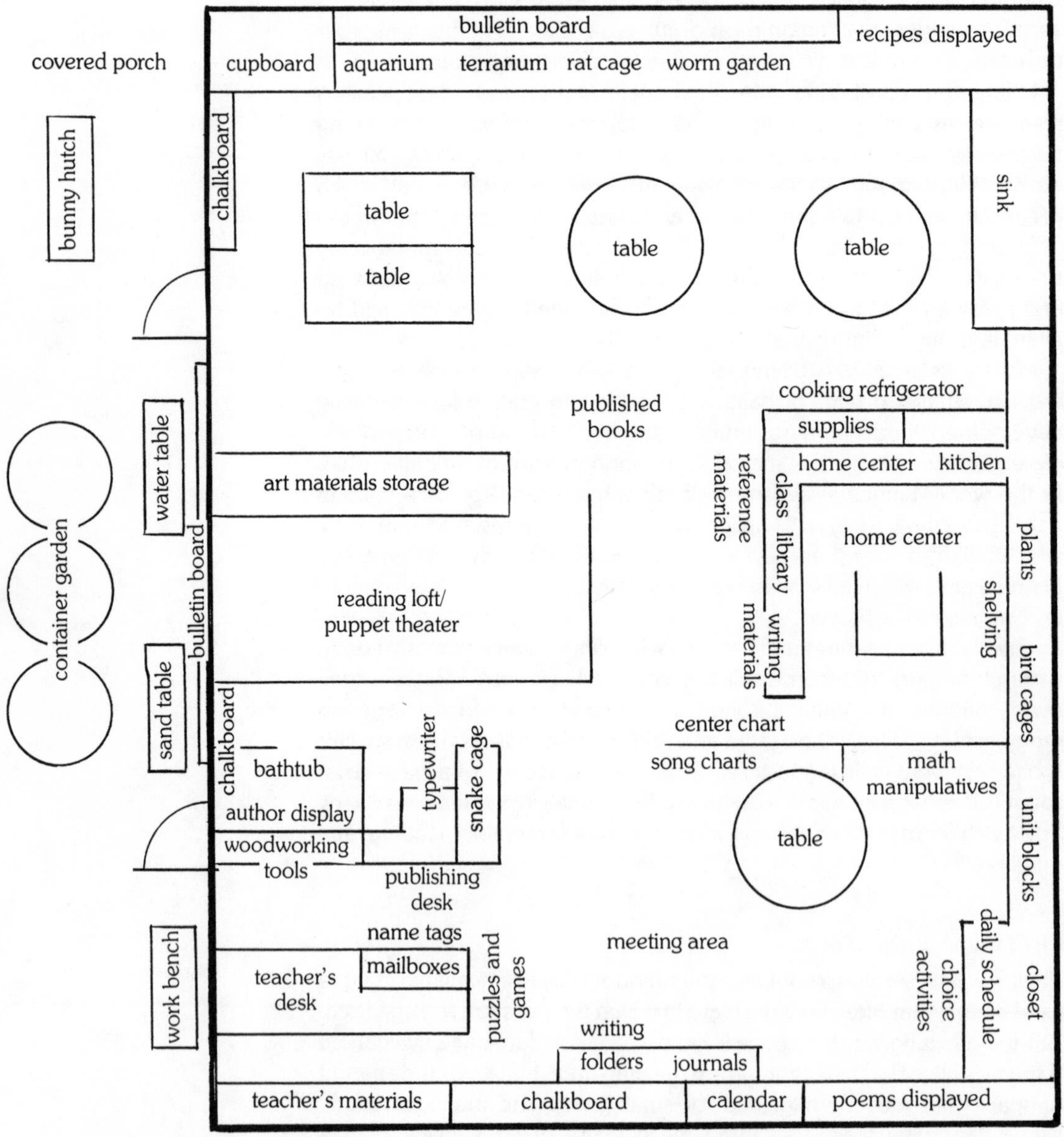

covered porch

cupboard

bulletin board

recipes displayed

aquarium   terrarium   rat cage   worm garden

bunny hutch

chalkboard

sink

table

table

table

table

container garden

water table

bulletin board

sand table

published books

art materials storage

reading loft/ puppet theater

cooking refrigerator

supplies

reference materials

class library

writing materials

home center   kitchen

home center

plants

bird cages

shelving

unit blocks

center chart

song charts

math manipulatives

chalkboard

bathtub

author display

woodworking tools

typewriter

snake cage

publishing desk

table

meeting area

daily schedule

choice activities

closet

work bench

name tags

mailboxes

teacher's desk

puzzles and games

writing

folders   journals

teacher's materials

chalkboard

calendar

poems displayed

activities onto a patio or into a hallway as needed. Providing children a variety of physical settings allows them to attend to their tasks and make use of a full range of appropriate strategies and groupings. By not restricting students' natural utilization of materials and peer interactions the teacher can ensure that a truer picture of their individual capabilities and growth will emerge.

Selecting appropriate furniture offers further options for facilitating learning. Individual desks take up a good deal more space in a room than grouped desks or tables. Round tables may offer more flexibility than rectangular tables in tight spaces. Shelves can be utilized as room dividers or activity boundaries while providing access to materials for specific tasks. Chart racks offer not only additional display space but more privacy as well.

The ongoing evaluation of specific lessons and activity structures within the physical environment provides information to teachers about how to improve the utilization of space. If possible, teachers and school planners must select carefully classroom furniture that best facilitates learning and meets the specific needs of a whole language classroom. Whole language teachers are creative in making do with less than optimal resources. But they need to help planners and purchasing agents rethink which furnishings are needed to facilitate whole language teaching.

ACCESS TO MATERIALS

Bob's classroom is organized to support children's growing independence in learning. Materials are organized so that the children can function without constant assistance from their teacher, and this accessibility aids learning. Bob evaluates the children's need for materials and space and then arranges the environment to facilitate access and eliminate dependence on the teacher. If the teacher's interactions with groups of students are continually being interrupted because the teacher is the sole dispenser of materials such as paper and art supplies, then a great deal of time is wasted, and students do not develop a sense of classroom ownership and responsibility.

Many opportunities for language use arise when students are responsible for maintaining and distributing supplies and materials. Children can use print and patterns of written language when sorting blocks or putting away painting supplies. Many literacy events occur as pupils obtain and store materials. For example, the teacher is able to observe how individual children respond to environmental print as they use written language for organizing and storing. After writing in dialogue journals, children can read labeled baskets that are within easy reach and deposit their journals appropriately. They read as they select materials such as Big Books and are free to reread favorite books when these are readily accessible. Accessible materials provide occasions for ongoing literacy events and for evaluating learning within the context of the events. Evaluation within this functional setting of environmental print use offers further insight into the prior knowledge and experience children bring to school.

The evaluation of materials themselves occurs in the context of their use. Which are the ones children reread frequently? Are the materials used individually or in group interaction? Can children use the materials easily on their own? Which are most often used as models for children's writing?

EXISTING FACILITIES

Some structures such as windows, doors, sinks, and electrical outlets are in fixed positions in classrooms. Thus groupings and activities must be organized around them. But both teachers and students can be ingenious and creative. Paints can be stored near sinks to facilitate clean-up, but pails or basins will serve as well when sinks are not available. Cooking areas are best set up near sinks and appliances (magnetic letters on the refrigerator can be used, as at home, to extend language play). Immovable light sources and writing surfaces need not limit the options. In Bob's class a grandfather donated a reading lamp for use under the loft and also cut up Masonite sheets for lapboards to extend the available writing areas. Chalkboards offer opportunities for written language play and can be supplemented by hand-held slates. This creative use of facilities within the existing classroom extends the opportunities teachers and children have for literacy activities. It allows written language to be encouraged in every nook and cranny in the classroom for a variety of purposes. It also makes the classroom a comfortable place for children in which to live, play, and work.

Carpet and linoleum dictate the types of materials and activities that will work most effectively and the amount of preparation required to facilitate clean-up. Sometimes specific spaces can be defined and extended with rugs or pieces of carpeting or linoleum to allow for that extra art area or padding for block building or meeting areas. This planned use of space establishes where certain materials will be used and allows the teacher to focus attention on evaluation of learning rather than on discipline.

The availability of a porch, patio, or hallway and the proximity of other rooms and facilities will affect decisions on extending the classroom space beyond the four walls of the room. Even displaying students' work is limited by the availability of surfaces to which it may be attached. The addition of bulletin boards, sheets of heavy cloth, or other makeshift display spaces can help extend the ability to show off student efforts. This provides the necessary audience for children to evaluate their work in an authentic setting and permits that self-evaluation to focus on what children can do when engaged in purposeful activities.

Bob and his students frequently evaluate the classroom facilities and their requirements for specific tasks. Just as students are able to select certain individualized tasks, so are they responsible for helping to organize the facilities to meet their needs. Throughout the process the teacher assesses the ability of individual students to plan, organize, and solve problems in collaboration with their peers for authentic purposes—activities that could not exist in a more restricted setting.

TEACHER SELECTION OF LITERACY MATERIALS

Bob is alert to the need to provide appropriate materials at the appropriate times for specific learners. His philosophy of learning involves students in evaluating materials and their optional uses in the classroom. Since students are assessed in a variety of social settings, he selects materials that will meet students' needs in a variety of social contexts as well.

Materials are chosen for the function or purposes they serve and the space and preparation required for their use. In Bob's class individual letters are not taught outside a functional context. Library books and lists such as the attendance book, physical education charts, and group graphs are kept in alphabetical order, as are other lists to which the children have access. An alphabet strip serves as a reference for the pupils in these functional tasks.

Evaluation of how children interact with resources often depends on how well the resources meet the needs and purposes of children in everyday use. A list of words and phrases brainstormed by the students on a subject they want to write about, such as cars, relates to authentic purposes in a way a list of sight-reading words cannot. The evaluation of resources is tied to the authentic use of the resources by the students. In classrooms with more accessible resources, including a variety of writing implements and types of paper, students use resources more frequently and write more than children in a less print-rich environment (Kasten, 1984). With a greater variety of materials, students have more opportunities to become engaged in a curriculum area that supports literacy growth.

THE EMOTIONAL-SOCIAL CONTEXT FOR LANGUAGE LEARNING

The emotional-social context for language learning in the classroom is vital to the issue of evaluation. Bob works hard to create a social context in his classroom in which children feel comfortable stretching their abilities. Key aspects of the emotional and social context necessary for evaluating students in a naturalistic setting include:

- School climate and influence of professional decision making within the school.
- Emotional environment.
- Social setting.
- Negotiated roles of teacher and student.

SCHOOL CLIMATE

The effect of the school culture on the language-learning environment is of great importance. Much has been written about the impact of school climate as it relates to evaluating a school as effective. Teachers in schools evaluated as effective maintain a high level of morale, trust, and professional respect; share common goals; work together to reach the agreed-upon goals; and are supported by a knowledgeable and accessible principal who encourages individual strengths and provides support for individual growth (Zumwalt, 1986). The degree of support received from the school administrator relates directly to the academic freedom and professional judgment exercised by the teacher in enacting the curriculum and choosing among a variety of evaluative measures.

In Bob's school the principal encourages teachers to expand their professional knowledge, supports them in using creative teaching strategies, and fosters learning through the use of a variety of evaluation techniques such as anecdotal records, interest inventories, writing samples, and audio tapes. Within this supportive and collegial environment Bob is able to extend his professional knowledge, open his classroom to the scrutiny of a researcher, share successes and concerns with his peers, and evaluate his own growth and abilities without fear of reprisal.

EMOTIONAL ENVIRONMENT

Just as the physical arrangement of the classroom facilitates large-group, small-group, and individualized activities, a framework of rules and expectations sets the criteria for ongoing evaluation. Developing goals negotiated by the teacher and students for classroom behavior allows for the rights of the individual to be balanced with the needs of the group and the programmatic requirements of the teacher. The children are then held equally responsible with the teacher for evaluating whether the rules are being observed and whether modifications are needed.

Bob wants his students to feel secure. The children must feel safe if they are to risk reaching out to attempt new activities, try new strategies, and express creative ideas without fear of ridicule or failure. The environment in Bob's classroom supports children's self-esteem by promoting the strengths and uniqueness of each individual's contribution to the group. This requires a continual group process of interaction and input to evaluate the common goals and concerns of the group as they pertain to individual needs. The emotional climate is tied to the social environment and cannot be evaluated independently, for Bob's students quickly develop the notion that they are responsible for themselves and one another.

SOCIAL SETTING

Bob has created a unique social setting in which teacher and children interact and learn from one another. An Adlerian interactive model for discipline (Dreikers, 1964) fits Bob's whole language classroom best in that the model recognizes behavior as purposeful and requires children to be responsible for their own learning. Bob creates an environment and introduces those activity structures that best require students to make conscious decisions pertaining to their learning and behavior. Thus children are naturally required to adhere to the agreed-upon social demands of general courtesy and to accept responsibility for their actions within the group. By involving the children in the process of decision making and requiring their evaluative input, Bob ensures that they begin to understand a system of rules tied to function and situation. Since the responsibility is in their power, they are answerable to the group and to themselves rather than the absolute authority of the teacher. It is within this social setting that Bob can measure growth in abilities and can constantly assess the strengths of the children.

This does not mean that Bob abdicates the professional responsibility of maintaining a rich and orderly learning environment conducive to intellectual, physical, and emotional growth. It does, however, require him to be sensitive to and aware of group dynamics in order to sort out the interactions in an event that best focus on the growth of individual children. It means that Bob must have a sound background in child development, learning theory, and evaluation and a willingness to read and risk the application of current research in his classroom.

NEGOTIATING THE ROLE OF TEACHER AND STUDENTS

In a whole language classroom such as Bob's teaching and evaluation become a shared responsibility among students, family, and teachers, even extending into the community through the participation of classroom volunteers who share their various talents and experiences. This further helps the students to consider the unique gifts each has to offer to the diversity of the classroom and enhances their ease in transactions with adults. Traditional power roles are minimized. Power over curriculum, knowledge, and the access to both is not hoarded by the teacher and rationed in small, unconnected pieces. Rather, the power to learn is shared by students and teacher alike. Adults and children become both teachers and learners, and growth can be monitored within this more natural setting (K. Goodman, 1986).

The teacher-learner relationship becomes less formalized and is better described in terms of a novice-expert relationship as promoted by Vygotsky (1987). Bob demonstrates his need to learn from the children, and the children collaborate extensively to learn from one another. Evaluation in this respect allows for greater insight into the child and into the activities structured for learning. The number and types of interactions in which learning takes place are extended, offering greater possibilities for the child to recognize and demonstrate competency.

The classroom must be organized in such a way as to support this collaborative work and encourage students to demonstrate their knowledge. The daily interactions with written language in Bob's classroom involve a variety of experiences and materials as well as teaching/learning and kidwatching strategies. Bob believes that literacy learning is best achieved through the child's meaningful and functional interactions with a variety of printed material. He works constantly to improve the physical, emotional, and social environment of his classroom through careful planning and assessment. This environment allows for and invites immersion in planned experiences. It offers sufficient depth to encourage concentration and sufficient breadth to involve all children within the range of their experience and development.

The literate environment in Bob's classroom promotes reading, writing, listening, and speaking in a wide range of ways across the whole curriculum. There is no isolation of skills from whole language or of language from its use in learning and communication. In Bob's class the physical, emotional, social, and literate environment always allows integration of the cuing systems of language: pragmatic, syntactic, semantic, and graphophonic (Edelsky and Smith, 1984). Bob assesses his students' knowledge within this environment as he builds on the many teachable moments that extend language development and build a new knowledge base from which his pupils operate. Within this setting Bob continues to evaluate the development of his students, his curriculum, the learning environment, and himself as a whole language teacher.

"ASÍ NO SE PONE SÍ"
(THAT'S NOT HOW YOU WRITE "SÍ")
René Galindo

Every school day presents an opportunity to learn, not only on the part of the students but also on the part of the teacher. Evaluation can be looked at as a two-way street. In one direction is the evaluation of the student's learning, in the other direction is the evaluation of the teacher's own learning. This particular account describes my own understanding of literacy development and the literacy events in which my students were participating. This two-way traffic provides a channel for communication in which information that is gathered from one side of the street can complement the decisions being made on the other side. What a teacher learns from his or her students about how children's knowledge of literacy develops helps that teacher become a better-informed evaluator of the students' learning.

Evaluation can also be looked at as an ongoing process that takes place during the children's actual involvement in literacy events. Part of the emphasis of evaluation as an ongoing process is the realization that most forms of evaluation are one-shot measures and might not be indicative of what students know. Ongoing evaluation gives the teacher the opportunity to observe the child learning on different days and in different social situations.

Evaluation of children's reading and writing should take place while they are actually reading and writing and not in situations that are supposed to simulate actual reading and writing. This makes it possible for the teacher to learn about how children use the many resources that are available to them from their classmates and from print material. Information obtained in these contexts not only helps the teacher learn about the students' use of written language but also provides information about how students apply their knowledge to expand their literacy.

The specific examples of evaluation and learning covered in this chapter are: the evaluation of a second grader's spelling strategies, the evaluation of children's choices of language use during literacy events, and the evaluation of the literacy event itself. Through a personal narrative of my own classroom experience spread out over two years, I describe my experience of looking at evaluation as an ongoing process on a two-way street.

After school one day, as I was reading through my students' journals, I began to notice that several students in my first-grade bilingual classroom were learning how to read and write in both Spanish and English. I was surprised because these students were receiving their reading instruction only in Spanish. My classroom was composed of twelve bilingual students and fourteen monolingual students. During "formal" reading instruction the students were grouped by their dominant language; out of four reading groups, two were learning how to read in English and two in Spanish. At different times of the day the students were also grouped in mixed language groups composed of children of different language and academic abilities. At that time I thought that a student had to learn how to read in one language before learning to read in another. But through what I was seeing in the students' journals my preconceived notions of how children develop biliteracy were challenged. My understanding of biliteracy did not explain how the children were learning to read and write in two languages at the same time.

My students challenged me with the question: How can bilingual children develop simultaneous biliteracy while receiving reading instruction only in Spanish? I decided to start looking for an answer. My students had been writing in dialogue journals containing a narrative of some kind. These were usually personal narratives, but sometimes the children wrote fictional narratives or a song that they liked. After they had finished their journal entries, they would read their journal to one other student. When each student finished reading, the other would write a question or comment. The two students would carry on an oral and written dialogue until they decided that they had finished. They would then repeat the procedure with the other student's journal. From the beginning of the school year I had also been writing in my journal and sharing it with a different student each day. But when I started thinking about the biliteracy question, I stopped writing in my journal and began close observations of the bilingual children's writing in order to begin to understand the literacy development that was taking place in my classroom.

PARTICIPANT OBSERVATION

Participant observation is a research method that is used in ethnographic studies. In participant observation the researcher participates directly with the people he or she is studying in the activities in which they are engaged. The purposes of this method are outlined by Peter Woods:

The central idea of participation is to penetrate the experiences of others within a group or institution. How better to do this than by assuming a real role within the group or institution, and contributing towards its interests or functions, and personally experiencing these things in conjunction with others? Access to all group activities is assumed, and one can observe from the closest range, including monitoring one's own experiences and thought process. Again, teachers are ideally placed for this, for they already occupy a role within their own institution. (1986, p. 33)

Participating directly with people in the activities under investigation is the central aspect of participant observation. In this way the investigator hopes to achieve a view of the processes involved in the activities that would otherwise not be possible. The perspective of the researcher in participant observation is more similar to that of the other participants in the activity. As Woods points out, the research methodology of participant observation is very suitable for classroom teachers because teachers already assume a real role.

The teacher is a participant in the classroom in the sense that he or she is there all the time and has a well-defined role in the class. The teacher serves as the leader or organizer of instructional activities. The teacher also participates sometimes by actually doing the activity along with the students. But there's a difference between being a participant-observer and being a classroom teacher. A classroom teacher does not become a participant-observer merely by occupying the role of classroom teacher. In order to be a participant-observer a teacher must first be aware of the differences that exist between being an ordinary participant in an event and a participant-observer. James Spradley mentions this difference in his book, *Participant Observation*: "The participant-observer comes to the social situation with two purposes: (1) to engage in activities appropriate to the situation and (2) to observe the activities, people, and physical aspects of the situation" (1980, p. 54). The second purpose is what differentiates participant observation from ordinary participation. In my case I was interested in noticing details that I might not have noticed had it not been for the questions that I was trying to answer about biliteracy. How, for example, did the choice of a writing partner influence the choice of the language in which to write? How did oral dialogue affect written dialogue and vice versa? Keeping these questions in mind while I observed or participated with the children made my participation different from the ordinary.

Another important difference is that "unlike most ordinary participants, the participant-observer will keep a detailed record of both objective observations and subjective feelings" (Spradley, 1980, p. 58). The records that I kept included audio tapes of the student's interaction, the students' journal writing, and observational notes. These notes included contextual information that would not have been recorded by the audio tape about the interaction that influenced what or how the children were writing.

Participant observation exists along a continuum moving from passive participation at one end (being present at the scene but not interacting with anyone else) to active participation at about the midpoint (doing what the other people are doing) to complete participant observation (studying a situation in which the researcher is already an ordinary participant). The continuum moves from only observing interaction to full participation in the interaction.

The classroom teacher is in a unique position to be a participant-observer. The students expect the teacher to be interested and to be paying close attention to whatever might be going on in the classroom. It is not difficult for the teacher to interrupt whatever is taking place between children as they work on an activity and to ask questions about what they are doing or learning. By contrast an outsider would need considerable time to be able to develop that type of relationship with the students. The students have come to learn through their school experience that teachers ask many questions and evaluate students' participation in the activities as well as the final product. When I participated in the activity of dialogue journals, I was not the leader of the activity. I was doing the same thing as the rest of the class; I was writing in my journal and sharing it with another student, or I was sitting next to some children, observing and writing notes. I set the tape recorder next to us and taped the interaction. I was not involved in observational note taking since I was writing in my journal. When I was writing, I was highlighting the participation aspect of participant observation.

When I became interested in the development of biliteracy, I decided to stop writing in my journal in order to observe the students more closely. I was interested in the interaction between the students and hoped to find out how that interaction affected what they wrote. During this time I was more of an observer than a participant. I didn't want to participate directly in their decisions about written language use. Since I was the classroom teacher, it was easy for them to assume that I would tell them what to do or would answer their questions. But I was interested in finding out how they would go about solving their questions about written language. So I would redirect the question back to them or suggest that they ask their writing partner or the other students who were sitting at the table with them.

Every day I selected a different bilingual student to observe. I would sit next to the student as he or she began to write. I then followed the student as he or she selected someone with whom to share the journal. I observed their interactions and took notes on their writing as they shared their journals.

After I had the opportunity to observe and tape the twelve bilingual students, I began again to write and share my journal with the students. I realized that writing in my journal alongside my students gave me an opportunity to interact with them in a manner not possible when I was only observing them. At the beginning of the year I had written in my journal as a way to introduce dialogue journal writing to the students and to show them the high priority that I placed on the journal writing.

Now I was writing in my journal again in order to become a direct participant in the interaction that I was interested in observing.

At the beginning of my observations I didn't want to interrupt the interaction between the students. But after several months of observations, issues besides biliteracy attracted my interest. I began to wonder about spelling strategies, the role of social interaction in written language concept development, and code switching in writing. Whenever I saw these issues highlighted in the students' interactions, I would question them about what they were doing. I felt that I had been a passive observer long enough to gain a sense of their interaction. Now I was interested in understanding their thinking as they wrote and talked about what they had written. I tried to do this by asking them why they wrote something a certain way or why they had decided to react the way they did to their partners' suggestions or comments. (Later in the chapter I list some examples of the kinds of questions I asked.) The children didn't find it unusual that I was asking them questions while they were writing. They expected the teacher to be interested in what they were doing. It would have been more unusual for me to be a passive observer, not asking any questions.

The students enjoyed and looked forward to their turn to sit with me at one of the tables to talk and share our journals. There would almost always be other students at the table who would join our conversation, and our writing time was full of talk about our topics and the events in our lives that we were writing about or other anecdotes that we shared.

Three examples from my classroom illustrate how these experiences also permitted evaluation to emerge as a part of this process. The first example shows my evaluation of the development of Don's spelling strategies. The second highlights my evaluation of code switching in children's writing. The last looks at my evaluation of the instructional activity of dialogue journals.

EVALUATION OF DON'S SPELLING STRATEGIES

I was concerned about Don's spelling development because his spelling ability was progressing at a much slower rate than average for the class. When it was Don's turn to be observed, I made a point of observing his spelling strategies. What I saw helped me understand and feel better about Don's spelling development.

The students in my class used a spelling strategy that made use of their knowledge of the initial sounds of their names and of popular childhood figures such as E.T. Don often used this strategy. He began by looking at the student name cards that were taped above the alphabet. Above each letter of the alphabet I had placed a card on which the students had correspondingly written their names. First names and last names were written on separate cards. As time went on, Don was able to make use of this knowledge of letter-sound correspondence without having to look at the cards. He was able to use the students' names as a mnemonic device in order to help him remember and use initial sounds. While writing, Don would exchange information about how to spell a word by saying, "*r* like in Richard," "*a* like in Anthony," "*t* like in Tony." Don also used the dictionaries in the classroom, and more often than the other students. In addition Don used as resources for his spelling his previous writing in his journal.

On one occasion Don wanted to spell my name in his journal. He was writing about the time I had given his rabbit some food. As he got to the place where he was going to write my name, he stopped writing and started turning pages in his journal. He found a page where he had previously written my name. He then copied my name onto the page where he was writing about his rabbit. I then asked him how he had been able to spell my name on the previous page. He told me that another student had helped him spell it. Don often made use of his classmates as resources for spelling, but this time he was able to spell my name without asking for help from his friends. After using his journal writing as a spelling resource a few more times, he won't have to turn the pages to look for the spelling of my name; he will have learned how to spell it without relying on any outside resources. Don's spelling strategy is an example of learning in the zone of proximal development. The zone of proximal development is that area of learning in which someone is able to do something with the help of more capable peers. "It defines those functions that are not yet matured but are in the process of maturation. It is the level of potential development" (Vygotsky, 1978, p. 86). Using this strategy Don moves from the point where he must ask his friends how to spell my name (help is provided by more capable peers) to where he is able to help himself by seeing how he had previously spelled it in his journal (help through the symbolic system of writing) to where he will be able to spell my name without having to look at his journal (Don as an independent speller of my name).

Another spelling strategy that Don used was to consult the writing in other people's journals. One time the girl with whom he was sharing his journal was writing about getting to use the reading loft in the reading teacher's room. Don wrote in her journal, "¿Qué es una loft?" (What is a loft?) As he was writing in his own journal he needed to use the word *loft*, so he looked for the place in his partner's journal where she had written the word. He then copied it into his own journal.

Observation of this kind yields richer information than a conventional spelling test. This information makes it possible to take more facts into consideration when I have to evaluate Don's spelling ability. A spelling test would have been able to tell me only which of certain words Don knows how to spell and which he doesn't. Instead I was able to learn about the different strategies that Don uses when he needs to spell a word that he doesn't know. Before evaluating Don's spelling ability I had been concerned about his slow spelling development compared to that of the other children. After learning about his spelling strategies I was relieved because I saw that Don was making use of different re-sources in the classroom—dictionaries, environmental print, his own knowledge of sound-symbol relationships through the mnemonic of students' names—and asking for help from his friends. When I learned that Don was making use of such a wide variety of strategies, I felt that his spelling ability would continue to grow because he had different options to try and because he was moving toward being able to spell the words that he was learning without the help of his friends.

EVALUATION OF CHILDREN'S CODE SWITCHING

Another area that I began to focus on was code switching in children's writing. (For an example of such code switching, see Figure 5–1.) Since mine was a bilingual class, the students were able to switch back and forth from Spanish to English as they were talking to one another or to me. There are many studies that look at children's code switching in oral language (Duran, 1981) but very few about code switching in children's writing (Edelsky, 1986). I decided to focus on this area because I thought that it might give me valuable information about the choices that the children were making in using English or Spanish in oral and written language. As a result I would have a clearer idea about their development of biliteracy. I was also interested in discovering how individuals varied in their use of Spanish and English in their writing, for I had noticed that some students seemed to code switch more than others.

An example of code switching in writing involved two first-grade girls. They were writing back and forth to each other as I sat next to them observing and audio-taping their interaction. Mary had just finished reading her narrative to Rosalinda. The narrative was written entirely in Spanish. Rosalinda then wrote back to Mary, "A mi me gusta la canción Yes o No" (I like the song yes or no). Rosalinda wanted Mary to tell her if she liked the song that they had mentioned in their writing. Mary was to indicate her answer either by writing her response or by circling the word *yes* or the word *no*. This type of opinion survey was widely used by the children in their journals. When Rosalinda read back what she wrote to Mary, she orally substituted the word *sí* for *yes* even

---

Figure 5–1 *An Example of Code Switching*

ANOCE mí PApA	Last night my father
me i va a dar	was going to give me
un dolr	a dollar
Y NO me do	and he didn't
DiNero	give me money
AND HiS	and he's
NNS mí DAD	nice my dad
THe eND Mar. 7	The end.

though she had written the English word *yes* in Mary's journal. Mary noticed that Rosalinda had written "yes" but read it as "*sí*." She told Rosalinda, "Así no se pone sí" (That's not how you write "*sí*"). Mary then erased Rosalinda's "yes" and wrote "*sí*." (Since the word *no* is spelled the same in Spanish and English and is pronounced almost identically, it was not an issue in their discussion.)

I then asked Mary why she had erased Rosalinda's "yes." Mary said, "Porque aquí era en Spanish" (Because here it was in Spanish). Notice that Mary code switched the last word, saying "Spanish" instead of "*español*." She meant that until Rosalinda had written the word *yes* in her journal, the whole narrative and written dialogue had been in Spanish. I then asked Rosalinda, "¿Cuándo escribes en español, puedes escribir en inglés?" (When you write in Spanish, can you write in English?) Rosalinda nodded her head yes. Without my having to ask her, Mary said, "Yo no" (Not me). I then asked Rosalinda, "¿Y por qué tú sí? (And why do you do it?) Rosalinda then answered, "Porque también es como una canción (Because it's also like a song). I'm not sure what she meant by that. Maybe she was saying that when you're talking in one language you can then start singing in the other, or she might have been referring to a specific song that contained code switching. I'm reasonably certain that by using songs to back up her opinion, she was saying that code switching was very common for her in oral language and was saying by implication that if you can code switch in oral language, you can also code switch in written language. She then said, "Porque si no quieres escribir en inglés puedes escribir en español" (Because if you don't want to write in English, you can write in Spanish). Here she was pointing out the role of choice in language use.

Later that day I asked Mary and Rosalinda separately about their opinions of code switching in writing. Both of them were able to summarize their views. Rosalinda said, "If I want to I can." Again she was saying that code switching in writing is a personal choice, like code switching in speaking. Mary said, "Cuando rayo en inglés o español no me gusta que me rayen en el otro" (When I write in English or in Spanish, I don't like them to write in the other one). Mary stressed the "no me gusta" (I don't like it) part of her answer. She was saying that when a text in her journal was written in one language, she didn't like the classmate with whom she was sharing to switch to the other language.

Both Mary and Rosalinda code switched very often when they were speaking. But in this case written language allowed Mary to be able to monitor the written conversation in a way that isn't possible in an oral conversation. She was able to do this because she had a graphic record of the written conversation in her journal. When Rosalinda wrote the word *yes*, Mary was able to see it and read it. She was also able to see that the remainder of the text was written entirely in Spanish. The word *yes* stood out. The written dialogue was also different from an oral dialogue because it was recorded in a journal. Mary owned the journal, and she could make decisions about what was going to be in her journal. Because she and her partner were writing in Mary's journal, Mary was able to erase the word *yes* and write the word *sí* without having to ask Rosalinda for permission. In other words, Mary "didn't like it," so she erased it.

This example demonstrates the difference of opinion that can exist between two students when it comes to code switching in writing. Both of the students were able to back up their position, Rosalinda by comparing code switching in writing to code switching in oral language (songs) and Mary by saying that she didn't like to see a switch in writing from one language to the other. I was surprised to learn that children as young as these first graders were able to express their opinions about language use as clearly as they did. These children had very clear and very different ideas about code switching. Being present during this interaction and being able to talk to them about it while they were writing and afterwards gave me the opportunity to learn their views on code switching, views I would not have been able to learn about through other forms of evaluation.

Code switching in oral language is very common in the Hispanic community in which these children live. The opinions that both of these first-grade girls expressed reflect common views in the community. Mary's opinion that one shouldn't switch languages is held by many people who feel that if someone is speaking in one language they should then complete what they are talking about in that language and not switch back and forth between languages. Other people hold more relaxed attitudes towards code switching similar to Rosalinda's, that code switching is a common part of the communicative behavior of bilingual speakers. Rosalinda and Mary helped me to think about the influence that language use in the community has on language use in the classroom, that the different patterns of language use found in the community are present in the classroom. They also helped me review my opinions about code switching. I code switch often in speaking and writing. My own oral and written language use in the classroom is also part of the community's language patterns. My students' opinions of language use helped me realize that I would have to look not only at what was going on inside the classroom but also at the literacy events outside the classroom. I interviewed my students' parents to find out about their experiences and their siblings' experiences with reading and writing at home. Those findings supported my growing understanding of emergent biliteracy.

EVALUATION OF DIALOGUE JOURNALS

As a participant-observer during the writing of dialogue journals I was able to evaluate not only the children's writing but also the use of dialogue journals as an instructional activity. (For an example of such a journal, see Figure 5–2.) One of the purposes of dialogue journals is to provide a context in which social interaction among students of different academic and linguistic abilities can take place. This context provides opportunities for biliteracy and the development of written

Figure 5–2 *A Dialogue Journal (Excerpt)*

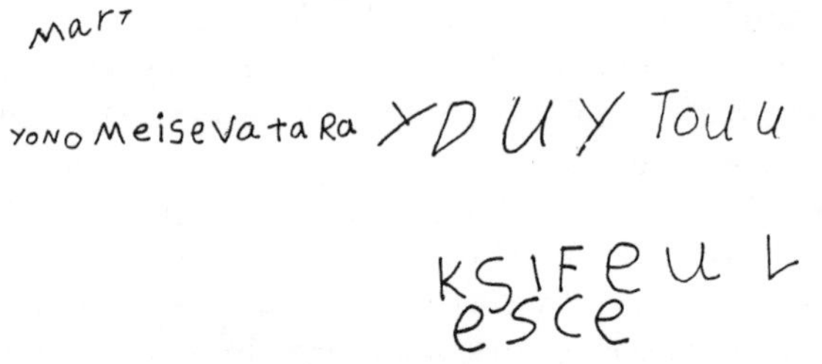

мАгт

yoно меiseVataRa ХР U Y Touu

KSIFеuL
esce

Lupe: Yo no me quise levantar en esta mañana.
       (I didn't want to get up this morning.)
Luis: Why didn't you want to get up?
Lupe: Because I feel lazy.

language concepts (Teberosky, 1982). It also provides an opportunity for the students to work in zones of proximal development with one another. In these zones the students are able to work on aspects of literacy learning in collaboration with more capable peers (Vygotsky, 1978). My observations of students writing together in their journals provided many examples of their sharing their ideas of the written system with one another. Such examples include the first exploratory use of cursive writing in their journals by some first graders as well as the exploration of the relationships between intonation and punctuation by second graders. The participant aspect of participant observation allowed me firsthand experience in the interchange of ideas about writing. This took place when I wrote in my own journal and then shared it with a student. When I was directly involved in writing in my own journal and responding to another, I had the opportunity to be directly involved in the interaction, not as a teacher observing my students but as one of the many people in the classroom writing and talking about one another's journal entries. This direct participation allowed me to evaluate the effectiveness of dialogue journals as a means for the interchange of written language concepts.

One such example involved Mónica and myself. Through this interaction I was able to get a glimpse into her view of adults as users of written language. Mónica had written in her journal about her three-year-old brother, José. In her journal entry Mónica had mentioned that she called her brother a "dum-dum." When Mónica had finished reading her journal entry to me, I wrote a question in her journal asking her whether her brother called her any names. We then initiated an oral and written conversation about her brother's language learning:

ME: ¿Le dijiste dum-dum a tu hermanito? (Did you call your brother a dum-dum?)

MÓNICA: Sí porque se miraba como un crazy. (Yes, because he looked like a crazy.)

ME: ¿Qué te dice tu hermanito a ti cuando se quiere reir de ti? (What does your brother call you when he wants to laugh at you?)

MÓNICA: Titopo. (baby talk)

ME: ¿Qué quiere decir eso? (What does that mean?)

MÓNICA: Yo creo que, ha-ha! Que fea! (I think, ha-ha how ugly!)

ME: ¿Y cómo aprendió decir eso? (And how did he learn to say that?)

MÓNICA: No sé pero mí papi le anda diciendo muchas cosas. (I don't know, but my dad is telling him a lot of things.)

ME: ¿Y cómo sabe lo que quiere decir las palabras? (And how does he know what the words mean?)

MÓNICA: Porque yo lo leyó. (Because I read them to him.)

ME: Pero yo estaba hablando de palabras cuando están platicando. (But I was talking about words when you're speaking.)

MÓNICA: Oh, yo no sabía, pero sí estás libre. (Oh, I didn't know, but you're free.)

ME: ¿De qué estás hablando cuando dices que estoy libre? (What are you talking about when you say that I'm free?)

MÓNICA: De que tienes muchas palabras tú. Pero no se que tienes mucho libre de palabras. (That you have a lot of words. But I don't know that you have a lot of free words.)

ME: ¿Cómo que libre? (What do you mean by free?)

MÓNICA: Pues libre de que tienes muchas palabras en tu mente. Pero no se que yo tendrá. (Well, free in that you have a lot of words in your mind. But I don't know if I'll have any.)

ME: ¿Sabes si tienes palabras en tu mente? (Do you know if you have words in your mind?)

MÓNICA: No se. (I don't know.)

ME: ¿Entonces cómo sabes que yo tengo palabras en mi mente? (Then how do you know that I have words in my mind?)

MÓNICA: Porque hablas mucho. (Because you talk a lot.)

ME: ¿Y tú no hablas mucho? (And you don't talk a lot?)

MÓNICA: Sí, pero no tanto. (Yes, but not that much.)

ME: ¿Y el José tiene palabras libre o de qué clase? (And José, does he have free words or what kind?)

MÓNICA: Babies' palabras, no más. (Only babies' words.)

ME: ¿Y entiendes palabras de babies? (And do you understand babies' words?)

MÓNICA: Pues no más de José. (Well, only José's.)

During recess, which followed our writing time, I asked Mónica more questions about what she meant by "free words." From that conversation, along with what we wrote about in her journal, I was able to piece together a rough idea of what she meant. She was using "free words" to mean the speaking, reading, and writing vocabulary available to a person from his or her knowledge without having to rely on outside resources such as dictionaries. Before this interchange with Mónica, I had never wondered how young children might think about what must seem to them the impressive number of words an adult can say, read, and write without seeming to have to consult any resources. I'm still not quite sure why Mónica chose to use the image of "free words" to describe her conception of adult knowledge of oral and written language, but it had some important metaphoric meaning to her.

Once again, as happened when I began to think about the development of biliteracy, I was presented with a question by one of my students. How do children view adults' knowledge of the written system (especially the influential adults in their lives such as parents and teachers), and how does it influence the way they view and approach literacy? I'm still thinking about that question. Mónica helped me evaluate the usefulness of dialogue journals as a context in which to challenge and expand not only children's written language concepts but also the teacher's. I could evaluate my purpose in using dialogue journals not only by observing what the children were learning about written language but also by being able to participate directly in the activity myself. This direct participation made it possible for me to expand my own knowledge of children's views of written language, and as a result I found out through firsthand experience that the journals were providing an effective context for the development of written language concepts.

CONCLUSION

The children's journals in my classroom introduced me to evaluation as a two-way street. They did this by forcing me to examine my assumptions about the way in which bilingual children develop biliteracy. Realizing my lack of understanding made it possible for me to assume the role of a learner and to allow my students to show me what they were doing during literacy events. Evaluation calls upon the teacher to learn not only about what his or her students know and are learning but also to learn about his or her conceptions about how children use and expand what they know. Becoming a participant-observer gave me the opportunity to learn about my students and also about my own ideas of the development of biliteracy. It put me into the interaction taking place between the children, and sometimes between the children and myself, as they were writing and talking about their writing. Throughout the school year, through this interaction I was able to learn about my student's literacy learning by observing and participating with them in situations in which they were using written language for meaningful purposes and in which they could make use of all the resources available to them. When I learned about Don's spelling strategies, I realized that he made greater use of different kinds of resources for spelling than most of the other students in the class. By using a wide variety of resources, he was expanding his knowledge of written language. When he used the dictionary, he used his knowledge of alphabetical order; his use of his classmates' names utilized his knowledge of letter-sound relationships; searching through his journal for a word that he wanted to spell made use of his knowledge of reading. Don helped me learn that spelling is not just a narrow use of written language knowledge but that it is tied to different aspects of our language knowledge.

The code-switching episode with Rosalinda and Mary helped me to learn about the variations that exist among speakers and about the ability of young children to express their views of language use. The exchange between Mónica and myself helped me to think about children's conceptions of adult literacy. My experience with my students has helped me to learn about the development of literacy in children. But equally important, it has shown me that I have much to learn about children's use of oral and written language and that evaluation is a two-way street in which teachers can evaluate not only their students' learning but also their own.

WHOLE LANGUAGE, TEXAS STYLE

John W. Woodley / Carol E. Woodley

In September Janet's second grade highlights the works of Tomie DePaola, author of *Strega Nona, The Popcorn Book*, and *Nana Upstairs, Nana Downstairs*. During the month the children learn about writing and illustrating books. DePaola books are read to the children; the children read them on their own and to one another; some children begin writing books of their own for "publication"; others relate to the experiences of characters in the stories and begin talking about books in a personal way. The class writes and sends birthday greetings to the author, whose birthday is in September.

Later in the year, Janet and the class visit an exhibit of the works of Chinese artisans at a local museum. This sparks a high level of interest. The children spend the next few weeks investigating topics that relate to China and Chinese traditions. By Chinese New Year the children want to expand their interest in China even further. In celebration of the Chinese New Year a Chinese speaker visits the class and discusses celebration of the new year in his homeland. A cooking experience allows members of the class to stir-fry and taste Chinese cuisine. A large Chinese kite streams across the room; samples of Chinese writing are examined by the children and later used to decorate the room.

Janet is completing her first year as a teacher in the state of Texas, though she has taught more than ten years at other grade levels in other parts of the United States. Her whole language program has evolved over the ten years she has been teaching. Like all effective teachers, she has creatively met and resolved many challenges. What Janet faces now in her new teaching position in a large school district north of Dallas is recent restrictive state-level legislation.

The laws and regulations established by the state legislature and the education agency in Texas reach into many aspects of education at all levels: what is to be taught, how often report cards are to be issued, the minimum number of minutes per week each academic area must be taught. In addition, the laws are extended and interpreted by each school district.

This is the story of how Janet maintains the integrity of her whole language program while still fulfilling the school district's version of the state regulations. It documents the approaches Janet takes to evaluating and reporting grades for her second graders.

THE CURRENT REQUIREMENTS

Teachers in Texas are required to teach "essential elements." These are goals that strongly influence the curricular framework whereby school districts develop the objectives for each grade level. Janet's district requires grades on report cards to be stated in percentages ranging from fifty to one hundred. Texas requires that school districts throughout the state issue report cards once every six weeks using either letter grades or numerical forms. Representing growth and development in percentages over so short a period in all language areas is very difficult. Janet faced a dilemma. Can a whole language teacher evaluate the progress children are making according to her own criteria while complying with such requirements for report cards? What types of records should be kept to serve as a basis for issuing report cards every six weeks while maintaining a whole language program?

This difficult task made it necessary for Janet to reconsider carefully the principles essential to her whole language program so that she could formulate decisions about evaluation in her classroom, meet state and district requirements, and remain true to the integrity of her whole language program—doing what's best for kids. Janet created guidelines based on her principles of whole language to help her develop her evaluation system:

- Language is essential to human learning.
- Reading, writing, speaking, and listening support learning in all curricular areas and support one another.
- Grading and evaluating are not the same. Grades are based on evaluations in the classroom, and the learners must understand how the two are related. Evaluation is ongoing—continuing from moment to moment, activity to activity.
- The context of language use is whole, meaningful, and natural. Kidwatching serves as the basis for further instruction and experiences.
- Language use is purposeful. In evaluation, the language context and process in which each product is completed are considered. Work is evaluated with regard to each child's purpose and the degree to which that purpose is met.
- Language learners generalize strategies from one situation to another. Evaluation emphasizes each learner's expanding competence as a language user.

- All language learners continuously develop language proficiency. Evaluation is based on each child's growth.
- Respect is the core around which the whole language classroom is built. Evaluation is based on respect for each learner. Criteria for assignments must be clear to the students. Those criteria must also be the criteria by which an assignment is evaluated.

THE CLASSROOM SETTING

Thematic units revolving around the works of Tomie DePaola or the Chinese New Year provide the children opportunities to engage in learning that far exceed the essential elements for the second grade. The children vary in how much they learn from each experience. When children write birthday greetings to an author, some may learn the form of a friendly letter while others become involved in discussions about U.S. geography, the United States Postal Service, the social function of letters, and writing for the specific audience of a letter.

As a result, plans for each lesson include several of the district's essential elements rather than only one. Planning becomes a matter of identifying the types of experiences some children are likely to have during any class activity and then noting how these correspond to the required objectives.

Each Monday Janet is required to submit written lesson plans to the principal's office. Each lesson outlined in the week's plans contains code numbers identifying the essential elements incidental to that lesson. This enables the principal to recognize that the teacher has addressed the required elements. Janet knows that the essential elements are not the mainstay or even a significant part of her program.

All children in Janet's class are able to learn from the instructional program to a degree appropriate for each one. Contracts (written agreements regarding what tasks are to be accomplished) between the teacher and individual children or groups of children become a way of encouraging the children to respond in their own ways. Janet uses individual conferencing and subsequent contracts to organize the children's learning. The children and teacher plan what will be happening in the classroom over a given period of time.

Whole-class instructional activities grow out of needs identified through individual or group conferences.

Janet's children are actively involved in language situations that promote questions about language that many children do not encounter until they are quite a bit older. At one point, when Janet was being formally evaluated, the children became involved in a discussion of how, why, and when quotation marks are appropriate. The discussion lasted several minutes and entered into a serious exploration of the differences between direct and indirect quotes. The evaluator, whose background was in secondary English, commented on how impressed she was by the discussion.

These discussions are not limited to only the "brightest" or "best" students. When accepted and respected for what they are able to do, all children, including children previously identified as "slow" or "low achievers," initiate such discussions.

STUDENT SELF-EVALUATION, PEER EVALUATION

In her discussions with the children, the teacher includes opportunities for the children to react to their own work. The procedures for self-evaluation vary from situation to situation. Some self-evaluations are conducted through oral discussion; others are written reactions. Some self-evaluations are guided by the child's criteria; other self-evaluations are guided by teacher-initiated questions.

Children can provide information on their own strengths and needs that is sometimes missed through kidwatching.

Late in the school year Janet showed her children their journals from earlier in the year and compared them with current journals. In a group self-evaluation session the children drew up a list of differences in their own journal writing:

1. Chris has become a better speller.
2. Damon has become a better writer. He writes more now.
3. Porsha saw a lot of writing.
4. Samantha is a better reader because she read it after she wrote it.
5. Michael is a good artist. He likes his journal.
6. At first Mina had lots of words wrong (spelling) and now she doesn't.
7. Linda has become a better writer.
8. Long likes to write in his journal.
9. Andy became a better writer because he writes more now. He doesn't skip big lines.
10. Emanda's handwriting became better.
11. At first Sheila didn't know how to spell a lot of words and she left off words so it didn't always make sense. Now she spells more correctly and it makes sense.
12. At first Rosa did not make sense. Now her writing does.

As the children finished this peer-evaluation period, Janet asked how many of them intended to keep journals during the summer. Most of them indicated that they would. If the purpose of education is to help develop independently motivated learners, readers, and writers, then perhaps the most important evaluation of this writing will not be completed for years to come.

TEACHER STUDENT EVALUATION

Janet carefully maintains files of the children's writings so that she can document the written language development of each child in several ways. For example, she examines each child's writing from a developmental perspective, looking for growth over time. She collects writing samples from each child and considers development across several samples rather than simply from one sample to another. She explains to the children that language performance involves many different abilities at one time; for example, as they write stories, they use their handwriting in telling the story. Yet they also select and organize their ideas, choose appropriate language to present those ideas, decide when and how elaboration of ideas or concepts is appropriate, spell words, use sentence structure—all as a way of sharing their ideas with somebody else.

To facilitate the frequent grading Janet is required to do, she has developed her own credit system. At least once a week she collects writing samples that the children know will be graded. The children are provided with the scoring system ahead of time. As she looks at the writings of the children she asks herself, "On a scale of one to five, what development do I see in this child's writing?" This scale becomes a holistic score for the children's progress. The holistic scores are based on the degree to which the children have completed the task they set out to do, their effectiveness in expressing themselves, and any growth or development that the writing demonstrates:

> This paper is from Susan. Compared to what some of the other children have done, it may not be great. But compared to what Susan has done before, this has to be 5 for her.

Janet keeps detailed anecdotal records. Observation checklists, quickly written notes of children's progress, and specific records of whether the children participated in an editing conference or completed a research contract all become part of the record-keeping system.

Differentiating between writing and reading for grading purposes becomes a difficult task when these two language processes are integrated as they are in the whole language classroom. It seems that whenever the children read, they also write. Certainly, whenever they write, they also read what they write.

Janet identifies certain activities that reveal information about reading processes. She lets the students know that these activities will count toward their reading grade. For example, when the children finish reading a book, she asks them to write a response to the book. Student book responses are available for other children to use in selecting what they will read. Janet uses her holistic scoring of the students' book reviews as a way of examining and documenting growth in reading comprehension.

Another example of an activity labeled reading is cooperative cloze, an activity that involves groups of children in completing a cloze passage through cooperative efforts. Oral discussion among group members recorded anecdotally often provides insightful evidence of comprehension.

GRADING STUDENTS

Janet is required to report a reading grade, a language grade, a composition grade, a spelling grade, and a handwriting grade for each student at the end of each six-week period. For the purpose of grading she must separate the language processes that are integrated in her whole language classroom and translate her holistic scores into percentages. Janet approaches this task quite simply.

The state of Texas specifies that 90 to 100 percent is an A, so a holistic score of 5 is assigned the percentage value of 95. A holistic score of 5, then, reflects a student's high level of performance. A holistic score of 4 is assigned the percentage value of 85 for a B, and so on down the scale of scores. As a matter of administrative policy, no score lower than 50 is assigned. The percentage values from each graded product are averaged to arrive at a percentage score for each grading period. Thus, the reporting requirement is fulfilled each grading period without Janet's having to change her teaching style or philosophy.

The integrity of the whole language program has been maintained; the teacher and students clearly see student growth; and students understand, have participated in, and can articulate the arbitrary grading process.

Students are able to use their report card grades to say to their parents, "I got 80 percent in reading this grading period. But I know that I'm continuing to grow!"

ADMINISTRATIVE TEACHER EVALUATION

The context in which Janet evaluates and grades her students can be better understood in the context of how she is evaluated as a teacher.

Though Janet is the first teacher in her school to refer to herself as a whole language teacher, the principal supports her whole language program. As the state requires, Janet is regularly evaluated by the principal and an outside evaluator. Support from her principal has proven to be a great asset as she works within the requirements for evaluation.

Texas calls its evaluation system a "model of effective teaching." Evaluation of teachers in Texas is based on performance in five domains: instructional strategies, classroom management and organization, presentation of subject matter, learning environment and growth, and professional growth and responsibilities. During the course of a single forty-five-minute observation period, the evaluator is expected to note fifty-five different characteristics of the teacher's performance during class and later rate the teacher on sixteen additional characteristics. These evaluations serve as a basis for decisions regarding contract renewal and advancement in a career ladder scheme.

The tool for evaluation of teachers leaves considerable room for interpretation. For example, one characteristic evaluated is preventing "off-task behavior." During one observation period, members of Janet's class were engaged in various stages of writing. Joey was a reluctant writer. In his writing process he slipped off his chair twice, regaining his seat after each occurrence. No other member of the class reacted to his behavior during these episodes. After this Joey settled down and started writing. Janet recognized Joey's activity as part of his process of getting ready to write. She did not comment or react to his behavior.

The evaluator saw only off-task behavior. This gave Janet the opportunity to discuss her evaluation of Joey with the evaluator.

Janet approaches her evaluation with two goals in mind. First, she is trying to educate those evaluating her. She shares information regarding the nature of a whole language classroom, her principles of whole language that provide the basis for her practices, the approaches she takes to encourage children to learn, and her ways of involving the students in continuous self-evaluation. She shares articles, provides written explanations of her approach to teaching, and discusses her class with evaluators in casual conversations. She also invites her principal into her classroom to become involved in class activities such as cooking and puppet shows and to participate in conferences with parents. Second, she tries to demonstrate to those evaluating her that what she is doing is based on sound knowledge and understanding of language learning and learning processes.

Any system of evaluation that emphasizes a narrowly defined act of teaching rather than what the students learn assumes that teaching is a system of easily defined behaviors. Whole language teachers emphasize learning and using language. Children's growth and development in language use or intellectual functioning are difficult, if not impossible, to identify every six weeks or by a measure of percentages. A basic tenet of a whole language philosophy is that children develop at different rates and in different ways.

CONCLUSION

The predicament that Janet faces is not unique but it is extreme. Unfortunately it is a common situation facing other whole language teachers in Texas as well as in other states and school districts with defined prescriptive programs and evaluation systems.

Teaching to mandated essential elements, being evaluated according to an arbitrary design for effective teaching, and strictly adhering to a program of frequent quantified reporting of children's progress present complications for any whole language teacher. Janet has struggled, and continues to struggle, with her situation. She continues to maintain her professional integrity and to do what she knows is best for her students.

EVALUATION:
THE CONVENTIONS OF WRITING
Orysia Hull

Young children in our whole language classrooms embrace writing with much enthusiasm. Their teachers delight in the progress they observe during daily writing activities. They can see from the daily writing that their students are learning. Yet occasionally a question from a colleague or parent raises doubts about the value of the work that is achieved by these young writers.

Other teachers want to know if students in whole language classrooms are really learning. They wonder what constitutes significant growth, where in students' writing there is data to show it, and what method can be used to analyze and record this observable data. Parents ask, "Will my child learn skills such as grammar, spelling, and punctuation in this whole language approach?" They notice that the teacher does not mark every error with a red pencil, and they wonder why. They want to see evidence of their child's growth in writing and the teacher's awareness of this development. Both groups want to understand how whole language teachers and their pupils know that what they are doing is valuable.

Those on their way to becoming whole language teachers also want reassurance that the conventions of writing will be learned through meaningful, purposeful writing activities in which the process of writing is as important for diagnosis or evaluation as the final product. In Manitoba many teachers have utilized a very simple technique to supplement their ongoing evaluation and show evidence of increments of progress in the conventions of writing consistent with a whole language framework.

The teacher collects samples of student writing throughout the school year but makes a special effort at the beginning to keep a copy of every piece of writing from every child. If a student wants to take a piece home, copies are made for the teacher's cumulative files. These early pieces are an important basis for later comparison. At the end of the month the teacher reads through the samples of writing, and from every file or folder selects one for later use. It is important to pick one in which the student chose the topic and had a reasonable degree of autonomy in writing the piece. Writing samples that are highly teacher directed or that are the result of much teacher intervention are not as useful for evaluation because they may not reveal the strengths of the pupils as writers.

In the middle and again near the end of the school year each student's original piece is dictated back to him or her. These rewritings are compared and contrasted with the original, and with one another, to determine increments of progress. For young readers and writers there are several strong indicators. They include awareness of wordness, indicated by spaces between words; awareness of orthography, indicated by increasingly appropriate use of lowercase letters; awareness of sentenceness, indicated by beginning use of punctuation, capitalization at the beginning of sentences, and relation of form to clause structure. Teachers keep these in mind as they carefully review each piece. The procedure becomes a more formal version of kidwatching: it is the same for every child—for the special needs, average, or gifted student—though each is looked at for personal progress. Individualization enters in the different starting point for each one. For evaluation purposes each student's work is compared to his or her previous piece but not to that of other students in the class.

Figure 7–1 *Eli, Late Fall*

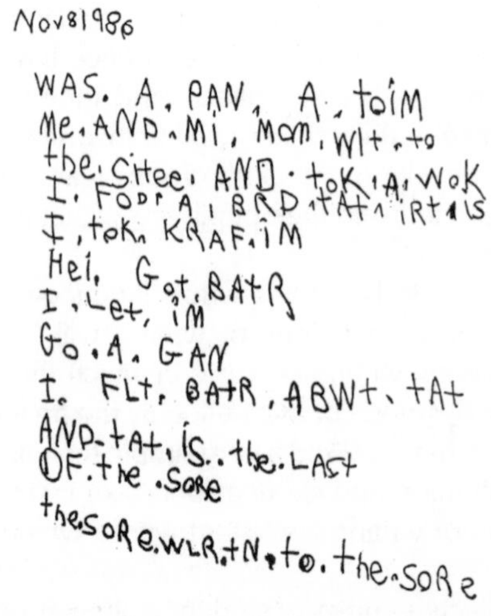

Figure 7–2 *Eli, Midwinter*

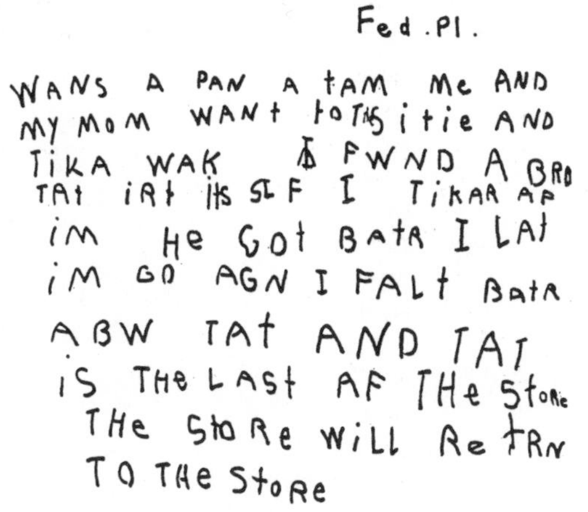

> Fed . Pl .
>
> WANS A PAN A tAM Me AND
> my MoM WANt toTHSitie AND
> TiKA WAK is PWND A BRo
> TAt iRt Hs SLF I TiKAR AP
> iM He Got BAtR I LAt
> iM Go AGN I FALt BAtR
> A BW TAt AND TAt
> iS THe LAst AF THe Stone
> THe StoRe WiLL ReTRN
> TO THe StoRe

Eli's writing samples illustrate how the technique is employed. At the time of writing he was a grade one student in Brandon, Manitoba. His teacher had some concerns about his progress, but she felt he was an enthusiastic writer and was pleased with his effort. Figure 7–1 shows his first example, written in his journal in late fall.

We can see that his story is written mainly in uppercase letters. We know that he has a sense of wordness since he is using a period to separate words. His spelling is mostly at the phonetic level. He knows that print is organized from top to bottom and left to right. From the way he begins and ends his piece, we know that he has an idea of how stories work. Eli wanted to write another segment to his story on the following day, but he couldn't remember "To be continued." Instead he wrote, "The story will return to the story."

In midwinter, when the piece was dictated back to him, he made some changes. (See Figure 7–2.) At first glance it is obvious that there are no periods between words. He now knows that conventionally, spaces separate words. He has moved from his invention for separating words to the social convention.

His spellings are now a closer approximation of the conventional form. Table 7–1 illustrates these changes.

Finally, at the end of the school year, the selection was dictated to him for the last time. (See Figure 7–3.) The appearance of Eli's writing had changed. He had better fine muscle control. The letters were not as large, and observation during the writing showed his effort to be less labored or difficult than it had been previously. Whereas virtually no punctuation had occurred in the second piece, in the last one the use of periods was conventional. Also, the move toward conventional spelling was dramatic. Almost every syllable now included a vowel. He knew

Table 7-1 *Eli's Spelling Changes*

November	February	Conventional Spelling
WAS	WANS	once
TOIM	TAM	time
MI	MY	my
WIT	WANT	went
Sitee	sitie	city
TOK	TIK	took
WOK	WAK	walk
FOD	FWND	found
is	its SLF	itself
A GAN	AGN	again
FLT	FALT	felt
SORE	STORe	story
WLR.TN	WiLL ReTRN	will return

that many words that end with the sound of the letter *e* are written with a *y*. "WANS A PAN A TAM" became "ONCE A Pohn a Time"; "Sitie" became "Sity"; and "WAK" became "Walk." Words such as *bird* and *self* now showed the use of a vowel where none had existed previously. Also, more lowercase letters appeared.

Figure 7-3 *Eli, End of School Year*

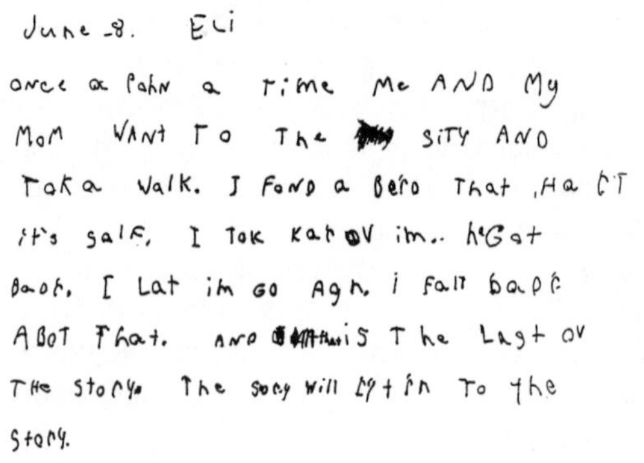

June 8.   Eli

once a Pohn a Time Me AND My
MoM VANt To The ~~bird~~ siTY ANo
Toka Valk. I FoND a Bero That ,Ha CT
it's salF. I Tok Kar OV im.. h'Got
Baof. I Lat im go Agn i Fall bapf
ABot That. Ano ~~th~~ is The Last ov
The story. The soey Will Lyt Pn To the
story.

Once upon a time me and my
mom went to the city and
took a walk. I found a bird that hurt
itself. I took care of him. He got
better. I let him go again. I felt better
about that. And that is the last of
the story. The story will return to the
story.

During the dictation, other significant occurrences were noted. First, he kept rereading or proofreading everything he had written. He kept checking to see if he had put down everything that was said. Second, when he came to the end, he commented that he should have used a phrase like "Tune in tomorrow" or "To be continued." He was critiquing his own writing.

As a final task, all three pieces were placed in front of him, and Eli was asked to comment. He became a self-evaluator; he could discern several significant improvements in his knowledge of conventions. Other changes that he did not notice were brought to his attention. He was pleased with his progress and through discussion was made more aware of what he was doing in writing. This self-evaluation procedure provided him an opportunity to revalue himself and to bring his knowledge of writing conventions and proofreading to a more conscious level.

This rewriting procedure is useful for evaluating progress in writing with all young children. Rochelle was a grade-one student in a suburb of Winnipeg, Manitoba. At the beginning of the school year, when asked to write in her journal, she chose to do her rendition of a Big Book that her class had been reading. It was a version of "Goldilocks and the Three Bears," written as a song. (See Figure 7–4.)

Much later in the year she chose to rewrite the same piece. The change was remarkable. (See Figure 7–5.) Her physical control over writing was much better, her spelling was conventional, and she made use of punctuation. She had gained control of the conventions of print through her reading and writing.

If pressured to show that children like Rochelle can spell words out of context too, the teacher, at three intervals during the school year, may take words from a child's story and use them as a spelling check.

Figure 7–4 *Rochelle's Version of "Goldilocks and the Three Bears"*

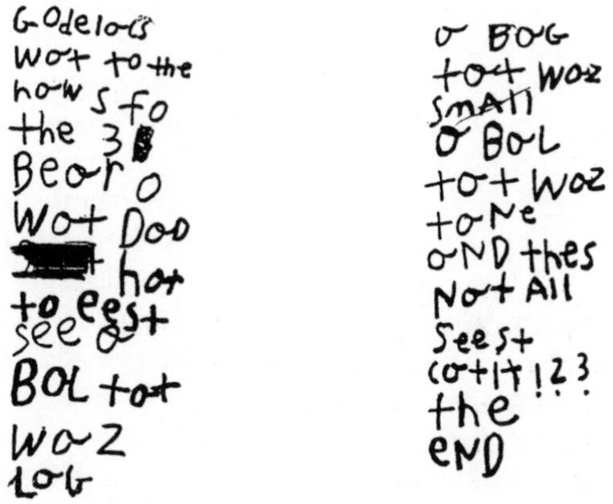

Figure 7–5 *A Later Version of Rochelle's Piece*

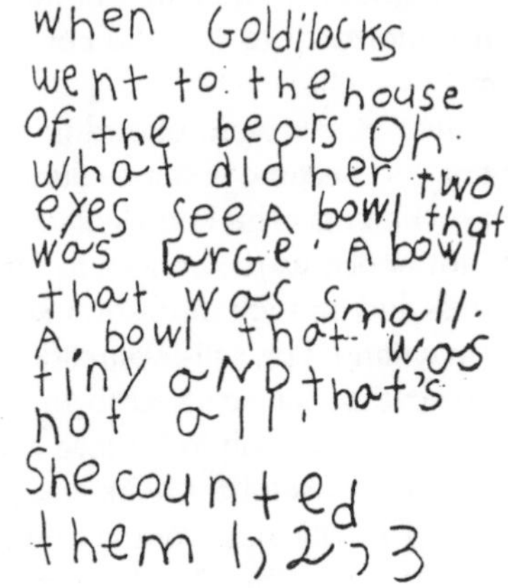

when Goldilocks
went to the house
of the bears Oh.
what did her two
eyes see A bowl that
was LarGe. A bowl
that was small.
A bowl that was
tiny anD that's
not all. that's
She counted
them 1) 2) 3

Usually these will include words common to traditional graded lists and others that show a personal, quite sophisticated vocabulary as well.

This is a quick way for the teacher to collect information that supports his or her belief that children are learning. With this data the teacher is able to convince critics that pupils are learning to spell in the context of writing and reading. He or she is able to show anyone who asks that the students are continuously developing conventional spelling while they are writing extensively and that memorizing word lists is not essential to improvement in spelling. If the students used only the words on graded spelling lists, their writing vocabulary would be extremely limited.

In collecting and examining these original and dictated samples, teachers are able to see what patterns are emerging in the classroom. If several students are putting dots between words to show that each one is a separate entity, the teacher knows that a minilesson on the use of spaces between words would be appropriate. He or she may choose to present the minilesson to the whole class so that other students can be peer tutors to those who might forget; more likely the teacher may form a small group specifically for this purpose. As the members of the group demonstrate the use of spaces in their writing, the teacher records this. The group is no longer called together for a minilesson.

Children's growth in the convention of writing can be recorded at the back of each pupil's writing folder. If other methods are used to collect student writing, teachers may wish to keep a complete central list and to record significant changes for each student. This list, in conjunction with close scrutiny of student writing, helps the teacher evaluate individual progress, class patterns, and the appropriateness of planning to meet student needs.

The dictated examples based on the students' original pieces are important for discussion with the children. The students become more aware of personal growth in the conventions of writing. This helps them to be more analytical toward their work during proofreading or editing.

These examples are important to the teacher. They provide information quickly through a technique that is easy to administer while validating the use of a whole language approach for literacy learning. This verifies for the teacher that what is happening at both the student and teacher level is working and can in good conscience be continued.

Perhaps more important, though, the dictated or rewritten examples illustrate to parents that their children are indeed learning. Instead of statistical data or grade-level scores, they are shown materials that they can readily comprehend. Any concerns or issues can be clarified or alleviated in discussion. Parents soon learn that whole language teachers don't forget about conventions in writing; they deal with them more effectively in their holistic activities.

Parents also learn that the teacher knows a lot about each child and is constantly working to meet student needs. This is probably one of the better public relations programs that any school could undertake. When parents are confident that their children are learning and that the teachers know what they're doing, they give tremendous support to the program.

Through the dictated examples based on a student's original efforts, teachers can demonstrate to everyone who is a stakeholder in a child's education that the conventions of writing, often perceived by the public as "skills," are being taught, learned, and assessed. At the same time, teachers continue to be consistent with a whole language point of view.

WHEN "SHUT UP" IS A SIGN OF GROWTH

Maureen Morrissey

After months of being exposed to English through stories, poems, songs, and a variety of other language experiences, third grader Manny still had not spontaneously spoken English. Our classroom atmosphere had immersed us in both English and Spanish. All the children, including Manny, were self-motivated and actively involved. On his own, however, Manny had not yet produced any English. I was afraid that our classroom environment was not stimulating Manny's second-language development. Then one day in our chaotic rush to get ready for lunch, when everybody was clamoring for a chance to do the before-lunch chores, Manny found his way to me and asked in plain English, "Can I pass the lunch tickets?" He must have misunderstood my surprised silence because he then looked at me with that knowing expression, rolled his eyes, and added, "Please?"

After complying with Manny's request, I quickly jotted down the date and this wondrous occurrence on a five-by-seven card with Manny's name on it. Already on the card were written other accomplishments of his:

9/28   Published first story.
10/19 Read Spanish schedule to John.
10/21 Pointed out new patterns to Carlos on patterned calendar.

As I replaced the card in the alphabetized stack along with the other kids' cards, I smiled to myself and thought, "I must talk to Manny about this later." I was pleased, not only for Manny but also for myself, because this occurrence reconfirmed my belief that the language-rich environment in our classroom supports all students' language growth in an encompassing yet individualized way.

How does this work? It starts on the first day of school, the very first activity of the year. Children wear name tags and are asked to fill in a short questionnaire with the names of classmates. The questionnaire is in English on one side and Spanish on the other.

> Find someone in the class who:
>   Is the same height as you.
>   Can read in Spanish and English, too.

> Escribe el nombre de alguien en la clase que:
>   (Write the name of someone in the class who)
>   No estaba en tu clase el año pasado.
>   (wasn't in your class last year)
>   Tiene la mano del mismo tamaño como la tuya.
>   (has the same size hand as you)

While I participate, I also note each student's reaction to the activity. Not only does this activity lead to engrossing discussions and graphing, but the completed forms also provide me with my first evaluative tool. David filled out the English side only, Jorge the Spanish side, Ana answered all questions on both sides, Manny answered one question only.

DOUBLE AGENDA

This is my double agenda (K. Goodman, 1986); students are so intimately involved in the process, they are neither aware nor concerned that I am evaluating their accomplishments or that they are involved in language learning. They are using language as a means to an end, and I am getting a true picture of their abilities at work. This insight on the teacher's part is the key to my classroom.

When the double agenda is in operation, the students' focus is on gaining and expressing knowledge and on solving their own problems, while mine is on guiding and evaluating academic growth in two languages and in the third-grade curriculum. For example, when we review the day's schedule, which alternates daily between English and Spanish, I notice that Jorge has begun to understand the English schedule. He asks questions about it in Spanish, but his dawning comprehension of English is obvious when he asks about the writing schedule for the day: "¿Puedo tener conferencía con Usted, Ms. Morrissey?" (Can I conference with you?)

The students listen to stories, literature, songs, poems, and text in both languages; read along on charts or in books; read silently and in small groups; write silently and in conference groups; discuss all kinds of subjects; write messages, stories, and letters.

Often students want to know what I'm jotting down, and I willingly share my views of their growth with them. They naturally delight in the positive attention to their achievements. It is thrilling to involve eight-year-olds in a brief discussion of one child's miscue. They learn in these discussions how to self-evaluate and discover that learning is an ongoing process and that errors are growth points. We laugh at one another and at ourselves, and then someone whom we consider an expert helps us learn. It never takes the class long to discover that, even though I am the teacher, I am certainly not left out of this process.

It is fun, and at times funny, to focus children on their own growth spurts. Mara is a good example. Since our classroom maintains a positive, encouraging atmosphere, it was natural for Blanca and Jessica to come running up and tattle that Mara had told them, "Shut up." I still laugh at the memory of the expressions on their faces when my eyes lit up and I exclaimed, "That's great!" These were Mara's first words in English. I explained my reaction to the two girls as we went over to tell Mara some nicer ways to say "Shut up" in English. She was receptive to our offers of new ways to express herself, and she also walked away armed with new English words to meet her need for quiet or to be left alone. Meanwhile, we had taken advantage of a teachable moment.

TEACHABLE MOMENTS, EVALUATIVE MOMENTS

Some teachers do not take advantage of teachable moments. They view such times as disruptions of their scheduled day. I see them as an important and integrated part of the curriculum. The key word here is *integrated*. In any classroom teachable moments happen often, and with them the *evaluative moment*, because the two are so closely associated that they are inseparable. Our classroom organization allows us to take advantage of most teachable or evaluative moments because they arise in the context of our activities. They generally start with a student's inquiry: "What time is it?" "Why did it rain at my Nana's house and not at mine?" "How does this work?" "How can I find a library book on horses?" Some teachable moments are followed through on immediately. Some I respond to quickly and jot them down in a notebook for further development.

By October my notes made it clear to me that many of my students could not tell time from a clock with hands. This grew into a unit on clock reading, a unit on multiplication of fives, and another unit on the history of clocks and the need for keeping time.

The teachable or evaluative moment is a growth point, a window of spontaneous insight for both my students and myself. The students' quest for immediate knowledge, and my encouragement, open doors that might otherwise never have been approached. This happens as often for individual students as it does for small groups and the whole class.

ANECDOTAL RECORDS

As these teachable or evaluative moments occur, I begin to expect more from each child, as well as from the class as a whole. The anecdotal notes that I keep on five-by-seven cards help me to know what the children know and can do. And they are an important aid in helping me guide progress. Mara's card reveals a sudden growth spurt two months after she arrived in our class from Magdalena, Sonora, Mexico:

11/4   First English words!!: "Shut up."
11/15 Named colors on the patterned calendar: orange, blue, black.
12/1   Shows a grasp of basic English words: numbers to 20, many colors, school words.
1/8   To Miguel, "That's my chair. It has my sweater."

Joe, a student I had labeled "predominant-English speaker" because of his lack of Spanish skills, has made marked progress in Spanish according to his card:

2/19 Volunteered to read schedule in Spanish.
2/25 Explained work to Favian in Spanish.
3/15 Shared a Spanish book with Antonio.

I now expect Joe to volunteer to participate in reading the daily schedule in either language and can depend on him to explain an activity to a Spanish-dominant student. He doesn't disappoint my expectations.

The anecdotal records come from the notebook I carry around all day. I jot down what I see the children doing informally. A day's notes look like this (brackets are for the reader's clarification):

4/21

Anel [average Spanish reading ability] and Marlena [low English reading ability] are partners in Lit. studies. Started with a tough English book, then switched to an easier Spanish one.

Joe and Antonio are Lit. studies partners in an English book.

Liz and Yamil picked too easy books in English. Need to conference.

Angelica and Laura tutored others in Math challenge activity in both English and Spanish.

The evaluation and noting of children's language use during informal moments shows true growth. When children are unaware that they are being evaluated, they tend to be more relaxed; I get a real view of their language growth. Since I do not follow students to lunch and recess and cannot hear their playground talk, I use the natural language events within the classroom in the context of our day. I listen to an unsuspecting group of mixed language-ability students learn to play a new math game, noting Blanca's use of Spanish, her second language, while Yolanda responds with attempts at English.

Students' growing control of the forms of writing arises from their understanding of the need for legibility, conventional spelling, and punctuation, among other means to better communication. As parents and teachers know well, children love to communicate. What better way to help children become more powerful communicators than to teach them to evaluate their own growth and that of their peers? Once children believe they own the process of their education, they strive harder to develop written expressions that communicate in a powerful way. Writing samples lead to minilessons and discussion of the writing process with kids.

When I saw that several students were at the beginning stages of developing the concept of periods and were ready to learn more about their use, six of us sat down together while other students were busy writing or discussing their writings or doing other writing-workshop activities. Our small group examined the use of periods in basal stories, favorite library books, and class-made books. We discussed why periods are necessary for the reader and how that makes it important to the writer as well. We went on to examine their own works in progress and inserted periods where they seemed necessary, on the basis of our previous explanations and discussions. I explained to the group that I now expected them to try to use their new knowledge even in informal writing and that they were free to come to a future lesson on periods if they, or I, felt the need.

I record which students attend minilessons on checklist sheets such as a class list with dated headings. I also make note of it on the students' five-by-seven cards and keep a close eye on progress in their future writing samples.

FORMAL EVALUATION

Formal evaluation also takes on many different faces, all of which affect future lesson plans. Writing samples photocopied monthly from stories, journal entries, and letters are formally evaluated as to mechanics and quality of first and second language. I keep an ongoing record of each child's writing. I record growth using a three-grade system: NE means there is no evidence of the skill in the piece of writing being evaluated; D means the skill is in developmental stages, showing a combination of appropriate and inappropriate use of the skill within the piece; and C means that the piece shows individual control over the skill being examined.

I evaluate growth in spelling by documenting the percentage of invented spelling and conventional spelling in each piece. I note changes in both high-frequency and low-frequency word use over time, as well as changes in second-language spellings.

Evaluating quality in writing is hard for me. I work very hard to separate my judgment of what I like from what is clear and concise and fits the child's intentions as stated in our conferences.

I document all this on a single form I've developed myself, adapted from the work of Barbara Flores (presented at an in-service in Tucson, Arizona, 1985). I am currently revising it to suit my changing needs.

Azucena is a Spanish-dominant bilingual child. The completed form in Figure 8–1 shows my documentation of Azucena's growth over two Spanish writing samples (Figure 8–2, A and B) as well as her first English writing sample (Figure 8–3). On the documentation form I use L1 to indicate the first language and L2 for the second. I evaluate each one for the qualities listed on the form and note additional significant features in the comments.

In September Michael wrote a very short, illegible piece with 5 percent conventional spelling. Writing samples from October and February show the change in handwriting, written expression, spelling, punctuation, and message. (See Figure 8–4, A and B). His growth is well documented (Figure 8–5).

Figure 8–1 *Evaluation Form for Azucena*

Name _Azucena_

	Date 9/4			Date 10/28			Date 1/88		
Writing Quality:	C	D	NE	C	D	NE	C	D	NE
Self-selected topics	L1			L2			L1		
Uses expansive vocabulary	L1			L2			L1		
Uses complex sentences	L1					L2	L1		
Experiments with different styles		L1		L2			L1		
Revision strategies		L1		L2			L1		
Writing Mechanics:									
Handwriting		L1		L2			L1		
Uses periods		L1				L2	L1		
Uses quotation marks			L1			L2			L1
Uses exclamation point			L1			L2			L1
Uses question marks			L1	L2			L1		
Uses capitalization	L1			L2			L1		
Grammar usage	L1			L2			L1		
Ratio and % invented spelling	2/17 (12%)			3/14 (21%)			22/182 (12%)		
Ratio and % conventional spelling	15/17 (88%)			11/14 (79%)			160/182 (88%)		

C = controls this   Primary language _Spanish_

D = developing this

NE = no evidence of this   Secondary language _English_

Comments: _Capitals after periods ~ Sept. cursive Oct._
English in diary ~ Oct. Question marks ¿ ? Jan.
No sign of accents ~ Jan.

Figure 8–2 *Two of Azucena's Spanish Writing Samples. A: September 1985. B: January 1986.*

Azucena Ochoa
Strawberry Shortcakes esta, en el campo.
Y la querian mator pero la salvaron.
Y isiero un pari.

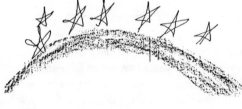

En el Rancho bibia una que
se llamaban Azucena y Manuel.
Ellos bibian alli y gorjito
el fartasma gorjito no espartaba a
nadie un dia los becinos salieron
y se les olbidó serar la
casa y unos ombres se metieron
a la casa. y se robaron las
cosas y luego los becinos bolbieron. y no encontraron nada de las cosas
nomas las cosas biejas ¿pero que pasa aqui
dijo Manuel ¿se an robado las cosa
dijo Azucena egue ablarle a la pole
dijo Manuel yo are algo dijo gorjito
el fartasma cuidado dijo lino el
gato se terdre cuidado le contesto
gorjito nosotras le ablaremos a
la policia dijo Manuel y le
ablaron a la policia bengan pronto.
dijo Manuel que pasa dijo el
policia ¿Nos an robado las cosa?
Dijo Manuel pero como dijo el policia
bera el bijo la la
Puerta bamos cragida
Dijo el pole cia y luego se puci
eron a buscarlo y luego lo atrar
y los echaron a la carcel y los
becinos les ajudaron a poner la
cosas y asi se acaba el cuento

EL QU
fin

A. Strawberry Shortcake is in the country.
And they wanted to kill her, but they saved her.
And they had a party.

B. Some people named Azucena and Manuel lived on a ranch. They lived there and Georgie the ghost. Georgie did not scare anyone. One day the neighbors went out and they forgot to close the house and some men went into the house and stole things and then the neighbors came back. And they did not find any of things only five old things but what happened here? said Manuel they have stolen the things? said Azucena we have to call the police said Manuel I will do something said Georgie the ghost careful said Lino the cat yes I will be careful answered Georgie we will call the police said Manuel and they called the police come quick Manuel said what happened said the police they have stolen our things? said Manuel but how? said the police we forgot to close the door we're on our way said the police and then they began to look for them and then they found them and put them in jail and the neighbors help them put their stuff and that's how the story ends
the end

Figure 8–3 *Azucena's First English Writing Sample*

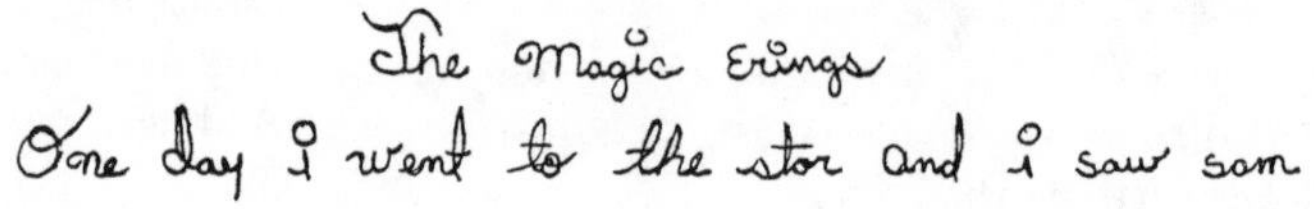

The Magic Erings
One day I went to the stor and i saw som

Shina entered third grade confident of her writing ability. During a conference Shina and I reviewed my evaluation of the September writing sample (Figure 8–6, A). Shina recognized her strengths and set goals for her own growth, documented in a sample collected in October (Figure 8–6, B). Shina's evaluation form is shown in Figure 8–7.

COMPLYING WITH DISTRICT AND STATE GUIDELINES AND TESTS

I have carefully adapted some checklists provided in prepackaged programs to the context of our daily activities in order to adhere to state- or district-mandated guidelines.

Figure 8–4 *Michael's Writing Samples. A: October. B: February.*

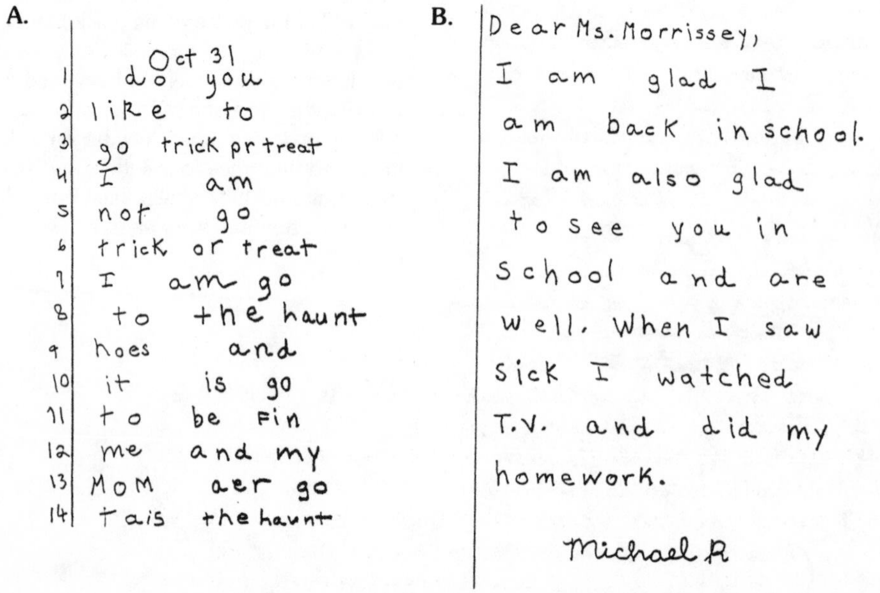

A.

```
            Oct 31
 1   do      you
 2   like      to
 3   go   trick pr treat
 4   I       am
 5   not    go
 6   trick or treat
 7   I   am go
 8   to   the haunt
 9   hoes     and
10   it    is  go
11   t o   be Fin
12   me   and my
13   MOM    aer go
14   t ais  the havnt
```

B.

Dear Ms. Morrissey,
I am glad I
am back in school.
I am also glad
to see you in
school and are
well. When I saw
sick I watched
T.V. and did my
homework.

Michael R

Figure 8–5 *Evaluation Form for Michael*

Name _Michael_

Writing Quality:	Date 9/87			Date 10/87			Date 2/88		
	C	D	NE	C	D	NE	C	D	NE
Self-selected topics		✓			✓			✓	
Uses expansive vocabulary			✓			✓			✓
Uses complex sentences			✓	✓			✓		
Experiments with different styles			✓	✓			✓		
Revision strategies			✓			✓			✓
Writing Mechanics:									
Handwriting		✓		✓			✓		
Uses periods			✓		✓		✓		
Uses quotation marks			✓		✓				✓
Uses exclamation point			✓		✓				✓
Uses question marks			✓		✓				✓
Uses capitalization			✓	✓			✓		
Grammar usage			✓	✓					✓
Ratio and % invented spelling	19/20 (95%)			7/40 (17.5%)			1/36 (3%)		
Ratio and % conventional spelling	1/20 (5%)			33/40 (82.5%)			35/36 (97%)		

C = controls this
D = developing this
NE = no evidence of this

Primary language _English_

Secondary language _Spanish_

Comments: _September – unintelligible sample, letter strings /conventional spelling_
October – use of word boundaries, numbered lines (?)
February – WOW! Control of period, use of comma after salutation, cursive name

One of our district-adopted English as a Second Language unit check-lists calls for certain words to be "mastered." The list includes *thirty, time, clocks, minute/hour hand,* and the numbers one through sixty. I used these words in the context of a whole-class discussion on time (previously noted as one of those teachable or evaluative moments). I wrote the word *clock* on the chalkboard and provided a manipulable teaching clock. I asked Karina, who is monolingual in Spanish, to point to the clock in our classroom. I drew a large circle on the board and asked several Spanish-dominant students to name the numbers in English for me as I wrote them. As we continued, students named the

Figure 8–6 *Shina's Samples. A: September. B: October.*

A.

Student:
> I Live in Silevbell road 'n a my apment number is 175# an I have a back yard My mom planted bean plants They Growed a Lot

Teacher:
> Have you eaten some beans from your garden yet?

Student:
> No I have not

Teacher:
> Fresh beans are the best! Is there anything else in your garden?

Student:
> No there if not

Teacher:
> One time I had a garden with radishes and carrots. We had so many radishes, I ~~can't~~ gave them away.

Student:
> I had a garden with sqase in it We had so much

B.

> Dear Serendpty,
> I read the book about you
> you were funny When you
> had the banana on your nose
> Did you have a mother when you
> cracked out of your egg?
> It seemed like your friends were
> nice. When you met the walrus
> how did you feel? I was so
> glad that you cleared all that Junk
> out of the sea So if I
> go to the sea I am not
> going to throw anything in the
> water because I know
> what is going to hapenn you
> will come out !!! and pick me up
> and thow me in the water Like
> you did to the fisterman and I
> do'nt want that to happen
> and I Like your book.
>
> Your friend,
> Shina

Figure 8–7 *Evaluation form for Shina*

Name _Shina_

	Date 9/87			Date 10/87			Date ___		
Writing Quality:	C	D	NE	C	D	NE	C	D	NE
Self-selected topics	✓			✓					
Uses expansive vocabulary		✓		✓					
Uses complex sentences		✓		✓					
Experiments with different styles		✓		✓					
Revision strategies		✓		✓					
Writing Mechanics:									
Handwriting	✓			✓					
Uses periods		✓		✓					
Uses quotation marks		✓			✓				
Uses exclamation point		✓		✓					
Uses question marks		✓		✓					
Uses capitalization	✓			✓					
Grammar usage	✓			✓					
Ratio and % invented spelling	4/47 (8%)			4/112 (4%)					
Ratio and % conventional spelling	43/47 (92%)			108/112 (96%)					

C = controls this   Primary language _English_

D = developing this

NE = no evidence of this   Secondary language _Spanish_

Comments: _September, no punctuation, large spaces between words._
October – self-correction on spelling (hapenn – happen)
use of ! mid-sentence

various times I showed on the clock face. We followed up the discussion by making clocks out of paper plates, fasteners, and paper hands. As children were making their clocks, I circulated through the group modeling clock language as we discussed their projects. When the students had finished, we talked about such things as lunchtime and school hours. That night the students were to find out the times of their favorite television programs. (I provided some old *TV Guides* for those students who have no television set and let them choose a favorite show.) The following day we created a display of the names of the favorite shows with student-made clocks showing the starting times.

In the context of the lesson I asked Spanish-dominant Manny to repeat certain words as they came up. I knew he was comfortable speaking in English. Karina is not ready to take risks in her second language. By asking her to indicate the corresponding pictures non-verbally, I was able to assess her receptive understanding of English. All levels of ESL were reached, all students were involved in the discussion, and the ESL lesson itself was incidental to the genuine exploration of time. Following the unit on time, I checked the appropriate boxes on the checklist.

My students' standardized test scores affirm that kids who understand language as a whole and the way it works can easily deal with its parts. The problems my students face when taking such tests is a lack of test-wiseness. Students in whole language classes are seldom familiar with either the test format or the type of information asked for. Although we cover far more during the school year than the skills tested, I find it helpful to spend time reviewing the labels for things that the kids use daily and take for granted, giving them names for what they already know.

One common test item is antonyms. In establishing our class rules, I stress the word *antonym* as helpful in predicting the second part of the rule: "If you open it, close it." "If you turn it on, turn it off." "If you break it, fix it." Sometimes I ask the students to rewrite the rules with synonyms instead, with rather funny results. "If you mess it up, clean it up" becomes, "If you mess it up, leave it dirty." Within the context of our discussion of rules, the children learn the rules, learn the concepts and labels of antonym and synonym, and, through their creative changes, I know that they understand what the rules mean.

I try to help my students see that, although the testing is very different from what we usually do in our classroom, all they lack is the testing terminology. In our daily math and language interactions I occasionally point out the labels that will help them shift into test mode.

During standardized testing students seeking to make sense of the test ask for clarification of test items. My response is usually, "Try to guess what the test makers are looking for. Imagine what they think a third grader would answer."

ADMINISTRATORS, PARENTS, AND OTHER TEACHERS

Administrators, parents, next year's teachers, and certainly the kids themselves are satisfied and excited by the growth shown in monthly writing samples and the other documentation. Administrators need visible evidence of students' growth in any school program. My principal is pleased with and responds enthusiastically to my writing program because of the constant development shown in the quality of the message and the technical writing abilities. It is not unusual for me eagerly to share writing development such as Michael's or Shina's.

Parents, accustomed to test scores and letter grades from their own school experience, appreciate the more solid, visible growth shown by their children's writing samples. Parents easily recognize learning and can accept our program when I explain in a professional way how the writing evaluation works; I do not send samples home without an explanation. Parents often agree that report card grades are, by themselves, not satisfactory explanations of their children's academic progress. They also appreciate the depth of my understanding of each child as an individual.

The following year's teachers, whether or not they continue our whole language approach, cannot deny the growth shown over the year in both the form of writing and its quality. They may in fact inquire about my program. They have commented on the high quality of critical thinking my students show in all subject areas, as well as the kids' abilities in subject-matter areas such as science, social studies, and math. One fourth-grade teacher claimed that in May, a whole year after they had left my class, students were still remembering, "Ms. Morrissey taught us to solve a problem by thinking it through."

PROBLEMS I NEED TO SOLVE

I am satisfied that the kids are learning academics and problem solving, processing language, and developing their language abilities, because I see it happening. The frustrations, however, are many. Principally the large class size frustrates my desire to work intimately with each child. I depend on the children to help one another. I often say, "There are twenty-seven teachers in this class." This poses another frustration, because the children are not used to viewing one another as authorities and experts and teachers. The flexibility of the whole language classroom does allow me and my students to find some ways to work out solutions to our frustrations. I have seen students become more independent and interdependent because we have discussed their need for help and my need for organization and my lack of time.

It is worth the extra effort to individualize and aim for students' self-examination (and my own). I learn something new every day about children or a child, about a topic of study or a language, about myself. No two days are ever the same. Kids are motivated and animated, and so am I. The class learns to help me deal with management and organizational questions, leading all of us to a sense of joint ownership. Visitors to our class often have to search hard to find me sitting on the rug with a small group or conferring intently in some corner with a student or two.

Although the school year begins with the frustrations of so many language levels, ability levels, and cultural differences, our classroom community comes to accept individual differences in language, ability, and culture. We as a class nurture our growth in academic and social areas. The atmosphere is close to that outside school; we use our first and second languages out of desire and need. Students grow and develop at their own pace in our challenging and encouraging atmosphere.

By the end of the year we are a community, a family, a whole. Students no longer view June as an end but just another window or door, part of an ongoing, continuous, spiraling educational experience. They have come to realize that evaluation, learning, and growth are one.

middle-grade
expansions

GUISE, SON OF THE SHOEMAKER

Mary M. Kitagawa

It is impossible to separate *valuing* from evaluating. The kernel of the word is also the kernel of the act. Helping students value themselves as readers and writers has an enduring impact on their literacy. Since reading and writing processes require the integration of strategies, the learner benefits most when evaluation of those strategies can be extended to serve wider, more complex purposes.

This is not an original idea with me, nor is valuing unique to whole language classrooms. Sensitive teachers, regardless of their philosophical stance, naturally build on student strengths. And whole language teachers hold no monopoly on appreciating students as individual learners.

Whole language teachers may stand out among such teachers as those who rely primarily on naturally occurring, ongoing evidence in the classroom to verify growth. We consider ourselves witnesses to phenomena rather than judges mediating between success and failure. We also use ourselves as subjects, determining what readers and writers actually do instead of blindly sending students over traditional obstacle courses. And because a whole language teacher is always open to being taught by his or her students, what others call mistakes we see as windows into the child's mind.

Therefore I was not dismayed when I read in fifth grader Eduardo's journal that he washed "cloughs." Like most of us, he does not pronounce the *th* in the word *clothes*, but he seemed to have remembered that the spelling is more complex than *close*. I valued his effort by a comment in the margin: "Bravo, you recognized the sound of *o* in *clothes* as being the same sound as in *though* and *although*!"

Every year Eduardo's spelling ability will be gauged in a state-mandated, standardized test. The task will be to pick out the nonwords from lists

101

of four. Eduardo's flexibility in recognizing the potential of *cloughs* to spell *clothes* may actually prevent him from seeing it as a nonword. But it is equally likely that our interaction helped him acquire a visual imprint of the conventional spelling of the word.

Appreciating the strengths that resulted in a misspelling like Eduardo's "cloughs," however, is not as critical a valuing as the evaluation that helped shed light on Mariella's problems. It is for perplexing students like Mariella that close observation is most vital. Although she had taken many tests of her language proficiencies and deficiencies, none had documented the revealing discrepancy between her strategies for reading and writing. Year after year it was her teachers, not her testers, who had used her writing proficiencies to argue against placing her in a special education class. When she was a fifth grader in my room, I noted anecdotally certain conversations that seemed to illustrate incongruity between her insecurity in reading and her relative confidence in writing.

Mariella was working on a report about Halley's comet and was having problems with the two resource books she had chosen. I had this conversation with her as she worked on a book about comets in general:

TEACHER: Hi, how's it going?
MARIELLA: Fine, I guess. Say, Teacher, what's this word?
TEACHER: *Wanderer.* What does that have to do with comets?
MARIELLA: I dunno. What does it say?
TEACHER [*after helping her read the answer to her question*]: What do you most want to know about Halley's comet?
MARIELLA: I dunno. What it's gonna look like, I guess.

Helping her locate that information in a middle chapter of the book, I reflected to myself that Mariella was not in control of the reading and research process. Later I found her struggling with the other book, trying to get through a chapter on Edmund Halley's childhood rather than asking herself how to find the pertinent information in the rather thick book. Even after I showed her how the table of contents would facilitate her search, I had to give her direct permission to skip to the relevant chapters.

At one point she told me that Edmund Halley seemed to have been the first person to sight this particular comet and that he had done so every seventy-six years thereafter! She laughed when I helped her figure out how long his life would have to have been to accomplish that. Finally, after a series of these redirecting sessions, Mariella clarified and sequenced her knowledge into an accurate oral report.

In contrast to Mariella's handling of material written by others, she was animated in producing her own texts. Here is a typical interchange, this one occurring as she wrote a description of her twin cousins.

MARIELLA [*tracking me around the room*]: Hey, you wanna hear it now?
[*Holding the paper herself, she read aloud a partial draft.*]

TEACHER [*after some response to content, and managing to look over her shoulder*]: What's this part you circled here at the beginning? I notice you didn't read that part.

MARIELLA: Oh, that's like an entry. That helped me get started but I'm not gonna use that part.

With her contrastive approaches to reading and writing in mind, I found an occasion to sit for an extended period of time with Mariella, listening to her read and discussing the miscues I recorded. We talked, for example, about why the word *immense* had been so difficult for her to understand. (The story's first sentence talks about being afloat on the "immense ocean.") I had heard her whisper to herself the word *ocean*, so I knew she was using the context, but to no avail. In trying to recapitulate I said, "If you were writing and you knew that you wanted to describe the ocean, but you had not decided how, what would you do?" She told me she would leave a space and later ask someone what sounded good. I praised her and suggested that skipping a word can be similarly used in reading. Getting on with reading while the ideas are hot is just like getting on with the story in writing. We continued to look at her miscues to find where she had used creative strategies such as those that strengthen her writing.

Matching Mariella's successful writing strategies with equivalent techniques for reading was an ongoing program during the rest of the year. Remembering how she held on to her own paper and sought me out while writing, I looked for equivalent signs of control in her mannerisms during reading. One of these signs was that she would "lay claim" to an author, like Patricia Reilly Giff, reading as many of her books as she could find and sharing the funniest incidents with me. When Mariella went on to the next grade, she could still become bogged down by overattention to graphophonics at times, but her attitude had become more positive. Mariella no longer claimed, as she had at the beginning of the year, "I only read riddle books."

THE LITERACY CLUB

Frank Smith (1986, pp. 37–38) advocates promoting in students a sense of belonging to a "literacy club," because the feeling of membership is an essential ingredient to owning the reading and writing processes. Mariella's problem had been that she had taken on a selective membership, considering herself a writer but not a reader.

One way to pin the badge of inclusion onto a student is to acknowledge the sense of expertise an individual has about himself or herself. "Jamie, the first time you read the phrase 'stifled a yawn' you had trouble with the word *stifled*. I thought maybe you had never heard that word, but the next time it came up, you pronounced it right. I wonder how you figured it out." Jamie could not really answer that and still was not sure what action that verb represented, but I could highlight the amount of attention he had given the word, a perfect balance between moving a story line forward and improving accuracy. Jamie also happened to have read the word *cash* as "money" and had corrected himself during the oral reading. When I asked him if he thought he would have bothered to reread the word had he been reading silently, I was being not a researcher but a teacher. I wanted to encourage his own text-creation role in reading, knowing from parent-teacher conferences that he had been criticized at home for such "misreadings." I wanted to verify to him that silent reading is a meaning search rather than a performance.

Jamie's comprehension score on that text was 92 percent, based on one critical question in my informal miscue analysis of his reading (See Goodman, Watson, and Burke, 1987). Each sentence of his reading of the text was evaluated on the basis of the question: Does the sentence, with his corrections, make sense in the context of the story? The number of such sentences divided by the total number of sentences provides the comprehension score. Combined with his successful retelling, Jamie's 92 percent indicates strength in reading a text that approximately matches his grade level. This is heartening, because he does not usually fare so well on questions based on short passages in commercially made tests.

Two-thirds of the way through the year Jamie informed me that he had been told in the past that he is a "slow learner." I do not think he would have brought the label to light if he had not realized through our many valuing interactions that I would heatedly disagree.

When I evaluated Jamie in terms of book handling, however, a problem emerged: there are descriptions of book handling for those just being initiated into the reading of books (See Clay, 1966; Goodman and Altwerger, 1981). I have used the following general criteria to evaluate reader control on the whole-book level with functional readers: (1) use of effective book-selection strategies; (2) apparent enjoyment of the "detective" role, especially in early chapters, when characters, setting, and plot are not yet established; (3) confidence to continue, pace, or abandon reading based on one's own intentions; (4) willingness to critique with specificity; and (5) preference for reading as an activity of choice. Before I discuss these criteria more explicitly, let's look at the contrast between some of the book-handling styles of Jamie and his classmate Andrew.

Jamie typically selects books based either on the number of pages (few) or some social factor such as the possibility of monopolizing a book someone else covets. He generally abandons books before the author has been given a fair chance to establish the necessary background information. Each book gets the same criticism: "It's boring." It seems that stories themselves do not live up to Jamie's expectations. His attention is not readily captured even when I read aloud or a master storyteller visits.

Andrew, by contrast, "lays claim" to authors, keeping track of those whose books he has enjoyed. When Beverly Cleary's varied format in *Dear Mr. Henshaw* proved disconcerting, he persisted because of his past experience with her books. If Andrew does abandon a text, he can usually provide criticism that is specific to that book. He seems to relish letting reading expand his world, as when he wrote about William Armstrong's book *Sounder*, "The author took me really into the book because he had words I wouldn't think of. It made me laugh when I read the word 'overalls' on almost every page."

Every time we have a silent reading period, I warn of the approaching time limit by saying something like, "Look for a good stopping place in the next five minutes." Jamie is one of several students who seem to consider any word to be a "good stopping place," for their books snap shut the instant I make my announcement. Jamie is not yet on course for a lifetime love affair with books. Although he resists writing in his response journal, we maintain some relationship as fellow readers through oral and written dialogues.

Andrew, meanwhile, often uses his response journal to make generalized pronouncements such as "People who read this book learn a lot about Martin Luther King, Jr.," or "Whoever reads this book will like it if they don't mind that it's a little sad and a little scary, for instance when Mrs. Calloway gets murdered." Besides taking on the fellow-reader role, Andrew also makes his responses to books a part of our interpersonal relationship. He was teasing me when he told me he wished he had never read *Jelly Belly* (Robert Kimmel Smith), and he got just the startled reaction that he anticipated. I gasped because he had given a glowing account of it in a book-sharing discussion. "That's right," he chortled, "I liked it so much I want to go back now and read it again for the first time!"

Testimonials and book-handling strengths are the sorts of evidence I would relish in a student like Jamie. Questions such as the following highlight the difference between the two boys and can be answered or inferred from observation, interviews, and written reactions, as in a reading log or response journal:

1. Use of book-selection strategies for free-choice reading.
    a. Does the student look to see if the author is familiar by checking the name or the list of that author's other books?
    b. Does the student check blurbs inside or on the back cover?
    c. What does the student consider while thumbing through a book? The student may mention some of the following criteria: number of pages, length of chapters, size of print, pictures, impressions of format, difficulty, ratio of dialogue to narrative, and so forth.
    d. Does the student consult another reader of that book?
2. Reader involvement in the text (the detective role, which is especially critical in early chapters).
    a. Inferencing: Does the student speculate and revise speculations as the author sets the scene, establishes characterizations and problems? Some students indirectly reveal this by the tone of their discussions or responses in journal entries.
    b. Predicting: Does the student anticipate character behavior and plot development?

3. Autonomy in the reader role.
   a. Pacing: Does the student read at variable speeds, including re-reading for pleasure or clarification and skimming ahead? Does the student use the index or table of contents to get at pertinent information in nonfiction reading?
   b. Persistence: Does the student persist on a whole-book level until purposes for reading are fulfilled? Does the student persist in meaning making on a conceptual level without allowing trivial problems (such as the pronunciation of a name) to disrupt the flow of ideas?
   c. Abandonment: Does the student abandon a text if, after a fair attempt, it proves inappropriate for his or her purposes?
4. Confidence to critique.
   a. Is the student able and willing to specify reasons for options, whether positive, negative, or mixed?
   b. If the text seems ambiguous, contradicts experience, or differs from data in another text, how does the student seek to resolve the problem?
5. Preference of reading as an activity.
   a. During silent reading, how long does a student maintain attention to the book? Do minor distractions readily draw the student's attention from reading? Does the student seem to have enough involvement to resist a sudden end to silent reading time?
   b. Does the student ever choose to read in school during free time?
   c. Does the student report positively about reading at home?

The hardest qualities to note are those of predicting, inferencing, pacing, and dealing with discrepancies. Pacing is more obvious when the students are reading for information than for entertainment. We can watch them skim, skip, and peruse parts of a nonfiction book looking for the data they need. A student often encounters apparent discrepancies about factual information when switching from a greatly simplified source to a highly technical reference book. Through conferences we can discover how confidently students weigh evidence for or against concepts for which they have ambiguous information.

If discussions are built into the teacher's read-aloud time, and if sharing sessions are built into literature study, students may reveal their inferences and predictions orally. Even incorrect assumptions can be credited when we consider that such delving into the unknown creates the excitement that makes reading fun. When a student read that Gwydion (in a Lloyd Alexander novel) came into town in the "guise of a shoemaker," he and his reading buddy agreed that the word *guise* meant that Gwydion was the *son* of a shoemaker. In the next few paragraphs they read about Gwydion's own shoemaking, and I overheard one say to the other, "He must have learned how to make shoes from his father." When the storyline later revealed that shoemaking was only Gwydion's cover, they decided that he thought up that disguise because of his shoemaker father! Their enjoyment of the reading process was not diminished by their misunderstanding. I bit my vocabulary-teaching tongue to keep from interrupting the success they were having with a difficult novel!

When I give students the choice whether to join an oral book-reporting group, it is significant that it is the avid readers who most regularly choose to include themselves in the audience. Apparently they utilize the listening opportunity as adults do the book review sections of newspapers and magazines. From comparing their voracious appetites for books with the attitudes of the Jamies and Mariellas of my classes, I have come to believe that the observation of book handling is more significant than formal testing. To accomplish this observation, of course, the teacher must make trade books, not basals, the primary focus of the reading curriculum.

Entries in students' response journals are a particularly good way of valuing student interactions with texts in upper grades because some preadolescents are reluctant to admit publicly to a love affair with a certain book unless it has the reputation of being "all bad" according to the current image of "cool." I encourage response-journal entries that have a letter-to-the-teacher informality by referring to them as "book-talk letters." I respond as a co-spectator to what the student shares of his or her experience with the text. Students sometimes make highly personal responses. This is helpful for me because there is a world of difference between a student who borrows heavily from the blurb on the jacket and one who relates some aspect of the book to his or her own life. One student reading *Operation: Dump the Chump* by Barbara Park amused me by describing how he planned to reenact the scenario in order to get rid of his own younger brother. As he neared the end of the book and found out how Oscar's careful planning backfired, he had to admit that perhaps he was stuck with his brother after all.

Besides the book-talk letters, which help me understand my students' reading experiences, there are also personal narrative entries, which provide an open-ended way to witness many aspects of writing and social development. Students take risks in journal writing because it is neither for public consumption nor for grades. They describe complex events, express themselves informally, and experiment with dramatic self-expression that might jeopardize their image if publicized in class. When the boys had to pay off a bet by providing a little party for the girls, Alejandro led a stormy meeting of the boys. Later in his journal he described the dilemma of leadership in which he had debated between encouraging the boys' rebellion (reneging on the bet) or promoting capitulation at the risk of his own image. It was one of the many times I saw through his journal a sensitivity that did not show in his normally tough classroom behavior.

Many students are more courageous in writing than in speaking, so we establish a dialogue relationship through journal exchanges that transcends the teacher-pupil one we have in public. Even though my responses on the margins and at the ends of entries rarely give direct praise, there is a valuing that pervades dialogue journal relationships. The fact that their agenda prevails as the topic and their seriousness or frivolity sets the tone of our dialogue seems to be a powerful incentive to encourage risk taking in this form of writing. In the preteen and early teen years these written dialogues help students develop and maintain their self-images. Teachers in a Japanese writing-education movement called *seikatsu tsuzurikata* claim that this role of self-actualization is basic to writing (Kitagawa and Kitagawa, 1987). James Britton (1977, pp. 36–37) also describes how students write autobiographically in ways in which they would like to be seen, especially when directing the text to a trusted reader. The power and vitality that flourishes in such writing may be the beginning of "voice."

In terms of proving writing development, there are usually observable facets of journal entries such as increase in fluency and descriptive precision. But the journal is not to be used as an example of edited writing.

Keeping writing samples of edited writing, whether self-edited or edited collaboratively, provides evidence of progress throughout the year. I prefer to let students collaborate during the writing process. If a punctuation usage or spelling success is the result of someone else's knowledge, the writer must still be congratulated for having consulted the right source. This is authentic because in real life poor spellers survive by the same means. The fact that they are poor spellers is so blatantly obvious that it does not need documentation, but successful compensations should certainly be credited.

On a special page near the back of students' journals I keep lists of language mechanics rules successfully followed. This list is not for my benefit but is rather an effort to nurture budding attempts. If the list claims that the student "uses quotation marks to set off dialogue," even though such is only rarely the case, it may become self-fulfilling prophecy.

In terms of noting development in the writing process, the journal and writing folder must be supplemented by observations in class. It is important to note instances of control, such as Mariella's in choosing topics based on her own interests, alternating between writing and rereading to satisfy her own purposes, seeking editing help only after the text matched her intentions, and exhibiting enjoyment in the writing process. The products were not always spectacular, but they clearly carried Mariella's voice, and they gave the reader, as well as the writer, a sense of satisfaction.

In spite of the after-school time they consume, anecdotal records seem to be the most accurate way to document the full picture of students' language development. Because of the time constraints, whole language teachers selectively record representative samples from the myriad of daily observations while constantly watching for those special moments. Many observations never find their way into written documentation and are only as available to outsiders as we ourselves are. I was glad that when Jamie's mother insisted that he could not read at all, I could use my miscue analysis coding sheet to read back for her how he had read a text and show her that most of his corrections and noncorrections indicated control of the reading process.

I used to put my fingers in my ears when I heard the word *evaluation*. I feared that only quantifiable data would be credited as evaluation. I came to grips with evaluation, I think, when I finally realized that it is not something I need to add to what I already do but that it occurs unavoidably, naturally, and simultaneously with every interaction.

I have to admit, however, that I'm still tempted to stick my fingers in my ears when I hear the word *accountability*. It sounds like a court-martial: "Can you account for your actions from 8:00 to 2:30 every day?" The school I teach in has been labeled a target school, supposedly meaning that we receive extra help in raising our desperately low test scores. Sometimes, however, we feel more like a bullseye than a focus of help.

The good news in Arizona, though, is our new state-provided guide to Language Arts Essential Skills. Under that direction it is possible to imagine local districts developing their accountability systems through such normal daily events as those I have described here. For the first time I feel that the ends of the spectrum—both state-level direction and teacher experience—are moving toward holistic evaluation. It is timely now, in Arizona at least, to be unyielding in insisting that isolated skills checklists and test scores do not represent students accurately. Kid-watching, writing folders, informal miscue analysis, and anecdotal records are the least intrusive and most representational documentation of language learning.

"WELL, WHAT ABOUT HIS SKILLS?" EVALUATION OF WHOLE LANGUAGE IN THE MIDDLE SCHOOL

Karen Sabers Dalrymple

Recently I had to hasten away from my classroom. My best friend was critically ill, and there wasn't time for writing extensive lesson plans. In my haste I left sketchy plans of a schedule and the advice "Trust the students; they know what's going on." Three days later I returned to the substitute's message: "Everything went well. I loved being here to see all the exciting things the kids do—you've worked wonders with some of these kids. Everything went perfectly with the eighth graders, too."

What better evaluation is there? If learning continues when the teacher is absent, what more can we ask of a program? Whole language teaching allows the students to become independent learners who acknowledge and enjoy a literate environment, and that is the primary goal of education.

Before I was aware of the term *whole language*, I knew of the work of Bruner, who advocated process education, and the work of Postman and Weingartner, who described a good school. As a young teacher I was impressed with these educators because their ideas were child centered and promised meaningful educational activities and evaluation.

A school is good when it moves away from factory-like processing procedures and toward more humanistic, individualized judgments. . . . The idea is to make evaluation a learning experience. . . . A school is good when its priorities are broadly conceived, rather than narrowly hierarchical. . . . A school is good when it does not use standardized tests, or uses them only with extreme caution and skepticism. . . . Testing should grow from what is taught, and what is taught should grow from who is taught. (Postman and Weingartner, 1973)

111

The precepts governing good evaluation are embedded within the philosophy of whole language teaching and learning. Assessing and evaluating learning is inherent within a whole language program; they are considered part of the teaching cycle; they are ongoing; and they are curriculum based. Testing and evaluation have traditionally been conducted after teaching; planning, teaching, and testing were described linearly. There is no gap between teaching and testing in a whole language program. Planning, teaching, and evaluating are continually intermingled as three interwoven cycles. The students are the curricular informants; as the classroom teacher observes and interacts with the students, he or she is making decisions about lesson plans and teaching strategies. Once those plans are enacted, the teacher observes and interacts and makes more educational decisions. Evaluation is the making of relevant educational decisions. As you can see from the description of the teaching cycle, evaluation is ongoing because it is embedded within the student-centered curriculum.

Knowing what I know about good teaching and its close relationship to good evaluation, I was somewhat concerned about my recent transfer from an elementary to a middle school. Middle schools are structured differently from elementary schools, as well they need to be, to help students bridge the gap between the self-contained structure of the elementary school and the departmental structure of the secondary school. Middle schools explore subjects in more depth than do elementary schools, but they are less specialized than high schools. My concern was that the success I had known as a teacher would somehow be threatened in a new environment.

Our middle school is more like a secondary school than an elementary school in its time structuring. As a former elementary teacher I was accustomed to and pleased with the large blocks of time I had with my children. In our middle school, class periods are arranged on forty-four-minute time allotments. Students in grades five and six are assigned to self-contained classrooms for most of the day. Two periods are set aside for "exploratory" courses and physical education. I was assigned to one sixth-grade classroom; our work involved the core curriculum courses of math, science, social studies, reading, and language arts. Another part of my contract was to teach one section of eighth-grade social studies.

In addition to the philosophical and time-structuring differences, the middle school curriculum was new to me. The curriculum guides gave information regarding the content of each subject area for sixth graders. Some of the guides—language arts, reading, and science—set out processes pertinent to each area as well as content requirements. I had to deal with the districtwide curriculum as well as the middle school guidelines. Our principal emphasized three components of middle school curriculum as he discussed middle school teaching with me during my interview: academic, affect, and activities. Although I could accept the premises on which the curriculum was designed, I was concerned that I might not be able to implement a meaningful curriculum while meeting the school district's curriculum requirements.

My success as a teacher was partially due to the use of an interdisciplinary structure (or integrated curriculum). The structure makes whole language teaching and learning possible. It utilizes units of study in literature, math, science, and social studies as vehicles for students to maintain and develop their literacy. An interdisciplinary program provides opportunities for students to comprehend while using a variety of communication systems, such as language, art, music, and drama.

The integrated curriculum model differs from most curriculum models; it is based on trusting the learner. Large blocks of time are allotted for students to pursue their questions and projects. There are many open-ended assignments to which students can apply their basic skills in a meaningful and exciting context. The definition of basic skills is very broad; rather than considering math facts, a minimal spelling list, or a controlled reading vocabulary, teachers using the integrated curriculum model believe that learning tools are basic and that students develop proficiency through activities such as silent reading, execution of science and math experiments, questioning, discussion, free writing (writing about any topic), focused writing (writing about a specific topic), and key-word usage (using the literary, scientific, or specific vocabulary related to a topic of study). My principal supports the interdisciplinary approach.

The following description of how I began with a new class of sixth graders is offered to demonstrate the cyclical relationship of planning, presenting, observing, assessing, and evaluating that occurs within an interdisciplinary model.

My previous experiences with sixth graders had been nine years earlier in an elementary school setting. I wondered what fascinated sixth graders now and what topics might engage them in learning. During the first day of school I asked about films they liked. Many of them spoke of the film *Back to the Future*. At the same time during my leisure I was reading *The Green Futures of Tycho* by William Sleator. Immediately I connected the film story to Sleator's book. When the children were leaving school that first day, I suggested that for homework they "Give some thought to the concept of time."

The following day Jennifer came into the classroom and said, "Do you think we could do a study of time?"

"I'm not sure, Jennifer. Let's come together as a group today and discuss the idea," I replied.

I wrote *Time* on the chalkboard and circled it. The children were quiet, yet I could sense some eagerness. Jennifer began the discussion with, "Just as I was going to sleep last night, I remembered our homework. So I started to think about time. What I think is that this isn't a fact, and it's not really a question, but . . . well . . . time can exist without people, but people can't exist without time."

Jennifer's statement began a discussion among the students which included fact giving, questioning, and more statements concerning concepts related to time. During twenty or thirty minutes the students composed, while I recorded, a list of questions, several statements that could be argued, and a web of facts. Given the students' interest, I was comfortable agreeing that we could embark on a thematic study of time.

Following the discussion-recording period I asked the students to make an entry in their learning logs based on the discussion. During their log time I recorded some of my observations about student behavior in the discussion-recording period. Later, after I had read the students' log entries, I recorded further observations and prepared strategy lessons for the unit.

We continued our study of time for three weeks. While some of the investigations concentrated on observing natural changes and phenomena in time, others became investigations in preservation or aging. Students were involved in scientific experimentation with molds, plants, and soil. Some students began reading the literature related to early discoverers who were searching for eternal life, and other students read about the origin of time-telling devices. A number of students became excited about the possibility of creating a time-traveling device. These students began designing their machines on paper, labeling the various parts of the machine and their special functions. It was during this time that Melissa suggested the students submit their drawings to a design review board, a simulation that reflected Melissa's father's work (he is a contractor and builder and was experiencing work with a design review board). Several students volunteered to serve on the board to review designs and interview designers of time machines. They tape-recorded all of their sessions so that I could participate in the work during after-school hours.

Other activities included reading and discussing literature related to the topic. *Tuck Everlasting* by Natalie Babbitt, *A Wrinkle in Time* by Madeleine L'Engle, *Into the Dream* by William Sleator, *The Lion, the Witch, and the Wardrobe* by C. S. Lewis, and *Half Magic* by Edward Eager were available in our multiple-copy library. Each student selected one of the books to read. Also I read aloud *The Green Futures of Tycho.*

For one of my strategy lessons I used a portion of T. S. Eliot's poem "The Love Song of J. Alfred Prufrock." The lesson was aimed at offering a new genre of work that dealt with the concepts of time we were studying.

Students also collected facts that included important time-related dates. These facts were written on a poster, and during various independent research periods I would notice several students discussing the implications of the dates and the world's recognition of time.

Another student read, reread, and reported on the classic "Rip Van Winkle." One student made a time capsule as a result of her interviews with students and various adults about their concepts of time. Her research was well designed; she used a questionnaire and tabulated the results specific to each age group.

Throughout the study of time I was observing, assessing, and conducting strategy lessons for small and whole groups. I encouraged students to "play with their ideas" while they were involved in the language

115
*"Well, What About
His Skills?"
Evaluation of Whole
Language in the
Middle School*

processes. I observed the students and made an evaluation of their work as scientists, social scientists, mathematicians, and literary critics.

Since that first unit study my sixth graders' studies have included the topics of "Inventions," "Outdoor Education," "The World as Seen Through . . ." (which encouraged the study of art, folklore, geography, and so on), and "Energy."

Themes for eighth-grade social studies (a one-period-a-day class) included "War," "The Sixties," "Local History," and also a study of George Orwell's *Animal Farm* as a comparison to the framing of our Constitution.

I discovered that middle schoolers, whether the topic is very general or quite specific, are able to read, review, and respond critically to literature. They are able to collect and organize data, question, generalize, and share information. Students are able to observe, make hypotheses, experiment, record data, and make deductions. They are grouping, comparing, ordering, and classifying. These abilities reflect the various disciplines and represent the skills about which I make evaluations.

Evaluation is a natural process within the interdisciplinary model; I am continuously making assessments and evaluations of the students as they are involved in their thematic study.

RECORD KEEPING

The ability to observe and record student learning, assess that learning, and make decisions about what experiences to offer a student is critical to my teaching. Good records allow easy reporting about an individual student; but they also reflect and store the many observations a whole language teacher makes about students. My description of the study of time is possible only because I have my records from that particular class.

A GROUP RECORDING FORM

The class roster form allows for charting numerous and valuable bits of information about individual learning. I place several clipboards around the classroom. These hold rosters on which I am able to record observations of students as they pursue independent and group work or as they respond to given tasks.

When I transferred from an elementary school to a middle school, I was concerned that I would have difficulty implementing a holistic evaluation process within a structure that required evaluation in the narrow sense of an A-to-F scale. After using my basic record-keeping forms the first few weeks of school, I found them very appropriate for assessing the learning of middle school students and discovered that they allowed for collecting information that could be translated into the standard grades. So even though I am not philosophically in agreement with grading a single subject area with a letter grade, I am able to translate my assessment and evaluation of my middle school students' work as I am required to do.

Recording, assessing, and evaluating are symbiotic processes that give support to teaching. Recording is a process of preserving data about student learning. Assessment is a process of gathering data about student learning. Evaluation is a process of making educational decisions based on that data. Figures 10–1, 10–2, and 10–3 demonstrate the use of the basic record-keeping form as a data sheet for recording the assessment of learning behaviors in the particular disciplines of science, literature, and social studies during the study of time. Note that the column headings indicate the type of task or process the student was performing.

Within a thematic unit study I might use twelve or twenty such forms. I specify the particular area (science concepts, science processes, problem solving, critiquing literature) that I am observing and write that title

Figure 10–1 *Basic Form Used for Science*

Time Study Sept. '86 Science	Time Line	Described OBSERVATIONS	Design of Experiment	Record of Data	Hypothesizing generalizing	Log Entries
Mark	✓+	+	✓ soil +	—	+	—
Todd	✓	✓	✓ soil	—	+	✓
Sue	✓	—	— beans	—	—	—
Marge	✓	✓	✓ soil	✓	✓	✓ —
Carol	⑦ ✓	✓ —	— leaf	—	—	✓ —
Don	✓ —	+	— water	—	—	—
Richard	✓ —	+	✓ + preserve	✓ +	✓	✓
Scott	—	✓	✓ oil	✓	✓	✓ —
Melissa	+	+	+ aloe	✓ +	✓ +	✓ +
Darrell	✓	✓ —	TM 1	0	0	—
Nancy	✓ +	+	+ aloe	+	+	+
Tye	✓	✓	TM 5	✓	+	✓
Peter	✓ +	+	✓ oil	✓	✓	✓ —
Kevin	✓ —	✓ —	— beans	—	—	✓ —
David	✓ —	✓	TM 3	✓ —	✓	✓
Derek	✓	✓	TM 3	✓ —	✓	✓
Dawn	—	✓	TM 3	✓ —	✓	✓
Maggie	⑦ ✓	✓	TM 6	✓ +	✓	+
Emily	✓ —	✓	TM 4	✓	✓	✓
Darin	⑦ ✓	✓	TM 5	✓	✓	✓
Trish	✓ +	✓	✓ — plants	✓ —	✓ —	✓ —
Ellen	+	+ ESSAY	0	0	+	+
Jean	✓ +	✓ +	✓ seeds	✓ —	✓	✓
Jane	+	✓	✓ seeds	✓ —	✓	✓

117
"Well, What About
His Skills?"
Evaluation of Whole
Language in the
Middle School

Figure 10–2 *Basic Form Used for Literature*

Time Study Sept.'86 Literature	Read-Aloud Log Entries 3 Assigned No.	Quality	The Green Futures Discussion of Text	Response to Poem J. Prufrock	Text Compared to "Back to the Future"	Film Response to Time Machine	Task: Respond to Own Lit Re: Time	
Mark	3	✓−	+	+ oral	+	+	0→+	
Todd	3	✓	✓+				W	✓
Sue	3	✓	−				0	
Marge	3	✓	✓−				0	✓−
Carol	3	✓	✓				0	✓−
Don	3	✓	✓+				0/W	✓
Richard	3	+	+		✓		0	✓−
Scott	3	✓−	✓−				0	+
Melissa	5	✓	✓+	+W			0	✓
Darrell	2	−	−				0	
Nancy	5	+	✓+	✓+W		✓	W/0	✓
Tye	3	✓	✓	✓ 0	+		W	✓+
Peter	3	✓	✓				W	✓−
Kevin	3	✓	✓−				W	−
David	3	✓	✓				W	✓
Derek	3	✓+	✓+				W	✓
Dawn	3	✓−	✓−				0	✓
Maggie	5	+	+	+ 0/W	+	+	W	✓+
Emily	3	✓−	✓−				0	✓
Darin	3	✓	✓				W	✓
Trish	3	✓	✓				W	✓
Ellen	3	+	✓+		✓		W	✓+
Jean	3	+	✓+				W	✓+
Jane	3	+	✓+		✓		W	✓+

0 = Oral   W = Written

in the upper-left portion of the form. As I move about the classroom, I am able to record on the various clipboards my observations of students as they pursue individual and group work or as they respond to given tasks.

For example, during an independent research period, when students gather information about a country or continent (selected because they like the folklore of that place), I move about the room observing students, perhaps stopping to ask, "How's it going?" "What are you discovering?" A student might wave me away, talk excitedly about some fact regarding population, or scowl and tell me, "There's absolutely no material on the country in any of these books." Any of these responses

Figure 10–3 *Basic Form Used for Social Studies*

Time Study Sept. '86 Social Studies	9.5 Webbing ?s- Informs 9. 9.	Read + Reviewing Literature ① → ②		Presented re: SS		
Mark	+ + +	+	+			
Todd	− ✓ ✓	✓	✓			
Sue	− − −	−	✓−			
Marge	− − ✓	−	✓−			
Carol	✓ ✓✓	✓	✓			
Don	+ + +	+	+	Ⓧ		
Richard	+ + +	+	+			
Scott	− − ✓	−	✓−			
Melissa	✓ ✓ +	+	+			
Darrell	− − −	−	✓−			
Nancy	+ + +	+	+	Ⓧ		
Tye	✓ ✓ ✓	✓	✓	Ⓧ		
Peter	✓ ✓ ✓	✓	✓	Ⓧ		
Kevin	? ✓ ✓	✓	✓			
David	− ✓ ✓	✓	✓			
Derek	+ ✓ +	✓+	✓+	Ⓧ		
Dawn	− ? ✓	−	✓−			
Maggie	+ + +	+	+			
Emily	− − ✓	−	✓−	Ⓧ		
Darin	✓ ✓ ?	✓	✓	Ⓧ		
Trish	Ⓐᵇ ✓ ✓	✓	✓			
Ellen	+ + +	+	+	Ⓧ		
Jean	+ + +	+	+			
Jane	+ + +	+	+			

is a bit of information about the child that I can record. Figure 10–4 is a roster with notations made during an independent research period. Each tick mark in a column means I observed the student engaged in the behavior described.

Figure 10–5 is a roster that summarizes the independent research skills of paraphrasing and use of resources. The numbers account for the facts expressed and supported in the focus writings.

I have rosters for specific behaviors; for instance, while one roster collects data on oral language, another is for written language, and still another for use of resources. The more I observe, the more I see, and the more information I can collect.

Using a roster to record observations of student behavior on a daily

119
*"Well, What About
His Skills?"
Evaluation of Whole
Language in the
Middle School*

Figure 10–4 *Notations During Independent Research*

Outdoor Ed. Unit–October Independent Research Time	Peruses Resources	Discusses Ideas w/Others	Reads	Writes in Log	Comes to Me for Perception	
Mark	II	ЖЖ II	III		II	
Todd	III	I	I	I		
Sue	II					
Marge	II	IIII	III	I		
Carol	III	III	III	II		
Don	III	IIII	IIII	I		
Richard	III	IIII	ЖЖ II	III		
Scott	IIII	IIII	IIII	II	I	
Melissa	II	IIII	ЖЖ II	IIII	I	
Darrell	I		I			
Nancy	ЖЖ	ЖЖ I	ЖЖ III	ЖЖ III	II	
Tye	II	III	III	II	III	
Peter	III	IIII	III	II	I	
Kevin	II	II	ЖЖ I	IIII		
David	ЖЖ	I	ЖЖ II	I		
Derek	II	II	II	II		
Dawn	II	ЖЖ	ЖЖ	III		
Maggie	ЖЖ	III	ЖЖ	ЖЖ		
Emily	ЖЖ II		ЖЖ II	III		
Darin	II	III	I	III		
Trish	I	III	I	II		
Ellen	II	IIII	I	II	III	
Jean	I	III	I	III		
Jane	III	II	II	I	I	

basis saves me time when report cards are due. When it is time for me to complete the report cards, I can pull out all the forms for a particular subject and make an evaluation. For example, if I am "figuring" a science grade, I would look at the forms labeled "science concepts" and "science processes" and use the data for the evaluation (the letter grade). Because I had collected the data over a period of time while observing a variety of activities—setting up experiments, group discussion, data recording in the learning log, questioning—I would have a view of the student as a scientist engaging in scientific behaviors. The science grade reflects a variety of experiences, behaviors, modes, and processes related to the discipline of science.

The record-keeping system I use accounts for many aspects of a

Figure 10–5 *Notations on Paraphrasing and Use of Resources*

Independent Research + Search: Energy	Focus Writings	① 4·20 ② 4·24 Paraphrasing	③ 5·5 Info	•Perusing •Use of Contents •Use of Texts for Purposes	Locates Sources (Additional)	
Mark	7	8	32	√+	+	
Todd	AB	AB	12	√	√	
Sue	3	2	4	√−		
Marge	2	3	6	√		
Carol	6	5	9	√		
Don	10	8	8	√		
Richard	7	13	18	√		
Scott	4	14	15	√		
Melissa	6	11	23	+	+	
Darrell	2	3	4	√−		
Nancy	9	22	37	+	+	
Tye	2	8	11	√		
Peter	3	11	5	√		
Kevin	4	5	6	√	+	
David	4	9	20	+	+	
Derek	7	13	15	√		
Dawn	AB	5	7	√		
Maggie	6	16	17	√+	+	
Emily	1	8	16	√+	+	
Darin	4	11	20	√+	+	
Trish	6	AB	20	+		
Ellen	6	5	13	√		
Jean	9	17	20	√+	+	
Jane	6	17	10	√		

student's learning. I am able to see the student as a listener, a writer, a speaker, a problem poser, a problem solver, a critic. Armed with so much information, I am able to attend special education staffing meetings or hold conferences with students, their parents, or school personnel without the need for additional paperwork or time. Preparing reports is not a time-consuming task.

I record a lot more than I need for the standard report card or for special education staffings and/or conferences, but all I have learned about each student is of great import. The information I have about the student allows me to communicate better with that student. And as a teacher I am most effective when I am a careful observer; the better an observer I become, the better I am able to offer students experiences for educational growth.

A FORM FOR INDIVIDUAL RECORDING OR REPORTING

Goodman, Smith, Meredith, and Goodman (1987) offered me assistance as I was developing a structure for using thematic units with my students. The text suggested a three-phase structure for comprehension—perceiving, ideating, and presenting. I use this framework and find it very comprehensive. During all of the phases I have an opportunity to observe my students and record information. When the unit of study is finished, I use an individual form for reporting activity specific to the three learning phases of perceiving, ideating, and presenting. Figures 10–8 and 10–9 (pages 129–30) are examples of the use of that form as I record my observations of individuals' work.

The form is also effective for individual students to use. Once the students are aware of perceiving, ideating, and presenting, they can begin to assess their own activities. Sometimes I ask the students to keep an account of their own work. Other times I might use the form to reinforce the process of comprehension through the phases of perceiving, ideating, and presenting.

One student began making a poster during an independent period; when I questioned his illustration, he couldn't explain why he had selected those particular graphics. As we spoke, it became obvious that he really had no concepts or ideas that he wanted to convey; he just wanted to use the new markers that had been placed in the basket that morning. I showed him the observation-assessment form and talked with him about comprehension and content leading to form. Then he smiled and said, "I get it—if I'm going to make a poster to teach other students about an idea, I'd better have an idea first."

ASSESSING STUDENT HOMEWORK AS A PART OF EVALUATION

I assign one homework task weekly. Most often the students are asked to respond to the unit study. Occasionally I assign a nonwritten task; for example, during the invention study I asked the students to invent something useful with one or more of the objects from their trash or wastebaskets at home. During the energy unit the students were asked to invent something that used energy and accomplished some work. Although there is some variety to our homework tasks, my objective is standard. I intend to offer the students an opportunity to play with ideas, display their knowledge and creativity, and extend their ideas on a topic being explored in the classroom. Furthermore, I hope to encourage communication between the students and their parents. Often parents become involved with homework tasks. This makes our work even more comprehensive and exciting because more minds and greater language use are involved with the homework tasks.

The particular responses described in the following paragraphs grew

Figure 10–6 *Melissa's Response, March 3, 1987*

```
                A MODERN-DAY FOLKTALE

                   Vocab Study-India
------------------------------------------------------------
           PROLOGUE
           Once upon a time, in India, there lived a girl who's
    family was very rich. They lived in the capital of India,
    which was Delhi. The family had many rupees, India's form of
    money. They had enough money to pay for an aya, or nanny. The
    girl's best friend's father was a subsistence farmer; he
    raised food for only himself and his family.
           Most Indians in India were Hindus at that and to this
    family Hinduism was a first. In the Hindu religion it is a
    tradition for many religious festivals.
           In India the social and religious groups we live in
    are called jatis. When the Europeans came to India they
    called them castes. Each caste has a different occupation,
    like the weavers' caste.
------------------------------------------------------------
------------------------------------------------------------

           Shieka's parents decided that it was high time for them
    to pick her a husband, but no one in their jati seemed
    right. Her family belonged to the weaver's caste, but they
    were very wealthy. The next day a handsome but snobby man
    rode into town on a elephant. Not knowing he was snobby
    Shieka's parents decided that he had to be the man that
    would marry Shieka. Sheika also did not know that he was a
    snob and it was love at first sight.
           A few weeks later they were married and living in the
    man's house in the outskirts of Delhi. Shieka soon found out
    that this man was a snob. She no longer liked him but in her
    jati it was illeagal to get a divorce, so she was stuck with
    this man for the rest of her life.
------------------------------------------------------------
    "IT JUST GOES TO SHOW THAT FOLKTALES DON'T ALWAYS HAVE
    HAPPY ENDINGS NOWADAYS!"
```

out of a thematic unit study called "The World as Seen Through. . . ." During the study we looked at the folklore, geography, people, history, and art of the world. We concentrated on one aspect at a time only to discover that such concentration is impossible because of the interrelatedness of historical, geographical, and cultural events.

Melissa submitted the piece in Figure 10–6 as a response to the homework assignment "Respond to Your Study." An examination of the piece offers much information about Melissa and her literacy development. Obviously she is able to use a computer and a word processor. Her use of a prologue demonstrates her knowledge of that literary technique that offers insights into a story. Melissa chose to write about her study using a Thurberlike twist on a folktale. The information about India is included in the tale; some fine content is represented here. The impressive fact is that Melissa designed and developed this task independently. An assessment of her work acknowledges her competence in integrating her knowledge and skills; and of course my observations of Melissa's competence are recorded.

During this same week other students used formats that differed greatly from Melissa's, although they displayed similar competence.

Joshua submitted ten analogies that described his study and compared the United States to Africa. Jennifer wrote a four-page report in

123
*"Well, What About
His Skills?"*
*Evaluation of Whole
Language in the
Middle School*

which she paraphrased her new information about Hawaii and the Pacific Islands. Holly's report was written about the Soviet Union; each paragraph compared some aspect of Russia to the United States. In fact twelve of twenty-seven pieces of work represented new formats— formats that had not been used in previous independent tasks. Other children submitted sentences, crossword puzzles, and stories sharing their study of a certain portion of the world.

What we as educators can learn from a study of the variety of responses to one standard task is that middle school students have a need for structure and a need for individual response and creativity. Middle school students appreciate making decisions about the use of their time and the type of work in which they are involved. Their repertoire of presentations develops throughout the school term as they become involved in evaluating their own and one another's responses to open-ended activities and tasks such as the standard homework assignment.

Students are also given many opportunities for independent projects in the classroom. The evaluation of such projects reinforces my belief in the strength of the program for producing responsible and literate students.

OBSERVING AND ASSESSING EXCEPTIONAL CHILDREN

Two descriptions of exceptionality are offered here to demonstrate the differences in evaluation of individuals. I could tell twenty-nine stories about sixth graders, and you might believe that each child is an exception. That's the strength of a whole language program; each child becomes focal, specific, special, and exceptional.

DARRELL

"Hey, Mrs. Dalrymple," Darrell half-whispered to me in mid-October after a whole class discussion about the use of a social studies text as a source of information. "Hey, are you ever going to teach us with real books here?"

Darrell is a thirteen-year-old sixth grader who is new to whole language programs. Since September he had participated in two units of study, "Time" and "Outdoor Education." The classroom had many resources for a third study, the study of Europe (begun when the town decided to institute an annual Oktoberfest). We used maps, pictures, artifacts, books from three libraries, and also the district's newly adopted social studies textbook. During a whole class discussion one of the students mentioned the use of the text as a possible resource for information.

One of the first activities of a unit study is to list questions students have regarding our topic. Building on that questioning activity and the student's reference to the text as a resource, I decided to give a quick assessment of the whole group regarding the use of the text. I asked the students to recall their specific questions regarding Europe. Each student took a text. After one student would state a question for all to hear, we would discuss the use of this particular text as a good resource for answering that particular question. One question a student posed referred to the size of European countries compared to the size of states in the United States. As we perused the text, students concurred that the text would give information related to the size of European countries but had no specific data about the size of U.S. states. After several questions I asked the students to think of situations in which the text would be an advantageous resource to a student.

It was after this activity that Darrell had posed his question to me about the use of real books. Perhaps he hadn't really questioned teaching techniques before; his use of "real" as a definition of textbooks is typical for students and parents who are not familiar with whole language. Perhaps it was this rather spontaneous textbook activity that triggered his assessment of the difference between our classroom and those he had known in the past. Later I recorded several entries regarding my conversation with Darrell. One of the entries noted Darrell's concept of at least two categories of books.

Darrell was sitting alone, so I attempted to continue our discussion. "We're using all types of literature, Darrell. I think we have to use whatever we can so that we can understand our questions and studies."

"Yea, I know, but I mean, are you ever going to teach the books?"

"Actually, Darrell, the way things have been here since the beginning of the year is the way I teach."

"I like it this way."

"Why?"

"I just do." He turned from me and continued to work on a map he was drawing.

A few weeks later I attended a special education staffing regarding Darrell's status as a special education student. The meeting came about because Darrell's record of low scores and misbehavior (fighting, swearing, creating disturbances) had followed him to our school, where he had been in attendance since May. Darrell is a foster child; his social worker, the school counselor, the school psychologist, the special education teacher, the principal, and I were at the meeting. The counselor began the meeting by citing Darrell's low scores on standardized tests and asked whether he should receive special education.

The principal reported that he had visited the classroom often and that Darrell's behavior had not attracted his attention. Darrell had appeared normal. The principal cited this as a very positive factor. I ventured that if we were to assign Darrell out of the classroom, we could be encouraging the behavior problems we were trying to extinguish.

"Well, what about his skills?" I was asked.

Skills? Generally, I bristle at the word. And it is a word used often at special education staffings. What about his skills? This boy was coping, he was generally well behaved, but a team of educators was concerned about his skills. Darrell hadn't hit any child, kicked a wall, knocked over a desk, or cursed anyone for more than two months. Isn't that skillful? When we help the whole child in a whole language classroom, it is obvious that skills are but one focus (and a minor one at that), especially

125
*"Well, What About
His Skills?"
Evaluation of Whole
Language in the
Middle School*

for the child who is obviously uncomfortable in a school setting. I knew the question was coming, and I had even prepared myself for it. Yet I was still angry that skills should be viewed as so important in this particular circumstance.

I took a moment to look at my records. Darrell had read four Choose-Your-Own-Adventure Books and had reported how he had fared in each story. "I got killed right away." "I made it nearly to the end of this story." "I found the secret." Those were the comments he had made regarding his reading. Darrell could spell well. The sentences he wrote were simple but comprehensible. When he wrote, his script was in all capitals but was very legible. Darrell didn't talk during classroom activities unless I called on him. When we made European flags for decorations at the local Oktoberfest, Darrell was meticulous in his work (he chose to work alone). He measured, used a straightedge, and kept referring to his resource, a traveler's guide to Britain. His behavior indicated his respect for accuracy.

Although he had never offered information during large-group discussions, he would smile, laugh, and even share some of his writing in a small-group setting. In the hallways he seemed confident and talkative, speaking easily with his friends.

I summarized Darrell's work as best I could for the staff at the meeting. In many ways Darrell is a beginning learner in a school setting. We can't really know his skills until we have given him an environment in which he is comfortable. The group agreed. Everyone in attendance at the meeting saw that for Darrell, the best we could do was to ignore his low standardized test scores from past years and capitalize on his obvious good behavior as an indication of a new beginning. Later we could evaluate his academic skills more specifically. It was decided that his needs were being met in a regular whole language classroom.

Every few weeks, Darrell asks, "How am I doing?"

I respond, "How do you think you are doing?"

Darrell and I talk about his work. It's obvious to me that he cares about what might happen to him. He has learned to use the calculator during our math sessions so that he can participate and not be held up because he hasn't yet acquired computation skills. He has participated in designing and presenting skits with a group of his classmates. He seems more attentive generally; if he values the work, he perseveres diligently. He has completed several of his own adventure stories during writing workshop.

Occasionally one of our unit studies will begin or end with a study of literature. For example, after a space study we read science fiction literature. Students assign themselves or are assigned to one of the various titles available. Multiple-copy novels are used during this type of study. During one of our literature studies I assigned Darrell the book *A Day No Pigs Would Die* by Robert Newton Peck. I thought he would like the hero of the story, and I liked the contrast between world knowledge and grammatical knowledge implied in the story and thought Darrell could relate to that idea.

Darrell laughed at Peck's first chapter as I read it aloud to initiate the study. He attended the small-group sessions and seemed to listen to the discussions and the questions of the students in the group. Although he didn't read much of the text, he did not want to drop out when I offered him the opportunity. Darrell told me he didn't like the book "that much" and so he hadn't read many pages.

Our classroom is rather cramped—twenty-nine students and I in tight quarters. When I meet with a discussion group or when I am conducting a formal lesson with a small group, we take over the places of six students who use the small tables at one side of the room. The students simply find another table or desk in the classroom. We have to "bump" Darrell during these times, since he sits at one of those tables. I've observed that Darrell does not move far from the group if the work concerns something he might want information about. If I ask him to join us, he refuses. Yet I think he is purposefully gathering information and language from the periphery.

Darrell needs the whole language program because within it he is accepted as a student. He is encouraged to build on his own repertoire of experiences and language abilities.

NANCY

Nancy has been a student in a whole language program for three and a half years. Nancy is a quiet, perceptive, and intelligent child who was tagged as "gifted and talented" (g/t) as a second grader. Students in the gifted and talented program spent one period weekly in a pull-out program. The idea of the sessions is to motivate the students and to keep their interest in school. Nancy was a student who rose above the standards set—she read aloud well, she tested well, and she was co-operative. As a third grader she was assigned to leave the classroom weekly for a session with the teacher of the gifted and talented.

Nancy enjoyed a whole language environment. She became interested in ideas through the structure of an integrated curriculum; she had time to devote energy to a particular interest related to the study. We began that year with a study of revolution (I had come upon a great sale of Jean Fritz's books) and thought it a good opportunity to study the genre of historical fiction. Nancy's linguistic abilities were apparent as she responded to her reading and other activities. She did continue to attend her weekly sessions with her g/t resource; once I noticed her frown as she read the schedule and realized that she would have to leave while the class would be designing and presenting dramatic skits as a response to one of our read-aloud books.

Several of the g/t students came to me during December of that school year. They complained that they "missed out on too much" when they had to go to their g/t class. In fact, one third grader sent a note to her g/t teacher via another student: "Dear Teacher. I am too busy. I can't come anymore. Love, Holly."

I collected the group of g/t students to discuss their concerns. We decided to invite their teacher to our room and get him involved with us as we pursued our studies. He was in favor of such teaming, and we were able to complete the school term by working together with the students. As third graders these students were involved with the evaluation process. They recognized their own learning and were able to discuss possibilities. Surely the heart of good evaluation is self-directed.

In October of this most recent term I received a call from another school district in Colorado. Two administrators wanted to visit our program to see how we "handled" our gifted and talented students. Their visit was on a day when I had no breaks except for a quick half-hour lunch period. When I told my sixth-grade students that visitors were coming, they wanted to know the purpose of the visit. After I mentioned the phrase "gifted and talented," both Nancy and Holly said they preferred the whole language program (locally referred to as the Integrated Curriculum Program) to the g/t program. I asked Nancy and Holly if they would like to talk with the visitors, explaining their experiences and answering questions. As it turned out, the girls thought that the Integrated Curriculum Program was in lieu of the gifted and talented program, which had been canceled by the school district after they became students in our whole language classrooms. (There had been no cause-and-effect relationship.)

I wish I had taped the interview. The educators were impressed with the manner, the competence, the language, the understanding, and the spirit of these two students as they responded to the visitors' requests. What better evaluation can there be?

Nancy as a sixth grader in her fourth year of a whole language program continues to develop literacy. She is an independent learner. She continues to enjoy school as she develops greater appreciation for herself and her world. In December she had an opportunity to compete in a statewide mathematics competition. Her standardized test scores are extremely high, and she is a fine mathematician. I talked with her about the opportunity for competition. Nancy questioned me: What was the purpose for this? What would she get out of it? How long would she be away from the classroom? What kinds of activities would be included in competition? I sent her to others who had participated so she could discuss her questions with former competitors. Later she came to me with her decision not to compete. She felt that it might be a waste of time; it didn't sound as though she'd learn anything. Why miss school to work math problems she might already know how to answer?

Nancy's poetry, her essays, her questions, her perspectives, her dramatic abilities, and so on demonstrate her intelligence and her creativity. She is a student who would have been successful in any program, but she deserves a whole language program because it takes the ceiling off and puts her in charge of her learning.

Figure 10–7 presents some of Nancy's entries in her learning log. These were written in a spiral notebook (a student's workbook) using a double-entry format (Berthoff, 1981). Figures 10–8 and 10–9 are records of Nancy's work in study units in September and January.

The information offered about Darrell and Nancy is specific to their learning and their experiences with schooling. Yet both children are in the same class with the same teacher who maintains high expectations

Figure 10–7 *Nancy's Entries
in Her Learning Log,
September 5, 1986*

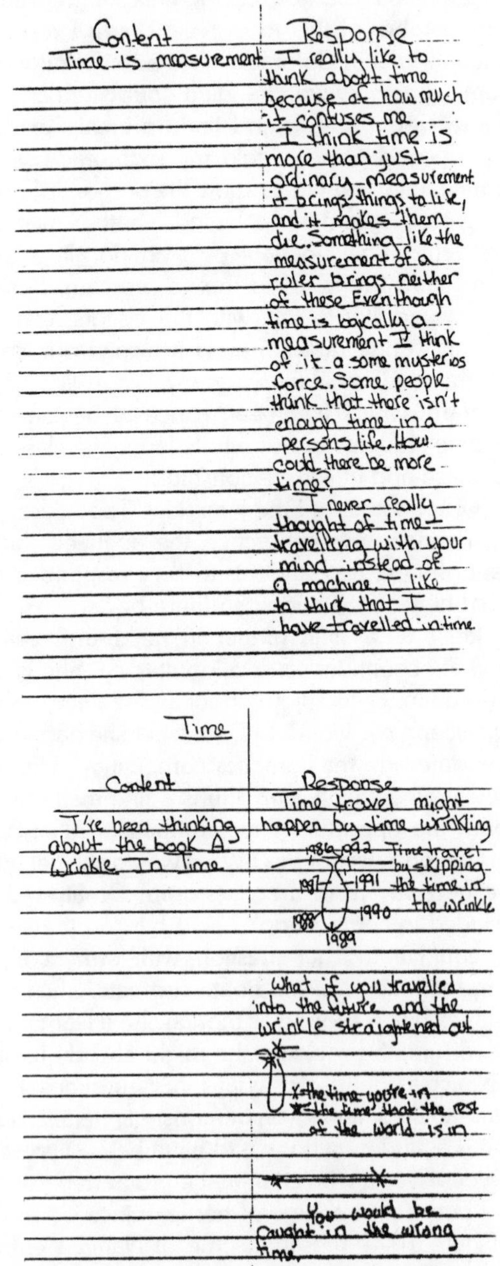

Time

Content	Response

Time is measurement | I really like to think about time because at how much it confuses me. I think time is more than just ordinary measurement, it brings things to life, and it makes them die. Something like the measurement of a ruler brings neither of these. Even though time is basically a measurement I think of it a some mysterios force. Some people think that there isn't enough time in a persons life. How could there be more time?

I never really thought of time travelling with your mind instead of a machine I like to think that I have travelled in time.

Time

Content	Response
I've been thinking about the book A Wrinkle In Time	Time travel might happen by time wrinkling

1986, 92 Time travel by skipping
1987, 1991 the time in the wrinkle
1988, 1990
1989

What if you travelled into the future and the wrinkle straightened out

x = the time you're in
x = the time that the rest of the world is in

You would be caught in the wrong time.

Figure 10–8   *Observation/Assessment Form for Nancy, September 1986*

Name of Unit _Time_
Date _Sept. '86_
Student _Nancy_

ACTIVITIES FOR:

1. PERCEIVING (gaining new facts, ideas, and impressions)
   Independent reading _3 novels, encyclopedias, science journals_
   Read aloud _Green Futures of Tycho, poem of TS Eliot_
   Conversation/Discussion _Participated in webbing, ?ing, Pro/Con groups_
   Presentations _Attended all student presentations_
   Films _Viewed Time Machine, Back to the Future_
   Photos, posters, etc. _Observed work of others_

2. IDEATING (responding to new facts, ideas, and impressions)
   Oral _Asked ?s, offered ideas during webbing, etc._
   Drawing (Illustrating) _Diagram of time wrinkle (being caught)_
   Writing _Logging re: all #1 and #2 activities independently_
   Experimenting _With plants and soil_
   Drama _____
   Other _Participated in all literature group discussions._
   Time line of self/historical event

3. PRESENTING (sharing facts, ideas, and impressions) _(re: Fountain of Youth)_
   Oral _Gave information on famous discoverers + explorers_
   Drawing (Illustrating) _Illustrated poster for poem ↓_
   Writing _Poem "The Reflection of Time"_
   Drama _____
   Other _Made a poster of facts re: Ponce de Léon_

and an enjoyable learning environment. Middle school programs must allow children their individuality.

AND SO?

I believe that whole language programs are not simply viable for middle grade education; they are a necessity. Whole language programs accept all students of varied backgrounds and dispositions toward schooling. The middle schoolers I am working with are becoming more responsible to themselves (and ultimately to others) through a strong whole

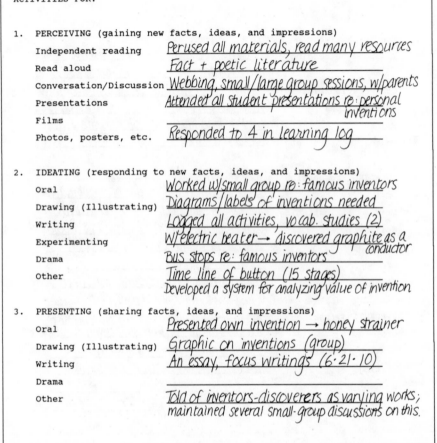

Figure 10–9 *Observation/Assessment Form for Nancy, January 1987*

Name of Unit _Inventions_

Date _Jan. '87_

Student _Nancy_

ACTIVITIES FOR:

1. PERCEIVING (gaining new facts, ideas, and impressions)
   Independent reading _Perused all materials, read many resources_
   Read aloud _Fact + poetic literature_
   Conversation/Discussion _Webbing, small/large group sessions, w/parents_
   Presentations _Attended all student presentations re: personal_
   inventions
   Films
   Photos, posters, etc. _Responded to 4 in learning log_

2. IDEATING (responding to new facts, ideas, and impressions)
   Oral _Worked w/small group re: famous inventors_
   Drawing (Illustrating) _Diagrams/labels of inventions needed_
   Writing _Logged all activities, vocab. studies (2)_
   Experimenting _W/electric beater → discovered graphite as a_
   conductor
   Drama _Bus stops re: famous inventors_
   Other _Time line of button (15 stages)_
   Developed a system for analyzing value of invention

3. PRESENTING (sharing facts, ideas, and impressions)
   Oral _Presented own invention → honey strainer_
   Drawing (Illustrating) _Graphic on inventions (group)_
   Writing _An essay, focus writings (6·21·10)_
   Drama
   Other _Told of inventors-discoverers as varying works;_
   maintained several small-group discussions on this.

language program that respects them and encourages them to participate. My record-keeping system enhances my work and helps me communicate the goals and accomplishments of each student. I feel that our work sets the stage for strong evaluation techniques: making relevant educational decisions for my students.

EVERYONE'S IN THE ACT:
EVALUATION IN A SEVENTH-GRADE
CLASSROOM

Toby Kahn Curry

Five years ago the word *evaluation* was synonymous with "stress" in my professional life. It brought to mind either a rating scale of my teaching performance, a batch of standardized tests that would determine my teaching success in relation to my students' scores, or the quarterly report card markings when I averaged grades for sixty or more pupils. Evaluation never meant analyzing my own behavior, observing my students' growth as writers, reflecting on my classroom organization, or challenging the mandated curriculum from a whole language perspective. That's the way it was, and thank goodness those times are long past.

After careful reflection I have come to understand evaluation as part of the continous learning process in my classroom, a process that is organized and facilitated by the teacher but requires participation by students, teachers, and parents. I still doubt that I'm an expert at evaluating my students' growth, but I am gaining more confidence with every passing year.

Last year I involved my students' parents as evaluators of their children's progress and engagement in the various aspects of our classroom program. At midyear I sent the following letter home with my fifty-seven students:

Dear Parents,

I would greatly appreciate some input and suggestions from you concerning our progress so far in seventh grade 407. I hope that you are aware of the many reading, writing, and research activities that we have been involved with in room 407 since the start of the 1986–87 school year.

I really need parental feedback about your perceptions and observations from "outside" the classroom. Your children can provide me with the data from within the classroom (along with my own observations), but only you have that special parental "window" that gives you that unique view of your child's growth and development over a period of time.

Please tell me what you think should be continued or discontinued and please explain why. Please address all *or* some of the following topics: our weekly current events; our 50 Book Club Reading Program; our student-written weekly spelling lists; our colonial research projects; our Equal Rights studies; etc.— Thanks so much for your help and feedback.

Sincerely,
Toby Curry

I received eighteen written evaluations and one verbal response. This meant that I had feedback from 36 percent of the parents. Since many of my students come from single-parent homes or homes where both parents work, I was pleased to get so many responses. I was also amazed and delighted at the depth and scope of the parents' evaluations. Imagine what a thrill it was for me to receive the following letter from Carrie's mother:

Dear Mrs. Curry,

Thank you for the opportunity to participate in Carrie's school life. As you know as children get older opportunities get less frequent.

Carrie has had great fun with the "50 Book Club." The competition she has going with herself has helped her through some otherwise lonely days. I like to see in her book reviews that she's learning to praise as well as criticize. I hope you will continue the "50 Book Club."

The colonial research project was great! It was Carrie's first introduction to how rich history is. She and I both enjoyed seeing the facts of history brought out in Carrie's imagination. I especially appreciated the way you handled the play reviews.

By writing their own spelling lists the children have lists that do not offend them. One of the common complaints at our house is "they always give us baby words." Carrie enjoys the challenge of finding new words and she often asks her father. So, it is good for the two of them.

With thanks,
Mary C——

Of course many parents had some questions and felt some trepidation about certain aspects of our program. Their concerns and doubts prodded me to make a closer analysis of my students' work and a more careful evaluation of the year's program. The following letter from Heather's mother was filled with a great deal of positive feedback along with thoughtful concern about Heather's spelling skills. Spelling is an expected part of my district's curriculum. After participating in a round-table discussion at the 1986 NCTE convention I decided to try a method that I heard about from a teacher in Maine. When I returned from the convention, I urged my students to select twenty spelling words each week and submit them to me with a letter explaining where they found and why they chose their words. Many students were unable to abandon the spelling text, but others were intrigued and excited by the new option. Although I felt comfortable with Heather's choices, her mother had a different perspective. I was pleased to receive her mother's evaluation:

Dear Ms. Curry,

The program you have developed for the 7th graders this year overall has been a successful one. I find many of the activities ones that stimulate growth and intellectual independence. The 50 Book Club offers a way for those students who do outside reading to obtain some credit for it, and those who are not used to reading outside the classroom may find some initiative to do so. The weekly current events is a must from my perspective. This forces these young adults to look at what is going on in the world around them and introduces them to the varieties of media (newspapers, magazines, etc.). I'm not sure the new weekly spelling method is one that really increases vocabulary and improves spelling. I find Heather looking for words just to have them rather than really looking for those words that are new and challenging.

There have been some good ideas presented in the Social Studies areas. The reports and research on Colonial America and the Civil Rights Movement were great. I feel it's particularly important at a time when so much of the world is interested in computers and electronics, that we still give our children a sense of history and an understanding of the events that make up the world we live in today. I often feel History and the Social Studies are areas this society gives little respect to.

Overall, I find Heather's 7th grade experience to be a very positive one. You have proven to be a teacher who cares, giving the students a sense of independence and responsibility. I believe your students come away with a feeling that education is important and could almost be fun. You instill in these young *impressionable* students that they are their own *thinking*, growing, worthwhile human beings. You will be a teacher they will long remember.

Thank you for sharing this experience with Heather.

Marcia C——

Each evaluation I received was filled with positive comments. I thought at first that there might be thoroughly disgruntled parents lurking in the shadows, waiting to make their criticisms known. But self-confidence and logic took over once again after I had had time to digest the nineteen responses that I received.

I realized two very important things. First, my classroom was probably the first whole language program that most of my kids had ever been exposed to. After six years of traditional, competitive, skills-based classrooms, a whole language curriculum approach seems like a breath of fresh air, even if it does promote some insecurities (such as abandoning spelling textbooks). Second, when parents see that their children are happy and excited about school, that they have some control over their own learning and a strong sense of ownership of their classroom, the parents are pleased and delighted. Imagine having a child entering adolescence who *wants* to come to school each day and willingly participates in reading and writing activities!

To top it all off, this was possibly the first time that many of the parents had been invited to evaluate their child's progress and classroom program.

Since discovering a whole language approach to learning I have also discovered the best teachers I have ever had: my students. By sharing the burden of classroom organization, planning, and evaluation with my students, I have realized how valuable their insights and perceptions are to my growth and development as a teacher, as well as to their own growth and development as learners.

My kids have taught me how to organize classroom materials. ("Put your paperback books inside the room and move the reference books and textbooks into the book cart in the hall. Nobody would bother stealing those." Shari, 1986.)

They helped me understand that a request from me that they organize their notes for their first research assignment was overwhelming. ("I'm having enough trouble just learning to *take* notes, for Pete's sake!" Judy, 1986.)

When I asked my students whether or not we should continue our weekly research and writing of current events articles from newspapers and magazines, my students were unanimous about continuing the weekly assignments. ("I think by doing Current Events it encourages us to look and focus on what's happening in our world. I know that before I got in the seventh grade I only looked at the Sports Section. But now I'm more aware that there are better things than sports in the newspaper." Troy, 1987.)

This year, as in the past, I chose not to use the basal reading program. Instead I relied on reading novels orally to my class, as well as whole group readings and discussions of classic short stories, and a teacher-designed "50 Book Club" reading program. In the "50 Book Club" the kids get credit for every book they read, as long as they give an oral or written book review. Each year over 90 percent of my students complete the requirements for the fifty required credits. I keep their parent-signed statement sheets on file during the school year. When I

135
*Everyone's in the
Act: Evaluation in a
Seventh-Grade
Classroom*

asked the kids at midyear to evaluate the reading program, an over-whelming majority recommended I continue using the "50 Book Club." ("The 50 Book Club? I love it! I don't like the Basal readers, I loathe it!!! [and workbooks too] I read a lot naturally. I don't know if I'm reading more now. It's the first year I've gotten credit for real reading." Melina, 1987.)

Carrie's response to the idea of the basal readers was probably the most emotional. ("The 50 Book Club is working terrific. If you start Basal Readers I'll probably go crazy. *I HATE RESTRICTED READING!* If I have to limit my reading I get frustrated." Carrie, 1987.) Carrie has a personal goal this year—to record two hundred credits for the "50 Book Club." She is in competition with herself and is enjoying notoriety as this year's most prolific reader in the seventh grade.

The program that has evolved in my classroom was inspired by a variety of sources. The skills-based mastery reading programs that my district has mandated stimulated my desperation for a real reading pro-gram. When I saw the "50 Book Club" idea in use in another teacher's classroom, I gradually worked out my own reading plan that revolves around student-selected literature, not skill-sequenced reading activities. Although the students may submit an oral review to the class, most of the book reviews are written and are kept on file in the classroom. Each review includes a brief plot summary and the student's analysis of what he or she liked and disliked about the book. The kids earn additional credits for every additional hundred pages that they read. (A two-hundred-page book is worth two credits.) Class discussions during the school year focus on standard literary terms (plot, theme, setting, characteri-zation). When I respond to the book reviews, I may ask students to explain their reactions or impressions. I try to get my students to focus on the author's purpose as well as *why* they enjoyed or disliked the book.

The major focus of my instructional program revolves around a teacher-directed writing program that integrates the teaching of language arts and social studies. I assign the broad topic for research (colonial America, Native Americans, and so on), and I brainstorm with the whole class to find possible subtopics (causes of the American Revolution, daily life in colonial America, the Cherokee people and the Trail of Tears). After the students have selected their topics, they use log books to follow a research format that I have created from a variety of sources.* My writing program takes them through several basic steps:

1. Brainstorming what they already know about their topic.
2. Developing a plan of work to decide how they will gather information (whom they will interview, where they will find written information, and so on).
3. Conducting their research by taking notes in their logs from their various resources.

*Discussions with Debi Goodman about Yetta Goodman's strategies; working with and observing David Bloome; and reading Macrorie (1984).

4. Writing a rough draft on their topic.
5. Conferencing with their study groups about their writing.
6. Revising their drafts.
7. Writing their final projects.

Evaluation during this process is continuous. I constantly confer with all my students by monitoring their progress in their log books. I try to keep them focused on their topic, guide them to a variety of resources, and teach them how to pull out the valuable information from their resources and develop their own note-taking style. I struggle along with my students as they try to organize the information they have gathered and come to their own conclusions about what they have learned. The most enjoyable part of the process is watching my kids produce their final projects, in which they show the whole class what they have discovered.

I've never considered myself an expert in the teaching of reading, nor have I had any formal instruction in teaching writing, but I can certainly recognize an original, meaningful piece of writing by a seventh grader. The most powerful evaluation of my classroom program stems from the "good works" (Macrorie, 1984) my students produce.

Instead of reading boring, partly plagiarized biographies of famous people, I see original short plays produced for the class. Heather's first dramatic attempt was *Benedict Arnold: An Anatomy of Treason*. Rather than correcting written essays that have no writer's voice, I am able to read the front page of Matthew's *Colonial Times* from July 5, 1776, a historical newspaper complete with an editorial, news stories, and a political cartoon. When Krystal and Holly researched slavery in the 1800s, they showed us what they had learned by presenting a dramatization of a conversation between two elderly ex-slaves. We were all mesmerized as we watched two twelve-year-old girls transform themselves into elderly survivors of the Old South. They reflected on their lives before and after the Civil War and ended the presentation by singing a song from their plantation days when they worked the fields.

I have come to realize that evaluation in my classroom is continuous and comes from a variety of sources. I am constantly listening to my students, learning from their questions, and watching them grow as writers. My kids are always editing one another's work and sharing their progress with their study groups. The parents of my students help their children revise their final projects and often participate in gathering resources for their children's work.

As a "becoming" whole language teacher I find that evaluation of my students, my classroom, and my teaching is easily achieved. What is difficult in a whole language classroom is isolating evaluation from the total program because it is such a natural part of all we do. As one can see in Judy's letter below, it is difficult to separate the impact of her evaluation from the joy of her wit and the strength of her writer's voice:

137
*Everyone's in the
Act: Evaluation in a
Seventh-Grade
Classroom*

Dear Mrs Curry,

I can't really think of much to say, I've already turned off my brain for the summer. It's been a good year, much different from last year. Along those lines, would it really matter if I told you what to change in your room? You change things every year. The new class is going to be so different that even if you seriously and drastically changed your program, it wouldn't matter. You are the one who's going to have to change to fit your class.

Anyway, you have all summer to plan. I think that whatever you do will be right. One thing that might help is trying to think like a twelve-year-old. You can't expect people to listen to you unless you have something important to say, so always be confident. That's it. Have an OK "vacation", and I was joking about the rat poison.

Jude

whole language in secondary and adult education

EVALUATION OF SECOND-LANGUAGE JUNIOR AND SENIOR HIGH SCHOOL STUDENTS

Yvonne S. Freeman / David E. Freeman

"The whole language approach may work for elementary classrooms, but can whole language work at the secondary level?"

"How can limited-English-proficient students handle whole language activities?"

"Even if I did try the whole language approach, how would I grade the students?"

These are some of the most common questions we are asked as we do in-service training with ESL and bilingual secondary educators. Teachers in secondary schools often feel limited by school schedules and traditional methods of teaching and grading. These limitations become even more overwhelming as they are asked to teach content-area materials to second-language students from a variety of linguistic and cultural backgrounds. Sometimes the teachers work with bilingual students in "sheltered content classrooms," where there are no native English speakers to compete with. At other times minority-language students are placed in regular content-area classrooms with students who have spoken English since birth. As the number of minority language students in schools grows each year, teachers look for the best ways to help these students succeed in school.

In Fresno, California, and in Tucson, Arizona, teachers working with students from a variety of language backgrounds have found ways to build on the strengths and potential of all their students, especially their second-language students, and to help these students succeed in school. These teachers organize their secondary content classrooms around six principles of whole language:

1. Learning takes place from whole to part.
2. Activities are learner centered.
3. Learning must be meaningful and functional.
4. Learners need language input from all four modes—listening, speaking, reading, and writing.
5. Learning takes place in social interaction.
6. Comprehension involves constructing individual meanings.

As the teachers are quick to point out, however, it is necessary to do more than talk about learning principles. It is necessary to share specific types of activities that reflect these principles and to devise a method of evaluating the students who engage in the activities.

Evaluation in the whole language classroom needs to take into account individual needs, differences, and interests. A system that allows students not only choices but also control of their own evaluation has proved successful in several classrooms. In this system students choose suggested activities and projects from among options with equivalent value and also negotiate their own options and credit. At the end of each grading period the credit is converted into a predetermined letter grade (the system that determines the conversion is agreed on by students and teachers from the first day). As the end of the period approaches, the students know what grades they can expect and how they can improve their grades. That takes care of the grading and makes it possible for both teachers and learners to concentrate on the more important aspects of self-evaluation and evaluation for planning.

In this chapter we will review each of the six whole language principles, describe specific whole language activities used by teachers in different content areas, and suggest an alternative to traditional methods of evaluation for each activity. We will also provide a sample system that teachers can adapt to their classrooms. Using the proposed system, students and teachers can work together to promote learning and at the same time satisfy the traditional evaluation demands of giving letter grades.

LEARNING TAKES PLACE FROM WHOLE TO PART

We believe that students learn most easily if they study concepts grouped around a general theme or main idea. As kids explore an idea, they become increasingly aware of specific details and how those details relate to the central concept. In evaluation, then, we think whole language teachers will be interested in finding out something about how kids are coming to understand these key concepts. As a result, rather than evaluating bits and pieces of information students may have acquired in the study of some topic, whole language teachers will instead evaluate students' understanding of the general content-area concepts.

For example, in one seventh-grade classroom in Tucson a bilingual class worked with the concept "Where we live determines how we live." Since bilingual students have often lived in two or more very different places, this topic drew on the strength of their experience. Instead of having the students memorize isolated facts about the geography, economy, and products of several countries around the world, as the textbook suggested, Melanie, their teacher, encouraged her students to focus on the larger idea that would encompass all those details. She also decided to have the students begin their investigations by studying their own community.

First, Melanie asked her students, "How does living in the desert affect how we live?" After the students had brainstormed in pairs and with the class, they looked at the answers they were already able to give and at questions they still wanted to answer. Questions that arose included: "How much water do the swimming pools around town use?" "How do we get all our water?" "Will we have enough energy in the year 2000 to keep our homes cool in the summer?"

Students suggested ways to explore the answers to their questions by forming groups to research, interview, and observe. They made comparisons of their community with other communities. Melanie and her students developed an evaluation system that gave them credit for organizing their research; doing the research; participating in teacher-student conferences; completing reports, both oral and written; responding to the reports of others; and completing a self-evaluation. As a result of their investigations the students had gathered different facts and details, but all of the students understood the overall concept and had learned how to discover facts on their own. Melanie was able to evaluate her students both on the process they carried out and on their grasp of the basic concept. At this point the students had a basis for returning to the text to explore the ways in which people in other countries have adapted how they live to where they live.

Felipe, a junior high school ESL geography teacher in Fresno, wanted his students to learn about the different kinds and uses of graphs, including pie graphs, bar graphs, and pictographs. Past experience had shown him that students disliked studying the graphs presented in the textbook and answering the questions based on the sample graphs. And at the end of the unit few understood that various types of graphs are appropriate for representing different kinds of information.

Felipe decided to help students focus on that central idea. The first step, he felt, would be for the students to gather some information that could most effectively be presented in graph form. Instead of beginning their study of graphs by looking at the charts of oil reserves and world population in the textbook, Felipe's students chose a topic they wanted to research. One topic the students were all interested in was their classmates.

First, the students gathered their own data about one another. Students interviewed their classmates to find out what their first language was, what percentage of the class spoke the same first language, what languages the students' grandparents spoke, and how many relatives lived in the United States and how many in another country. In self-selected groups students gathered and organized their data. At this point Felipe showed them different types of graphs, and they decided which type to use to present their results.

Then they made large graphs and put them up around the room.

These graphs served as the basis for lively discussions. Credit was assigned to students for their participation in the process of gathering information and discussing it as well as for their completed projects. By the end the students understood how the data they had gathered could be displayed in different kinds of graphs. They also had a deeper appreciation of the varied linguistic backgrounds of their peers.

ACTIVITIES ARE LEARNER CENTERED

Both Melanie and Felipe planned learning opportunities that drew on the background knowledge and interests of their students to provide the content of their lessons instead of relying solely on their textbooks to provide that content. Whole language teachers also involve their students in the process of evaluation. Rather than giving tests of facts and details that other teachers and textbooks choose for the students, whole language teachers have their students make up their own tests and allow them to devise alternative ways of evaluating themselves.

A successful summer program in Tucson for high school students labeled "limited English proficient" proved that students can evaluate themselves and one another (Freeman, Freeman, and Gonzalez, 1987). Though the students had all failed at least three content-area classes during the school year, they were told that their teacher would work with them to help them succeed in the U.S. history class they were taking. Rather than centering the first day of class on what they had to do to pass the class, their teacher, Ron, explained how everyone would work cooperatively toward common group-set goals.

Ron's classes were not watered down in any way, but he used several techniques to refocus attention from the texts to the concepts and make a variety of oral and written material more comprehensible. Ron showed movies, read stories, brought in pictures, and held group discussions before students read. Groups worked together reading aloud, brainstorming, doing projects, and discussing the main points. Working in small groups, students made up test questions themselves and tested group members. Often Ron set up a sort of game show in which one group asked another the questions they had made up. Then Ron incorporated these questions into his unit exams.

When students discussed the class in their journals, their responses were extremely positive:

> I enjoyed when we got into group today and how we thought of what to write on the board from what we could remember

> . . . it seemed that in this class . . . I learned more than I learned last year and on the first test I took in here was the best test I ever had done and I thank you teachers for the help

> I think this class is very different from others. Group working has helped me a lot.

> This is the first class I ever took where I passed a test without cheating.

145
*Evaluation of
Second-Language
Junior and Senior
High School
Students*

These journal entries formed an important part of the students' self-evaluations. In addition, the groups rated themselves on a checklist, which included such things as how well they had cooperated with one another, how consistently they had stuck to social studies topics in their discussions, and how much their group had contributed to the success of the class as a whole. Thus Ron was able to involve his students in evaluation at two levels, with both their formal tests and their informal self-assessments.

LEARNING SHOULD BE MEANINGFUL AND FUNCTIONAL

In classrooms where they are involved in choosing the content of their studies as well as the ways they are evaluated, students can better set their own purposes for learning by becoming engaged in activities they find meaningful and functional. In these classrooms rather than deciding what students need to do, teachers invite students to explore subjects building on their background knowledge and personal expertise and then to share their knowledge with others in the class.

For example, during an in-service day a group of ESL content-area teachers looked at a U.S. history book written especially for ESL high school students. The teachers discussed together the many possible topics that students could choose to explore the focus of the chapter "Westward Movement from 1848 to 1890." The chapter listed facts and dates, but the teachers decided that they wanted their students to do more than memorize those facts. They hoped their students might gain an understanding of the times and the reasons for the movement and then, perhaps, be able to compare the movement with their own immigration to the United States and possible effects of their migration on the future history of the United States. They discussed potential projects: the California gold rush, the building of the railroad, the importance of the Homestead Act, and the search for silver in the West.

As the discussion evolved, the teachers realized that their goal was not so much for the students to produce a finished report as for them to choose an area of U.S. history that might have significance for them and become an expert in that area. Since second-language students are usually aware that their presence in the United States is not always welcome, the teachers thought it would be important for their students to understand the effects immigration has had in the past and will probably have in the future. The teachers proposed that the students themselves decide how to gather and present information about immigration and determine how to evaluate their work.

At another in-service, ESL English teachers complained that their students did not take composition assignments seriously, especially on topics the teachers chose. Discussion led to the suggestion that instead of assigning topics, teachers might invite students to write to one another about topics they found interesting. For beginning students short messages could be exchanged or kept in dialogue journals. In these instances note-passing would become a legitimate classroom activity. Students would use English to communicate with one another in writing. Beginning students could read their own messages at first to be sure they were clear. Out of these activities students would begin naturally to help one another with vocabulary, spelling, and grammar because they would want to communicate.

Once students were writing longer texts, pen pals could be established between classes or schools. Lonna, an ESL content reading teacher in Fresno, has been having students from the two high schools where she teaches exchange letters. She observed, "Students put much more time and effort into getting the letters edited carefully for each other than for compositions they write for me! Not only that; they want to write!" Lonna has noticed the excitement and interest generated as students receive and respond to pen pal letters. When students write for a real audience and for a real purpose, the assignments take on meaning and have a function that calls for a real response. Lonna has found that students share their letters with her and one another and thus improve their writing through discussion. This type of activity is meaningful because students have become involved in the writing process as a communication tool.

LEARNERS NEED INPUT FROM ALL FOUR MODES

In all the classes we've described the teachers involved their students in activities that included speaking, listening, reading, and writing. For example, Ron's students read the text to one another, discussed the text in groups, and wrote down what they considered to be the main points. When evaluating his students, Ron gave them credit for their speaking, listening, and reading activities as well as for what they wrote in tests and journals. Rather than basing their grades entirely on the results of written exams and compositions, he gave his students credit for activities that involved listening, speaking, reading, and other kinds of writing. In this way teachers applying whole language can include in their evaluations both the processes their students go through and the final products they create.

Bill teaches high school biology in Fresno to classes of limited-English-proficient students. At the beginning of the year Bill and his students devised a grading system in which students are credited for engaging in different activities. For example, students get credit for keeping science logs detailing their observations; doing and demonstrating experiments; doing research in groups and presenting the results in an oral report to the class; attending special lectures, programs, and science fairs and reporting back to the class; interacting with a special guest speaker; tutoring other students; keeping daily or weekly journals; and responding to other students' journals. The students themselves kept track of their credit activities and their own progress in the class. By including all these different factors in the grading system, Bill ensured that his students understood that he valued all the different kinds of listening, speaking, reading, and writing in which they were engaged.

147
*Evaluation of
Second-Language
Junior and Senior
High School
Students*

LEARNING TAKES PLACE IN SOCIAL INTERACTION

In many classes students sit quietly in straight rows most of the day. The students in the classes we've described spend most of their time working in groups. It follows, then, that rather than giving credit on an individual, competitive basis, teachers also credit group efforts and products. Cooperative learning techniques seem to be especially successful with minority students (Kagan, 1986). In cooperative learning students are grouped heterogeneously, and a "positive interdependence" is created as group materials are shared and group recognition is given for group products.

When activities are set up that allow them to work together, students cooperate enthusiastically. Carol, an ESL teacher, reported that her groups worked together much more productively after she began to assign and value group projects. Once students realized that their teacher gave credit for the work the groups produced, they began to organize and plan carefully. Carol told other teachers that she had found, for example, that skits were more effective when students received a group grade. All the students were motivated to participate to produce a quality product. In order to include students with different interests, the students themselves negotiated different kinds of participation, including writing and editing the skits and organizing props.

David, a high school science teacher with a large number of language-minority students in his biology class, explained that, frequently, shy second-language students who would never speak up in class discussions became very involved in small-group projects. In their groups they were able to demonstrate their understanding of the subject to their classmates and could contribute to the success of the group. By evaluating his students' activities in these group situations David was better able to assess their knowledge of science. At the same time the native English speakers in the groups came to value more highly the abilities of the second-language students.

COMPREHENSION INVOLVES CONSTRUCTING INDIVIDUAL MEANINGS

Teachers applying whole language value students' ability to construct meaning as they read. This is especially true for teachers with language-minority students since those students bring very different backgrounds and experiences to their reading. Rather than reading the chapter and answering questions at the end, students in whole language classrooms construct their own questions about the text and find the answers not only in the text but in other sources. The authors of textbooks often write questions that require a simple, literal repetition of a portion of the text. When students do that type of exercise, they construct no personal meaning. They simply copy the part of the text that contains a key word from the question. Even when questions ask for main ideas or key concepts, there is no opportunity for students to explore ideas and construct their own meaning.

In Tucson, Ron was aware that his students were answering textbook questions by matching key words in the questions with the text. They could do this without much comprehension of the questions or the answers. Ron was able to make a change by having his students work together on the content of the textbooks. In this way they helped one another construct a meaning from the text. The students' background was different from that of the textbook authors and the teachers, so it was important to give the students a chance to work with the text with their peers, ask questions about the text in class discussions, and respond to the text and class discussions in their daily journal writing. Ron gave students credit not only for student-constructed questions but also for their discussion participation, pair and group work, and the personal journal responses. Ron's goal was to have the students explore the ideas in the text and to learn how to construct meaning from text.

In her content-reading class in Fresno, Lonna's students choose their own books to read from literature sets available in the classroom. Each set consists of five or six copies of paperback books that are interesting to teenagers. Students discuss the books in groups. In their literature journals they respond to the parts of the book that they especially like and tell why, or they write about the parts that remind them of their personal experiences. Lonna's goal in this class is not to have students answer comprehension questions about the books or write traditional book reports but to have them read English for enjoyment and to respond to the parts of the text that have significance for them. Thus the students construct individual meaning for the text by reading, discussing, and writing. Lonna evaluates them by giving credit for participating in this process rather than by asking them comprehension questions about their books.

A SAMPLE SYSTEM FOR ASSIGNING CREDIT

While a credit system is not necessary in many whole language classrooms, it is a convenient means of charting student progress in many secondary classrooms and a method to which many secondary students are accustomed. As students engage in a variety of activities, they get credit for both the processes they engage in and the products of their learning. It is important, however, that earning credit does not become the motivation for learning. And the amount of credit should be agreed on by the teacher and the students.

Melanie's class of bilingual seventh graders who examined the relationship between where they live and how they live provides an example of how a system can be set up. The students in her classroom engaged in the following activities:

1. They brainstormed in pairs to answer the question "How does where you live influence how you live?"
2. They shared their answers with the class and participated in the ensuing class discussion.

149

*Evaluation of
Second-Language
Junior and Senior
High School
Students*

3. Through the class discussion students raised questions, and students in pairs or groups of three chose questions to research.
4. The students listed resources and methods they planned to use in researching their topic. They also formulated an action plan and a time line and gave these to the teacher.
5. They carried out their research. While activities varied depending on the topic chosen, students kept group logs of these activities in which they included observations and interviews.
6. The students held conferences with the teacher to share their logs and evaluate their progress in terms of the time lines they had set up.
7. Pairs or groups of students presented oral and written reports of their research to the class.
8. The students listened to the reports of the others and filled out response sheets to those presentations.
9. Students filled out self-evaluations on their own reports and responded to the evaluations made by the other students and the teacher.

During the four weeks the students worked on this unit the teacher charted the progress of individual students. Credit was allotted for each activity as follows:

Activity	Possible credit (percent)
1. Participating in brainstorming.	2
2. Sharing answers with class.	4
3. Choosing questions to research.	2
4. Making preliminary list of resources for research.	5
5. Writing a time line for the research.	3
6. Engaging in research for fifteen days.	2 per day
7. Participating in three conferences.	10
8. Oral report.	15
9. Written report.	15
10. Listening to others' reports and filling out response sheets.	4
11. Filling out self-evaluation.	5
12. Conference response to evaluations of classmates and teacher.	5
Total	100

While it is not necessary to have the credit add up to 100, the number is commonly used in grading and is easily understood by students. Over the course of a quarter a teacher could make the same amount of credit possible for each week. In this case a four-week unit adds up to 100. In a nine-week quarter there could be 25 a week for a total of 225.

Students should help to establish the grading scale before beginning the unit, and teachers should allow students to negotiate credit for activities and participation. There should always be the possibility of making a case for more credit for creative or unusual efforts. And there should always be the possibility of students regaining lost credit through extra effort or redoing past products. If students understand the system, they can keep track of their own progress. Then, during the final conference between the teacher and pairs or groups of students, agreement can be reached on the credit earned.

Several things are important in using a credit system such as the one we have just described.

1. The system should be easy for both the teacher and the students to understand.
2. At least as much weight should be given to work in progress as to final products.
3. The students should be involved in negotiating the system.
4. Awarding or taking away credit should never become part of the discipline system. It should be clear that the system is simply a convenient way of facilitating assigning grades and not an end in itself or a system of rewards and punishments.
5. Finally, the focus of the class should be on the content, not on the evaluation. This is facilitated by presenting the system briefly at the beginning and end of the unit and referring to student credit as little as possible during the weeks the students are engaged in learning about the topic. It is particularly important that earning credit does not become the motivation for engaging in learning.

CONCLUSION

A whole language approach to teaching secondary language-minority students draws upon their interests, strengths, and background. Teachers can involve students in whole language activities and evaluate their work using a system that students understand and believe is fair. Since the system can be converted to letter grades, the teacher, student, and administrator can be satisfied by the evaluation procedure. Rather than evaluation being the sole goal, it becomes part of the shared process of learning.

GRADE EIGHT STUDENTS COPE WITH TODAY AND GET READY FOR TOMORROW

Richard Coles

"Hi there, Mr. Caldwell, where do you want us to sit?"

"Hey, Miss Di Pede, I like your blue sweater."

It is the first day of school. As grade eight teachers greet their classes, they realize that these students are in a unique position. They are about to complete one phase of their schooling and are looking forward with excitement and a little apprehension to their years in high school.

The teachers also are thinking about this transition. They want their students to have a successful year, but there are concerns about reporting students' progress and the expectations of secondary schools.

Some teachers implement whole language activities and evaluation techniques in the lower grades. Sometimes, however, they feel the need to be more traditional in the last year of middle school or junior high to prepare the students for high school.

Such comments often voiced in casual conversation in the staff lounge or at grade meetings remind me of one of my favorite "Peanuts" character posters. "Education Prepares You for Tomorrow" can be seen on the blackboard. Poor Charlie Brown, with his head on the desk and a forlorn look on his face, comments, "I'm not even ready for today."

For several years I have been teaching in a multicultural inner-city community in Toronto, Ontario. Drawing from our past teaching experiences, graduate study, professional reading, discussions, and attendance at conferences, we have developed a curriculum with a theoretical rationale based on whole language principles (Goodman, 1986).

Our daily teaching practices reflect our knowledge of psycholinguistics, literature, curriculum implementation, evaluation techniques, cognitive psychology, the composing process, biological and neurological devel-

151

opment, our students, and the world of early adolescence. In our whole language teaching we are always aware of the need for evaluating and communicating progress to our students, their parents, and our colleagues at several different high schools.

In our grade eight classrooms as teachers we are cheerful, well organized, understanding, and energetic. Frank Smith (1986) talks about the need for students developing literacy to feel that they are part of the "literacy club." Whole language teachers don't just teach reading and writing; they demonstrate with excitement and enjoyment the advantages of such membership. They enjoy reading themselves and reading to their students. Sharing personal thoughts, ideas, and feelings about the readings is a daily occurrence. As members of the class, whole language teachers are seen as fellow writers. They extend an invitation to the young teenagers to join or renew their membership in the literacy club.

Whole language grade eight classrooms are colorful, literate environments where learners feel comfortable engaging in a variety of reading and writing experiences. Teaching strategies, materials, and learning experiences differ from the prescribed language arts curricula in current use in many middle schools or junior highs. Students are actively involved in decision making and in their learning. They self-select reading materials and have time in class for reading and discussing literature with friends. Compositions are written for different audiences and for a variety of purposes. Their responses to literature are displayed throughout the classroom.

The adolescent world is a busy place. In addition to their classes the students are involved in extracurricular activities, sports, clubs, part-time jobs, family responsibilities, Heritage Language Programs,* and just hanging out with friends.

They seem to be in a state of perpetual motion and change. One day they are sophisticated socialites preparing for a school dance. The next day a small stuffed animal takes its place on a desk. Some appear to grow before your eyes. They switch culture groups—from "Head Bangers" to "Preppies" on a day's notice. It is a time to try new fashions and to experience different feelings. No one is more self-critical than an adolescent.

The young people bring with them different life experiences, expectations, learning styles, and attitudes toward adults and learning. Many students in our urban Toronto school are new to our country, culture, and educational system. English is often their second or third language. Some learners have attended school in two or three countries, in refugee camps, or in as many as six or seven other school districts in Ontario. The customs and values of their homes are often quite different from those of the prevailing peer culture.

From our experiences it is evident that a whole language approach

---

*In a Heritage Program students have an opportunity to maintain or extend their first language other than French or English. These voluntary classes are in addition to the school curriculum. For our students these classes take place after school or in the evenings.

not only meets the varied needs of our pupils but also enables them to be successful in grade eight and in secondary school. As teachers we try to capitalize on the excitement of the literacy development of this diverse school population.

The remainder of this chapter describes methods of evaluation we employ in our classrooms.

It is essential that methods of evaluation assess the ongoing development of the learners. James B. Macdonald (1974) concluded after examining evaluation for fifteen years that "evaluation is at the present the major disaster area in education." If Macdonald is correct, there are means to halt this trend and to prevent future disasters. Despite numerous articles and research many administrators, school boards, and parents still maintain that a number such as a 7.4 reading score is an accurate, valid assessment of progress.

Rexford Brown (1986, p. 123) compares this practice with the use of economic indicators that "are gross estimations open to flagrant misuse and multiple interpretations." He continues, "Many people are convinced that standardized tests though far from perfect, are good enough estimates of what is going on in school and school districts."

I believe that a number score is an ineffective method of assessing and reporting the complexity of the reading and composing processes. What does a holistic writing score of 8 mean to a grade eight student or to the parents? How does this score help an adolescent become a better writer? What does it tell a teacher at another school?

Our method of evaluation involves teacher observation, interviews, and anecdotal records to assess and record development.

Students are actively involved in record keeping and self-evaluating. Each student has a reading and writing folder. Atwell (1987) and Coles (1986) describe various methods for using reading folders. Reading interviews permit a teacher to employ a variety of questions and probes to determine a reader's comprehension of and personal response to what has been read. Students are also encouraged to evaluate the text and their ability to understand it and to ask the teacher questions. Classroom time is also available for discussion and evaluation of personal readings with other students. A variety of grouping and discussion strategies enables the readers to interact with many of their classmates in small groups.

To record my observations of reading in class or after an interview I use a plain notebook with the student's name at the top of a double page. On the left-hand page are comments about the student's reading process. I list the reading strategies the pupil successfully employs to obtain meaning from the text. On the right I record notes about books or materials the pupil requires or possible strategy lessons for the reader. (See Figure 13–1.)

The second double page belongs to the same student. On the left is a simple checklist for assignments. For example, when Fiona has finished her poster advertising a favorite novel, the assignment's name and any other pertinent comments are recorded. (See Figure 13–2.)

Figure 13–1   *First Double Page*

Student's Name: Fiona

Left-Hand Page: Reading Process	Right-Hand Page: Materials
Selects a variety of novels dealing with friendship and feelings. Uses prior knowledge to predict the story's events. Self-corrects when necessary. Has developed a sense of story for these novels. Able to analyze the character's actions. Compares the story events with her own life experience. Compares book to others by same author.	Wants to read the new Gordon Korman book. Needs cardboard and markers to make a character poster. Is completing a list of books we need for our class library.

On the right I record observations of the student during discussions or group work or while he or she is working on reading activities. I also record unobtrusive observations (Webb et al., 1986) of behaviors that demonstrate that the pupils may be becoming readers for life. For example, Rui, an active, athletic pupil, comments that books and reading are boring. In January he tells everyone that a new adventure book is the best novel ever written. He then disappears into a quiet corner and reads for a whole period. By the end of two weeks he describes and discusses three other novels by the same author.

Paula and Julie arrive at school with two small stacks of new novels.

Figure 13–2   *Second Double Page*

Student's Name: Fiona

Left-Hand Page: Assignments	Right-Hand Page: Observations
1. Character poster 2. Book advertisement 3. Post card 4. News story for a novel	Is reluctant to participate in group discussions. Reads during spare time. Takes books home regularly. Suggests new books for our class and to her friends. Prefers to work alone.

They have joined a local library and have bought three new books at a nearby bookstore. A complex exchange network is quickly established to aid in the circulation of these materials.

I also observe students who select a book to read during spare time in class or who recommend a book to a classmate. In our class students sign out novels to read at home. Usually over half the class decides to take a novel. The sign-out list gives me some insights into reading habits and interests.

Each grade eight student also has a writing folder. Graves (1983), Giacobbe (1984), and Atwell (1987), among others, describe procedures for using these folders.

To record my observations I use another plain notebook. Each student is assigned four pages. (See Figure 13–3.) On the first page I write my observations of the students as they are writing in class or after a conference. The second page contains a list of the things the student can do as a writer. On the third page I note certain goals we have agreed to incorporate into the next piece of writing. The final page contains a list of the writer's work.

Figure 13–3   *Four Pages of a Notebook for Writing Observations*

Student's Name: Tylor

Page 1: Writing Process	Page 2: Skills as a writer
Has many interesting story ideas.	Uses paragraphs.
Discusses his story with several people before writing.	Variety of sentences.
Writes with several drafts spread out on a table.	Well-developed characters.
Revises the conclusion until it sounds right.	Uses a title.
Prefers to do his final copy on the computer.	Uses periods, question marks, exclamation marks.
	Proper use of capitals.

Page 3: Goals in Composition	Page 4: Titles
Use quotation marks before and after a character's exact words.	Skateboard Blues
Eliminate some overused words and clichés.	Lifestyles Of the Poor and Unworthy
Provide more information about the story's setting.	Dorfs Revenge
	The Cremation Of Orville Redenbacher

Before the end of a term I have an interview with each student. The pupils bring their reading and writing folders, and we discuss their progress, review their work, and talk about how they are developing as readers and writers. I also ask them to evaluate themselves and ask questions concerning their development.

These methods of evaluation permit me to move about the class recording my observations; they do not require a great deal of valuable class time. Since development is personal, observations and comments vary throughout the class. By reviewing these notes I can easily trace the literacy development of each student. The student is already aware of that progress, and I can discuss this process with parents and teachers from other schools.

Many of our parents appear to be reluctant to visit school. Education in North America is different from their experience. They often do not feel comfortable expressing themselves in a second language. When parents visit our school, we have the students act as guides, explaining displays and acquainting their parents with reading and writing folders. Translators from the community assist in the parent-teacher interview. A teacher's warmth, caring, and knowledge of a student is easily discerned by parents despite the language barrier. With the involvement of our students it is not uncommon to interview a family representative for each member of the class.

Students from our school have an opportunity to choose among seven different high schools. During class visits or on professional development days we meet with members of the secondary panel to discuss curriculum, specific students, and methods of helping our pupils make a smooth transition to high school.

Representatives from the various secondary schools usually inquire about students' reading levels and their writing experiences. Anecdotal records and reading and writing folders help shift the discussion away from number scores and toward what our students can do as readers and writers.

High school teachers in all subject areas find this information useful when planning their teaching strategies. For example, grade nine English teachers know that our students discuss literature in small groups and are familiar with conferencing with peers or a teacher. Geography and history teachers can examine several written assignments, from simple research reports to eyewitness accounts of an event in history. Our talks also outline the procedures the writers followed to produce these final reports.

At the conclusion of each school year the local high schools send us a printout of our students' grade nine marks. It is most encouraging to discover that our students are generally very successful in English classes and in other areas of the curriculum.

A whole language grade eight classroom requires daily organization, enthusiasm, and knowledgeable teachers. Suitable evaluation procedures give the pupils, their parents, and the teacher a clear, valid indication of each student's literacy development.

USING EVALUATION
AS AN INSTRUCTIONAL STRATEGY
FOR ADULT READERS

Ann M. Marek

Adult readers who want to improve their reading ability often have misconceptions about the nature of the reading process and their accomplishments. Extensive research has shown that for proficient and nonproficient readers alike, reading involves constructing meaning from print and, in the process, making miscues. Thus, even for good readers, reading is not a perfect rendering of text resulting in a complete, unabridged recollection of what has been read. Unfortunately adult readers "in trouble" often ascribe unrealistic qualities to good readers: good readers know all the words they encounter, they never make mistakes, and they remember everything they read. Measured against this mythical good reader, many adults find themselves lacking. Perhaps because readers in trouble are consciously aware of their inadequacies, many become immobilized in their attempts to grow as readers. The challenge these readers present is clear: How can teachers help them move toward more effective use of reading strategies and more positive and realistic perceptions of themselves as readers? How can they help these readers to revalue themselves?

One strategy that I have found particularly useful in working with adult readers is called retrospective miscue analysis (RMA). This strategy is designed to involve readers in self-evaluation of their own reading, and the self-evaluation becomes instructive. The technique provides readers with a method for evaluating the quality of their own miscues so that they may begin to see error as a qualitative rather than quantitative issue. This awareness of the reading process and of their own strengths and weaknesses brings about a positive change in the reading strategies they employ. And as readers assume control of the evaluation process, they begin to take control of the reading process itself.

157

READERS WHO NEED TO REVALUE READING

The scenarios are familiar. In Tucson, Carmen, a young mother in her late twenties, calls the university and asks for help with her self-described "fourth-grade reading skill." Another woman in her early forties, faced with the challenge of finding employment, calls for help from the Reading Center at the University in Reno. Gloria describes herself as "a fraud, a cheater who has spent years covering up" her reading difficulty. And Marianne, a twenty-one-year-old woman who has been in special education classes since third grade, contacts the Truckee Meadows Community College in Reno, willing to try another in a long series of efforts to remediate her "dyslexia."

What these women had in common when I met them was their certainty that they were bad readers; that the strategies they used when reading were nothing like those used by the good readers they knew. Here are some of their responses to questions from the Reading Interview (Goodman, Watson, and Burke, 1987):

ANN: Who is a good reader that you know?
MARIANNE: My mom.
ANN: What makes her a good reader?
MARIANNE: She reads a lot. She helps me.
ANN: Does she ever come to something she doesn't know?
MARIANNE: Yeah.
ANN: What does she do?
MARIANNE: She looks words up in the dictionary.
ANN: Do you ever do that?
MARIANNE: Not really, because I can never find the words.

ANN: Who is a good reader that you know?
CARMEN: My brothers are good readers.
ANN: What makes them good readers?
CARMEN: They all went to college in Guadalajara. They are all intelligent.
ANN: What do your brothers do when they come to something they don't know when they read?
CARMEN: They never come to something they don't know. They're very smart.

The women all believed that learning to pay closer attention to the letters and sounds within words held the key to improving their reading.

ANN: If you knew somebody who was having trouble reading, what would you do to help that person? What would you recommend?
CARMEN: Help them sound out words.
GLORIA: I would let them read, and I would point out things. You know, "What does that word say?" All the time. Like you do when you're teaching a child. Say the word over and over again; maybe get them to write it down. Maybe just sounding it out and saying it to you. I think that's all.

MARIANNE: [The readers] would sit down and read along with a teacher and if they got in trouble the teacher would have them say the word and keep going on. But if they kept missing that word, they would have to stop and spell the word, and say it, and go through that way.

Analysis of their initial reading ability using the Reading Miscue Inventory (Goodman, Watson, and Burke, 1987) suggested that these three women were somewhat ineffective as readers. But I doubted that a program focused on skill building through "practice reading" would be helpful. Rather, I suspected that in order to grow as readers they needed to become risk takers. And in order to become risk takers they needed to revalue themselves as readers. It seemed that self-evaluation was a promising approach to use in demonstrating that many of the strategies these women used were effective, even if they did involve making miscues, while others were less effective. We know from miscue analysis research that all readers make miscues; but in their focus on making sense good readers tend to produce the kind of high-quality miscues that result in minimal loss of meaning. We also know that even poor readers use some high-quality strategies as they read, whether they are aware of that strength or not. In retrospective miscue analysis, readers become involved in analyzing their own miscues and making determinations about which strategies seem to work well and which do not. As they become more aware of effective reading strategies, they begin to incorporate more of them into their reading. For readers like Carmen, Marianne, and Gloria whole language teachers may wish to incorporate retrospective miscue analysis into their instructional repertoire.

THE TECHNIQUE

Retrospective miscue analysis is a technique that allows readers an opportunity to analyze the quality of miscues they made during an earlier reading. The technique described in this chapter has been used with a teacher and reader working one to one, although it can also be used by readers working in pairs or in small groups. In a typical RMA session a reader is asked to read a self-selected text, unaided by the teacher, into a tape recorder for the purposes of conducting miscue analysis. Following a retelling of and discussion about the text, miscues from the tape recording of the previous week's reading are analyzed by the reader.

THE RMA QUESTIONS

The following questions are asked by the teacher during the RMA session in order to guide the reader in evaluating the quality of the miscues. Note that while these questions serve as a guideline, adults who are participating in RMA sessions very quickly internalize the questions and begin to ask them of themselves. Because the readers are frequently in control of the direction the discussion takes, the questions are not always asked in the exact order presented here.

Always ask:

1. Does the miscue make sense?
2. Was the miscue corrected? Should it have been?

Consider asking:

3. Does the miscue look like what was on the page?
4. Does the miscue sound like what was on the page?

Always ask:

5. Why do you think you made this miscue?
6. Did that miscue affect your understanding of the text?

Here is an excerpt from Gloria's fourth retrospective miscue analysis session. The miscues she was analyzing are listed as figures.

[Gloria and I are seated at her kitchen table. A tape recording of her previous week's reading of "The Boy and the North Wind" is being listened to at points where miscues have been selected for discussion. The RMA session itself is being tape-recorded for transcription at a later time. Gloria is able to hear herself reading on the tape recording, and the typescript with her miscues marked is also in front of her on the table. The first miscue is shown in Figure 14–1, A.]

ANN: Does that one make sense?
GLORIA: It does make sense in a way; it could be like me being a mother and I'd say, "Go and get some meal for your porridge."
ANN: Is that one you corrected?
GLORIA: No, I didn't.
ANN: Do you think you needed to?

Figure 14–1 *Gloria's Miscues*

A. Go to the storehouse and bring me some meal for *your* ~~our~~ porridge.

B. He *sat* seated himself and said, "Cloth, cover the table and serve a fine meal."

C. In the middle of the night she crept to the room where the boy was *sleeping* ~~asleep~~ and took the cloth from him.

GLORIA: Not really. I think you could still get the gist of the story. But it was a mistake.

ANN: Do you think it affected the meaning of the story?

GLORIA: No.

ANN: What we're trying to focus on again is the efficiency with which you read—the fact that you don't need to correct things that make perfect sense. That's what good readers do. And you are beginning to make more and more corrections on things that don't make sense.

[*The next miscue is shown in Figure 14–1, B.*]

GLORIA: I didn't say "He seated," did I?

ANN: You said, "He sat himself." Does that make sense?

GLORIA: "He sat himself down" would have been correct. "He sat himself. . . ." It might make sense to me, but I don't know if it is correct grammar.

ANN: I don't know either. I think speakers of varying dialects of English would be able to say different things there. What we tend to do is to manipulate text to suit our own dialect.

GLORIA: I think maybe you're right. I think I said it how I would say it.

ANN: Does it have any meaning variation at all?

GLORIA: No.

[*The next miscue is shown in Figure 14–1, C.*]

GLORIA [*laughs as she hears the tape*]: Asleep . . . sleeping—well, that makes sense. I'm putting my own things in.

ANN: Any reason to correct that one?

GLORIA: No.

ANN: It's precisely the kind of miscue good readers make and don't bother to correct. They're so adept at predicting and sampling the text to confirm whether they're right. If we read letter by letter and then crunched it into words, we could never read as quickly as we do.

GLORIA: I guess not.

ANN: So reading isn't letter by letter, put it together, make a word, say what the word is, and then go on.

GLORIA: I think that's what I used to try to do. But I must be getting better at that.

ANN: Because now you're paying attention to sense, and that's the only thing that matters in reading.

It is clear from this excerpt that as RMA sessions progress (this was Gloria's fourth), the teacher begins to assume the role of co-evaluator —extending the observations of the readers and sharing professional knowledge about the reading process. The importance of the teacher's knowledge base must be stressed. That knowledge is what guides the whole language teacher in capitalizing on so-called teachable moments inherent in RMA sessions and leads to opportunities for readers to revalue their strengths in the reading process.

THE SELECTION OF MISCUES FOR ANALYSIS

Approximately fifteen miscues can be analyzed in an RMA session lasting one hour. Typically the teacher reviews the tape recording of the previous week's reading and preselects miscues for the reader to analyze during the RMA session. A critical feature of retrospective miscue analysis is that it encourages readers to become more self-confident about their reading skills by revaluing the extent to which the strategies they use are effective. For this reason teachers can select a majority of miscues (about ten to twelve) that show strength in the reading process and allow readers to release themselves gently from the notion that all miscues are bad and require correction. Some guidelines for selecting RMA miscues follow, based on individual reader characteristics:

Reader Characteristics	*Suggested Miscues*
Low self-confidence.	Select miscues that are fully acceptable semantically and syntactically and are uncorrected.
	Select miscues that are unacceptable and corrected.
Holds a text-reproduction model of the reading process.	Select miscues that are acceptable and have little or no graphophonic similarity.
	Select miscues that are acceptable and contain insertions and omissions.
Needs to focus on making sense.	Contrast miscues that do make sense with those that don't.

As readers become more confident of their abilities, comparisons between higher- and lower-quality miscues can strengthen their understanding of the qualitative differences among miscues. The selection of miscues for a particular session may also become more thematically oriented as sessions progress. The teacher may notice interesting patterns of miscues across a text and design a session where readers are encouraged to evaluate those patterns. For example, a session might focus on contexts in which *then* is substituted for *when* or on comparing the quality of insertions and omissions throughout a text. It is in these RMA sessions that the technique may work most like a "strategy lesson" (Goodman and Burke, 1980).

Certainly as readers increase their confidence and become comfortable with the RMA technique, they may begin selecting for themselves the miscues they wish to analyze. They may also begin to work in pairs or small groups, and the role of the teacher may move from co-evaluator to session facilitator.

RMA RESULTS

Several research studies have documented the effectiveness of RMA techniques in improving readers' self-perceptions (Woodley and Miller, 1983; Stephenson, 1980; Worsnop, n.d.). In my own research (Marek, 1987) conducted with Gloria and Marianne, each of them moved from what appeared to be a text-reproduction model of the reading process to a model focused on meaning construction, on making sense. Consider the following responses made by Gloria and Marianne at the close of our four months spent together:

ANN: When you are reading and you come to something that gives you trouble, what do you do?

GLORIA: Well, now if I'm into the story I try to read on and I try to get the word later. I try to look at the next couple of words. The other day I actually went on, then I went back to it and I realized it was such a simple word—I should have got it really. Wasn't simple, but just because it was long I didn't get it. Then I went into the sentence and got it right. So that's what I try and do now.

ANN: Do you have any different attitudes about reading than you had at the beginning?

GLORIA: I find now that I am looking around for something to read. Used to be when I was in a doctor's waiting room, I would just sit there. And now I will try to find a paper or a book to read. Anything, rather than just sit there and be bored. Before I wouldn't touch a piece of paper with words on it. It would either be scary or I knew I couldn't even read "The cat sat on the mat." . . . I find that it is quite interesting to read, I must admit. I am surprised that people write such a lot of rubbish, though. And I never knew that before.

Marianne expressed similar thoughts:

ANN: If you knew somebody who was having difficulty reading, what would you do to help them?

MARIANNE: Encourage them to read, practice reading.

ANN: What if they came to something they didn't know?

MARIANNE: Tell them to ask someone to help them.

ANN: What if they were all alone?

MARIANNE: Tell them to skip it.

ANN: What should they be thinking about the whole time they are reading?

MARIANNE: Just making sense of the story and understanding what the author wants them to understand.

ANN: How do you feel about your ability to continue to improve your reading?

MARIANNE: I can do it. It will take a lot of practice and reading a lot on my own.

My research with these two women also confirmed that those positive changes in self-perception were accompanied by an increase in effective use of reading strategies. During the four months I spent with each of them they received no instruction other than being involved in RMA sessions. For the most part they self-selected the texts they read each week, and I used the Reading Miscue Inventory to analyze those readings. The texts ranged in difficulty from about third-grade through college level and included fiction and nonfiction. At every level of difficulty each of these self-described nonreaders was able to demonstrate an improvement in the quality of her miscues, accompanied by a decline in the actual number of miscues made. In a sense a cycle of revaluing had begun. As the readers began to view themselves more positively as readers, they found the confidence to focus on meaning instead of letters within words. The focus on meaning resulted in more effective reading and higher-quality miscues; and the RMA analysis of those high-quality miscues served to strengthen the readers' confidence.

A FINAL NOTE

Individualizing instruction and evaluation is a cornerstone in whole language theory, whether the classrooms are in school buildings or in suburban kitchens. Readers proclaim themselves to be "in trouble" for a myriad of reasons. A businessperson may sense that she is a poor reader because she is unable to keep current in reading the dozens of trade journals that cross her desk. A student failing in college English classes may be certain that he reads poorly when in fact his difficulty is in writing the required five-paragraph essay. It is possible that neither of these difficulties would be associated with the kind of ineffective reading strategies revealed through miscue analysis. As a result the techniques a teacher might use to help each of these readers would probably not include retrospective miscue analysis. But when a twenty-one-year-old dishwasher like Marianne describes herself as a dyslexic nonreader, and miscue analysis confirms the presence of ineffective reading strategies, then RMA may serve as a catalyst in the revaluing she must accomplish in order to begin improving her reading. In this context the process of evaluation has become a process of instruction, and the two processes work in tandem to support the development of the reader.

revaluing
potential
losers

"... OF FLYING TO THE STARS AND LOOKING AT THE DIPR": WHOLE LANGUAGE EVALUATION ON THE NAVAJO RESERVATION

Susan Howe-Tompkins

Chinle, Arizona, is situated in the heart of the Navajo Nation, ninety miles from the nearest town of Gallup, New Mexico, where the Navajos go to shop, visit doctors, repair vehicles, and trade.

Many Chinle children, grades K–3, attend Chinle Primary School (a public school). Ninety-five percent are Navajo. Most of them speak Navajo as their first language.

For Navajos communication and teaching have historically been in the form of a strong oral tradition. For many families this is still the case. Grandparents traditionally teach the young ones sheepherding, use of herbs, rug weaving, jewelry making. They teach Navajo ways through example, participation, and storytelling.

Beulah and her family live in tribal housing, a basic low-rent house with electricity and plumbing. Her father is employed, while her mother stays at home with Beulah and her siblings. Much of Beulah's time is spent with Grandma at her hogan nearby. Grandma speaks only Navajo and lives by traditional Navajo ways. Beulah and her classmates have heard many traditional stories. Navajo storytelling is seasonal. During the winter months, when the animals are asleep and before the first lightning, many legends and fables are told for teaching purposes. Among these stories are Coyote Tales. The coyote holds special cultural significance and purpose.

Integrating Navajo culture throughout my program, for example by using Coyote Tales as a springboard for oral and written activities during the appropriate season, establishes a foundation for trust, communication, and success.

For the first several months of her third-grade year Beulah was quiet and reluctant to use English. Her excessive absenteeism those first months was a strong hint of her attitude toward school. On the days she did attend, I made a point of saying, "Beulah, I'm so glad you're here today." Through our use of whole language and positive affirmations in our classroom Beulah grew to overcome her apprehension in sharing language. Her attendance also improved notably.

The third graders who attend Chinle Primary School come from many backgrounds and interests. Travis, one of eight children, lives in Nazlini, a remote rural community southeast of Chinle. Travis's father is employed in Chinle. His large extended family maintains a traditional Navajo lifestyle. They live in a hogan with no running water or electricity. They care for livestock (sheep, cattle, and horses), speak predominantly Navajo, and maintain Navajo ways. Travis's fondness for horses is apparent in his art. His drawings of horses display great detail and intimacy. Horses capture his interest in books and art and in his ideas for writing.

Ranae lives in a blend of modern and traditional ways. Her father is a butcher in a large market. Her mother is an office clerk. Like Travis, Ranae lives in Nazlini. Unlike Travis's family, however, Ranae's family lives in modern tribal housing and speaks English at home.

Spanish-American Laila lives one-half mile south of school in a trailer that has electricity and many modern conveniences. Her father raises livestock and is the leader of Chinle's Future Farmers of America. As the eldest of four children, Laila spends much of her out-of-school time caring for brothers, sisters, and animals. English is predominantly spoken in the home, but Spanish is spoken as well. Laila says she speaks very little Spanish.

Beulah, Travis, Ranae, and Laila represent a sampling of the 64 percent of third graders who had scored a grade equivalent of 1.9 or below on the ITBS Language Usage test at the end of second grade.

My immediate job as a teacher of a pull-out third-grade Chapter I English as a Second Language class was to determine which children out of that group should be selected for the program.

After becoming familiar with the Language Usage portion of the ITBS, I realized that this score didn't tell me anything about the competence of these children in oral or written English. What the test told me was what the kids know about identifying aspects of English grammar. The absurdity of the scores was even more apparent when I compared the students' reading level (in English), determined by a Ginn Basal Reader Placement Test, with the ITBS grade-equivalent score. Some students showed a language-usage grade equivalent of K7 (seventh month of kindergarten). Most did not score above 1.5 (fifth month of first grade). Their reading scores were considerably higher.

The discrepancy between test scores and ability is illustrated by Laila's work. When the time came for her to submit her first writing sample, Laila was reluctant to write anything. I invited her to tell her story on tape. She liked this idea and was excited although anxious. I was astounded at how well she created her story on the spur of the moment. I transcribed the story after our session:

A fox came and when they were asleep the fox came and got one of the sheep. And the next morning the boy got up and he counted and he saw one missing. So he hunt all evening and he couldn't find the sheep, so he went to sleep again! And the fox came and got another one! And the boy start . . . [*pause*] and he. . . . [*pause*] So the next day when he was sleeping, the boy stayed awake and looked. And the fox came and took one of the sheep and the boy saw it. When the boy saw it, when he took one, the boy left the sheep. And then he went off and started hunting. And when he went off hunting the wolf came and the boy saw it. And he had a sharp, sharp stick and he threw it and it stabbed the fox. And the sheep never got killed any more. And the boy didn't have to go hunting no more. And he lived happily ever after.

Later Laila confirmed my suspicion that her literacy background included much storytelling.

I realized I needed something more than test scores to come up with a sensible way to select the kids who needed my program most.

ORAL RETELLING

Keeping the whole child in mind, I wanted to capture the child's most natural oral language through a retelling of a story that contained predictable, repetitive language; creative, imaginative, stimulating vocabulary; and rich contextual and pictorial clues that would advance the plot. I selected the story "The Hungry Giant" (Storybox Books, 1986) to use for fall and spring retellings.

The Hungry Giant

"I want some bread!" roared the giant.
"Get me some bread, or I'll hit you with my bommy-knocker."
So the people ran and got the giant some bread.
"I want some butter! . . . (the pattern repeats)
"I want some honey! . . ." (the pattern repeats)
The people found a beehive.
The giant looked at the beehive.
"That's not honey!" he said, and he hit it with his bommy-knocker.
The bees zoomed out. They zoomed after the giant.
"Ow!" he roared, and he ran and ran, ow, ow, OW, all the way home.

I introduce the book to each child, saying, "I'm going to tell you a story called 'The Hungry Giant.' All of the words are covered up because I just want you to listen to the story. When I'm through we'll go back to the first page and I'll ask you to tell the story back to me the best you remember. I'll turn on the tape recorder so that we can tape your story."

Following each retelling the children are able to hear a portion of their retellings. Then we talk about their strengths. For many students this kind of feedback is a new and enjoyable experience.

FOUR RETELLINGS IN FALL

Laila:

Get me some bread. So the people ran and got him some bread. Get me some butter, the hungry giant said. So the people ran and gave him the butter. The giant wanted some honey. The people look . . . wanted . . . ran. Looked everywhere but no honey. I want honey, the giant said. Get me some honey. The hungry giant said get me some honey. The people found a honeyhive. This is . . . this is honey. The giant said this is not honey. So he banged it with his bonk [?] . . . bonker [?] The honey ran . . . the . . . all the flies zoom, zoom, zoom and followed the giant. The giant was running home.

Focus for discussion of strengths: "I think making up other words like 'honeyhive' and 'bonker' is a good idea."

Ranae:

He was hungry and he said he wanted some bread. Then the people ran and ran and got him some bread. And he yelled again and said get me some butter. And the people ran and ran and got him some bread. And he said he wanted some honey and the people ran and ran and ran and got honey. They looked everywhere and then he yelled again he wanted some honey and his bommy-knocker and they found him some honey. He said it's not honey and he hit it with his bommy-knocker and the bees started biting him and biting him and the giant ran and ran home.

Focus for discussion of strengths: "I can tell that you have read books often. You tell a good story."

Travis:

Giant man. Giant . . . [response unclear] bread. Ran. Said give me some butter. And . . . [response unclear] Giant said honey. They ran. They ran. Said honey. Giant. Give me some honey. Here's the honey. He's looking . . . he's hitting it again. Ran. Giant ran away. Bees. [Most of Travis's responses followed probing questions.]

Focus for discussion of strengths: "I can see that you understand what the giant wanted and what happened to him."

Beulah:

Giant. Let me have some bread. I'll hit you with my . . . [no response] The children ran to him. And let me have some bread . . . I mean . . . the butter. And the children are crying and they run away. And let them have some honey. I'll hit with my stick. The children are ran to somewhere. The children are crying and digging, they're just sitting, they're crying. He said don't do that. [Probe: What does the giant still want?] The butter and the bread and the honey. And here's the bread and the honey and he smelled it and that's bees house. And then this is not a bread with honey. And then the bees went out and then they're going like that.

Focus for discussion of strengths: "You used the pictures to help you tell the story. That's good."

EVALUATIVE NOTES

Following each retelling, after the students leave I write anecdotal evaluative notes. In this way there is no anxiety or interference from the teacher taking notes during the interaction. Yet it is important to record in writing while the thoughts are fresh. The success of retelling depends on the close interaction between the teacher, the book, and the child. Probe questions—questions intended to initiate more language about the meaning of the story—are often used to help stimulate the flow of thought and language. The tapes of the retellings are kept on file for further analysis, to share with teachers, administrators, and parents, and as basic documentation.

I use the same outline to evaluate each retelling. In italics is the basic outline; following that is my evaluation of Beulah's retelling.

1. *Comprehension*
   a. *Main idea:* Supported by student's comment after question: What else does the giant still want? "The butter and the bread and the honey."
   b. *Supporting details:* Student retells details of the children crying, running away, digging, sitting, the giant smelling the honey.
   c. *Logical sequencing:* Student indicates sequence of what the giant wants (bread, butter, honey) and in what order the children get these things.
   d. *Use of dialogue:* Giant: "Let me have some bread. I'll hit you with my . . ."
      "And here's the bread and the honey."
   e. *Book talk:* No indication of book talk in this sample.
   f. *Expressiveness:* Some use of expression in the giant's dialogue.

2. *Syntax:* Sentences convey meaning but are often short and simple. This shows me her need to hear and use English more.
3. *Semantics:* Student communicates a meaningful message with additional descriptive phrases for personal interpretation.
4. *Fluency:* Student often uses Navajo language structure when speaking English. Needs more exposure to oral and written English.

THE WRITING SAMPLE

Following the retelling, I offer the children three story starters from which they are to choose one for writing:

- One morning I woke, looked out my window, and there was a giant cornstalk as high as I could see. So . . .
- As I lay asleep under the stars, I dreamed . . .
- One day the shepherd boy was out with his sheep, when all of a sudden . . .

Though I wouldn't normally give story starters in a creative writing program, owing to the time constraints of evaluating many children, I use them in this manner.

Before selecting a topic, we read through the choices together. I sit with the children as they write their stories to give support and to observe their writing behaviors. I encourage them not to worry about constraints but to "write their thoughts on paper."

THREE WRITINGS IN FALL
Barry:

So I ran out the house
and tole the
Pepole ran out the huoes
and thay took off a nother
huoes the corn stalk went to
the bee huose

Lemix:

I dreamed . . .of flying to the stars and
                    looking at the dipr.

Ranae:

As I lay asleep under
The stars, I dreamed . . . giant.

EVALUATING WRITING SAMPLES

In evaluating the writing samples I want to look at three specific strengths:

1. Fluency: How much language was written and with how much ease?
2. Semantics: Does the story make sense?
3. Message quality: Is there evidence of beginning, middle, and end? Is there a sense of story? A sense of audience?

To help my evaluation in these three areas I selected two evaluating systems. Both the Clay Scale (Clay, 1975) and the T-Unit (O'Donnell, Griffin, and Norris, 1967) enabled me to answer my questions and to put the evaluation into a numerical format that would facilitate selection into my program.

According to Marie Clay one may observe change and development in a young child's written work at appropriate intervals. The samples should be analyzed according to:

1. Language level: What is the linguistic organization used by the child?
2. Message quality: Does the child have the concept that a message is conveyed? How much language is used to convey that message? Are the sentences arranged in some sort of order with one or more main ideas?
3. Directional principles: Does the child use spaces between words and sentences? (Clay, 1975)

A T-Unit is defined as a single independent clause together with any attached dependent clauses. A clause is a structure containing a subject and a verb (O'Donnell, Griffin, and Norris, 1967). The T-Unit measurement is an appropriate tool because I am looking primarily for cohesive language, which is especially important for second-language learners. I was not looking for correct grammar so much as I was looking for a cohesive text.

Barry's fall story about running out of the house reveals four T-Units in thirty words, averaging out to a mean length of 7.5. On the Clay scale his story rates Language 4, Message 3, and Direction 3. By evaluating the children's writing in this way, I am better able to see and compare strengths and weaknesses.

PROGRAM SELECTION

After evaluating the oral retellings and scoring the writing samples, I am able to distinguish those students whose oral and written English are limited from those whose English-language abilities are relatively adequate. Children with weak retellings as well as kids with scores below 5 on the Clay scale and a T-Unit length below 7.0 are selected for my program.

The results of the fall oral and written samples are reviewed and explained to the classroom teacher. During this conference I discuss the interpretation of the samples as well as the basic philosophy and content of my ESL program. Further insights into the students are shared with the teachers. Through our shared analyses we are able to make fairly accurate selections.

THE ONGOING PROGRAM

In the winter and again in the spring both the oral retelling and a written language sample are collected from each child. By comparing the early samples with the later ones I am able to document growth. A midyear conference with the classroom teachers focuses on evaluating progress as well as making referrals for students to continue or discontinue my services. I am also able to show the classroom teacher how growth can happen naturally in a whole language setting without explicit drill on grammar or isolation of language skills.

The oral and written samples, kept in the students' folders along with other writings throughout the year, are shared and discussed with the kids, affirming their growth as writers and speakers of English. Out of this positive affirmation their confidence and trust in themselves as communicators grows.

Travis's winter retelling and Ranae's winter and spring writing samples exemplify that growth.

Travis:

Giant. The giant said give me some bread. Ran to the giant. Give me some butter . . . peanut butter. And ran to giant. Give me some honey. Ran way. Looking to find honey. Get some more honey said giant. I'll hit you . . . I'll hit this . . . He get honey. He look un honey. He hitted the honey. The giant ran away the bees.

Ranae's winter writing sample:

So I went to tell my mom and Dad
That I saw giant corn stalk. When I
When I woke up.

Ranae's spring writing sample:

In a little town near the sea there were
lots of peple even there were too
mush house but all the houses were
full. Thay need some more houses in the
town. Thay had to live to geter
untle a that can fix some house. and than
A prson came the town he said he was
from the city. He said some of you
can come to the city. Who have no
houses so thay went to the city but
thay did look so nice. But in the town

175
*". . . Of Flying to the
Stars and Looking at
the Dipr": Whole
Language Evaluation
on the Navajo
Reservation*

thay look funny when thay come to
the city peple said thay are funny
but when the peple from the city
can to the town the peple of the
town said the city peple look funny.

Significant positive change has occured by the spring. Students have
written and published several books and a monthly school newspaper
and have participated in puppet shows, choral readings, and storytellings
for selected audiences. Had I relied on the ITBS pretest scores alone
to determine the selection and evaluation of my students, not only would
I have had a false representation of their level of proficiency but I would
also have been ignorant of their English-language development. Eighty-
two percent of the students in my program showed an increase in their
grade-equivalent language-usage score on the ITBS posttest. I had documentation of significant language growth for all my students.

The intention of my program is to create a learning atmosphere that
is centered on children's language strengths rather than language def-
icits. I try to create a place where children receive support in creating
and sharing language and sharing their Navajo heritage. The success
of my program, while documented in the collected language samples,
is most evident in the children's attitudes as they ask daily, "Mrs. Tompkins, are we having language today?"

THE EVALUATION PROCESS—
IN PROCESS

Debra Jacobson

At the beginning of school while cleaning out the files I found IEP (Individual Education Plan) forms that listed phonics tests and the Woodcock and other skills-oriented testing devices. I was preparing for my second year as a second and third grade Chapter I reading teacher in an urban southern Arizona school district. I had been told that each child would need an IEP. But what I needed was an IEP form that would reveal information important to me as a whole language teacher. Counting on administrative respect and support (support I felt for the first time in eight jobs), I designed an evaluation system that would be in the students', parents', classroom teachers', and my own best interests. I kept the same IEP form but changed all the categories. Information for the IEP would come from whole language evaluation measures: some published, like the Reading Miscue Inventory (RMI) (Goodman, Watson, and Burke, 1987), and others that I developed myself.

Just as we expect children to grow and change, my evaluation process continues to evolve. In order to show the evaluation process I use, we'll follow one student, Jesús, from our first meeting through different times in the school year. Through a variety of documentation tools, you will see Jesús's growth. I will also be commenting on my rationale for using the selected tools, my own growth in implementing them, and my plans for future change.

DOCUMENTING JESÚS'S GROWTH

Jesús is a second grader who was referred to me by his teacher because he appeared to have very low "reading skills" compared with the rest of his class. I met with Jesús in the first days of the school year. At our first meeting I asked him the questions in Figure 16–1 and recorded his responses.

What is important for me is information that reveals a student's attitudes and self-concept as a reader or writer. In my quest to understand and document student attitudes I have used four different questionnaires about attitudes and interests but found them too cumbersome in our school, which has a high student turnover rate. This year I boiled the questions down to the thirteen most useful to me.

Jesús's responses helped me decide which passage to start with for the second part of our initial interview. His low self-concept as a reader led me to choose a simple, predictable language story. I followed the

---

Figure 16–1 *Jesús's Responses to the Reading Questionnaire*

1. Do you like to read? _Sometimes_ Why? _I just don't got that much books._

2. What kinds of books do you like to read or listen to? _Little Red Riding Hood; Berenstain Bears; Dinosaurs_

3. What do you do when you're reading and you come to something you don't know? _Tell my mom and dad._

4. Do you think reading is important? _yes_ Why? _So you can learn to read._

5. Do you go to another library besides the school library? _no_
   Which one? _—_ How often? _—_ With whom? _—_
   Do you have a card with your name on it? _—_

6. Is reading hard or easy for you? _7_ Why? _Some I know, some I don't. Some words are easy, some are hard._

7. What's your favorite subject in school? _music_ Why? _Because we get to do things there._
   (Note: didn't understand "subject.")

8. What do you like to do in your spare time? _Watch TV (lots), play outside hide and seek with sister_

9. Are you a good reader? _Not that much_ Why? _'Cause I don't know how to read that much._

10. Are you a good writer? _Sometimes_ Why? _Some things I don't know how to spell._

11. What languages do you (or your parents) speak at home? _Dad— Spanish Mom— Spanish a little   Jesus—English_

12. Is your family a reading family? _Mom—she's not. Dad— isn't either. Sometimes they read to me, sometimes they don't. Dad likes dinosaurs, Mom likes Berenstain Bears*_

13. Is there time and a place for you to read at home? _Sometimes Mom and Dad say no. I have to ask._

Other comments:
   (#12 cont) They read mine. They don't have their own.

Reading Miscue Inventory procedures (Goodman, Watson, Burke, 1987). I told Jesús that he'd read from the book while I listened, jotted down some notes on my paper, and taped what he read. I also told him that I wouldn't be helping him and I'd be asking him to tell me about the story when he was finished reading.

What Jesús read is shown in Figure 16–2.

When I asked Jesús what the story was about, he said, "The boy liked his wagon for a bus. He went on a hill and put it in his bed. He let his dog sleep in it."

I get a lot of information from being an active participant-observer, a kidwatcher, when children are involved in actually reading and writing authentic and extended texts.

Before students came to school this year, I selected several stories,

Figure 16–2 *What Jesús Read for* Rudy's New Red Wagon

Rudy's New Red Wagon

A boy and a its his at
Rudy got a new red wagon.

S be a bus driver
He liked to sit in it.

S
He liked to put toys in it.

S
He liked to ride in it.

S people too
He liked to take his dog (for) a ride (in it.)

S at
He liked to go to the park in (it.)

S in riding down the hill
He liked to go down the hill in it.

He liked to go fast.

day he made a bus
One night Rudy put his wagon in his bed.

He got into
Then Rudy couldn't get in the bed. The wagon starts to move

He took it at he liked to make red but not (?) he sleeping it.
I like my new red wagon. But not in bed with me.

typed them up double-spaced, and made several copies of each in order to mark the typescripts of the stories during students' reading following the procedures of miscue analysis. Knowing that I'd have readers at many levels of early development, I chose several predictable texts including some well-known stories such as "The Three Little Pigs" and others at greater levels of difficulty, according to my own judgment, but keeping in mind that the texts should contain language patterns and concepts familiar to the children. *Rudy's New Red Wagon* (Scott Foresman, 1971), the story Jesús read for me, is one of these texts.

Jesús's reading and retelling indicated that *Rudy* was a difficult story for him. When students have a hard time with even the most predictable passages, I ask them to tell me a story and I write it down, using a piece of carbon paper in order to produce an instant duplicate so that I can mark the miscues on the copy as the students read from the original. Then I have them read it back following miscue analysis procedures. Figure 16–3 shows Jesús's story and miscues.

I noticed that while he was reading his dictated story, Jesús paid more attention to the written text at the beginning of the story than he did at the end. The meaning remained basically the same. I noted this observation to enter later onto his IEP.

After each initial meeting, either my aide or I entered the responses from the questions onto each student's IEP. (In an effort to save time, I toyed with the idea of writing the questionnaire responses directly onto the IEP form.)

I also dated any passages read and jotted down initial comments and observations. Figure 16–4 shows what the front page of Jesús's IEP looked like after I had reflected on our first meeting.

Once my program got under way, I continued doing evaluative work with students during our regular sessions within small groups as we introduced ourselves and became familiar with books in the room and other materials. I introduced students to our class library and how it is organized. I asked them to spend some time browsing, reading if they wanted to, and choosing three books to check out and take home. I told them I'd be interested to know why they made their choices.

Figure 16–3 *Jesús's Story and Miscues*

my go tell say
After I watch the show I want to watch I tell

Seek I goes
Monica to play Hide and Go Seek. But she never

didn't she went to tell my Dad
finds me. She goes and tells my Dad about that.

Figure 16–4 *Jesús's Individual Educational Plan*

Name _Jesús_ Grade _2_ Teacher _Ms. Smith_ Date accepted _8/19/86_ Date left____

ITBS Date _5/86_ Referral Date _8/15/86_ Gates-MacGinitie Date_____ Date_____

% Score _2_

	%ile	GE	%ile	GE
Vocab	___	___	___	___
Comp.	___	___	___	___
Total	___	___	___	___

Chapter 1 Teacher _Jacobson_

B = Browsed   LAP = Looked at Pictures   PBQ = Put back quickly   RR = Reading

	Entrance Testing	Observations	Instructional Plans
① 8/19 ORAL READING ② 8/19	A Boy, A Dog, A Frog The Bus Ride Rudy's New Red Wagon My Name is Tommy The Empty House The Three Little Pigs Are You My Mother? The Missing Necklace The Little Knight Willaby The Chimp and the Dinosaur Dictation	① _Some attention to print, but mostly making up meaning from pictures; some lack of meaning._ ② _Initial attention to print; less at end of story._	_Begin with simple predictable books._ _Shared reading with pointing at words._
READING STRATEGIES	Something you don't know: _Tell Mom and Dad_	_8/19 Used pictures; made up own text._	_Help Jesús develop independent strategies._
INTERESTS	Books _Berenstain Bears, dinosaurs, Little Red Riding Hood_ Spare time _lots of TV, play_ School _Music_		_Call Jesús's attention to predictable book section. Contact Jesús's parents about how much support Jesús has at home for choosing to read rather than watch TV._
INTERACTIONS WITH BOOKS		_9/86 Picked several B. Bears. B, LAP, absorbed._	
SELF-CONCEPT	Hard or easy _Easy/hard_ Good reader? _Not that much_		_Enhance self-concept._

When we began this activity, Jesús made a beeline for the *Berenstain Bears* books, pulled out about seven of them, sat down by himself, and started to browse. I noted this observation in section 3 of his IEP under "Interactions with Books": "9/86   picked several B. Bears. B [browsed], LAP [looked at pictures], absorbed." Toward the end of the session I asked students individually which three books they'd like to check out and why. Jesús picked out three *Berenstain Bears* books and said that he was going to show his little sister the books. I noted his intense interest and absorption in these books on his IEP as well as his lack of any attempt to read the text.

It is important to me that every part of the evaluation process be meaningful and purposeful to both the students and me. In an evaluative writing activity I explain to students that I want to know what they know and think about writing.

I show them some of my own writing that I am working on and point out that my early draft is sloppy with crossing-out and misspellings. I tell them that they will begin by writing their own sloppy copy about anything they want and that I won't help them with their spelling because I want to see what they can do. I explain that after this they will have the option to read their piece to a group, fix it up, and finally copy it over for the final draft. They write the first draft with black pens so that I can see what they cross out and self-edit. I tell the students I want them to use black ink because I intend to photocopy their work after school. Jesús's initial sample looked like the one in Figure 16–5.

The next day I hand back the originals and ask if anyone would like to read to the group. I talk briefly about how we can help each other make our stories clearer. For those who decide to read to the group, I ask if there's anything specific they'd like us to listen for and help them with. I keep notes on what the reader and audience say.

For the next step I give students a thin green marker and tell them to make any changes they want; to mess up their sloppy copies before they recopy for their final draft. Before I distribute the green pens, I demonstrate on the chalkboard some ways that I use marks to revise my writing. Figure 16–6 is Jesús's revision. (Note the only two changes are the addition of 2 A's.)

As students use the green markers and later copy their stories for final drafts, I make notes, recording student comments and behaviors in the writing section on the back of the IEP. Figure 16–7 is what Jesús's IEP looked like at this point.

Throughout the year I keep the IEPs handy during class to jot down any observations that come up during the course of our work together

---

Figure 16–5 *Jesús's Initial Sample*

A long time ago there was
a dinosaur named Tyrannosaurus Rex, who is in the
museum and everybody was laughing at it.

Figure 16–6 *Jesús's Revision*

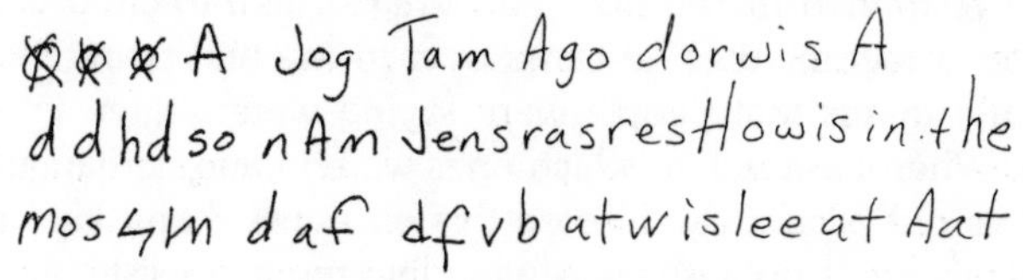

> XXX A Jog Tam Ago dorwis A
> d d hd so n Am Jens ras res Howis in the
> mos 4 m d af dfvb atwislee at Aat

that seem interesting or in some way point out where the students are
in their literacy development. Sometimes I record puzzling occurrences.
In the context of everyday activities I find that students make significant
and revealing comments. I use the comments on the IEP to see if there
are patterns to what is happening. Such evaluation helps me plan for
each child.

One day early in the school year the students were reading books in
pairs. I was noting how they decided between themselves who would
read. When Jesús's partner told him to take a turn, he said, "I can't, I
don't know how to read." I knew I had to continue to work on boosting
Jesús's self-concept as a reader.

I frequently take time to sit back and observe students, reflecting on
their actions, behaviors, and choices rather than rushing in to direct what
they're doing or to steer them to do things that I think are productive.

Figure 16–7 *The Reverse Side of Jesús's IEP Form*

	ENTRANCE TESTING	OBSERVATIONS	INSTRUCTIONAL PLANS
AT HOME	#5 library *no* #11 language *English/Spanish* #12 reading family *no* #13 time/space *?*	9/15/86 Jesus has regularly checked out books from the classroom library. Jesus speaks English as his primary language.	Encourage Jesus's parents to take Jesus to the library.
READING ATTITUDE	#1 like to read *Sometimes* #4 important *yes*	9/15/86 Jesus listens avidly to stories read to the group. He appears to have a good attitude about books.	Reinforce positive attitude.
WRITING	#10 self-concept *Sometimes*	writing sample 8/29/86 Used invented spelling, unconventional word boundaries, attempted revision — very little, was not able to read story to the group, but did so w/my help. Wrote willingly.	Encourage more writing.

Jesús was spending a lot of time looking at the last page in the book *The Biggest Cake in the World* (Cowley, 1983), which shows people standing around eating slices of cake and commenting in little comiclike bubbles. I restrained myself from encouraging him to choose another book. After a few minutes he came over to me and pointed out that some of the things that people were saying were written in another language. When I asked him which ones were in another language, he pointed this out accurately! I noted this on the IEP and later realized that from this point on Jesús was attending more consistently to print and really making an effort to read rather than to construct a story almost exclusively from the pictures.

In December and January I focused on more formal reevaluation of the progress the students were making. I met with individuals during class time and together we looked over their IEPs and addressed areas of concern.

My students have learned that I am very interested in their thoughts about their transactions with the reading and writing processes, and consequently they have become more comfortable sharing their insights. This helps me a lot in evaluating their progress, and it helps them move ahead in their learning as they verbalize their insights, questions, or confusions.

Sometimes I have students reread texts that they read at the beginning of the year as well as more advanced ones. In most cases they show great improvement, which I point out, explaining to the students some of the things I've learned about their reading from the miscue analysis so they can see what they're now doing differently and more effectively.

When I met with Jesús on January 5, I asked him to read *Rudy's New Red Wagon* again. After he read (very successfully!) I showed him how he'd read it at the beginning of the year. He was very pleased with his improvement. This time when I asked him what he did when he was reading and he came to something he didn't know, he said, "Skip it." I jotted this down on his IEP form. I was glad that he felt he had an independent strategy to use in dealing with impasses in his reading.

I also asked Jesús how he thought he was doing with his reading and he said, "I'm doing better. I can read more and I know more words." I noted these entries on the IEP.

I continue to attach dated writing samples as well as any miscue analysis texts to students' IEPs. At the end of the school year, during a final formal conference, I ask each student the thirteen questions again and do one last reading miscue inventory. I also keep an end-of-the-year writing sample, following the same procedure as I did at the beginning of the school year.

Jesús's final writing sample, revised after reading to the group, is shown in Figure 16–8.

When I compared his final sample to his first, I noted the following indications of growth on his IEP:

- Conventional spelling of high-frequency words.
- Concept of wordness, use of word boundaries.

Figure 16–8 *Jesús's Final Writing Sample*

my BroTh yowsT To Rid my
grandmoes 'chicKin and my grand-
mo youst to smack him.

My brother used to ride my
grandma's chicken and my grandma used to smack him.

- Use of punctuation—hyphen and period.
- More consistent use of capital and small letters.

SHARING JESÚS'S GROWTH

All the documentation is useful during the course of the school year when I participate in child-study meetings. Other teachers find much worthwhile information in looking at writing samples or listening to a child read. My colleagues find it informative to follow along in a text while I use the miscue coding to read a story the way the student did. I can point out strengths and other insights about the student's reading.

I sat in on a child-study team meeting for Jesús in November. His teacher described him as a nonwriter, but as we looked at his first writing sample and the other writing he had done, we could see together that this was hardly the case! The teacher was interested to see the kinds of things that Jesús could do, and she was eager to hear any ideas I had for helping him.

I keep in touch with parents and call them on the phone; I have a home liaison aide make home visits or make my own visits. Fortunately I don't have to give grades or participate in the report card system. I feel that the contact I have with parents provides them with a lot of evaluative information and creates a valuable two-way exchange. The interaction usually starts with a positive "good news report."

I ask parents the questions: Does ——— read at home? Have you heard ——— read lately? How do you think ——— is doing? What do you tell ——— to do when he gets to something he doesn't know? Depending on the depth of discussion that any one of these questions triggers, I save some questions for another conversation. Lots of useful information surfaces. In one telephone conversation Jesús's mother asked if it was bad that his father yelled at him whenever he missed a word. We discussed the importance of boosting Jesús's self-image and encouraging his taking risks as a reader and how his father's tactics could be counterproductive.

Another conversation led to his mother asking for books to be sent home since they didn't have many books at their house and it wasn't easy for them to get to the library. I usually let students check out one book at a time, but after this conversation Jesús took several books home at once and then returned them for a new batch.

EVALUATING MY OWN GROWTH

At this writing (it's the summer before my third year on this job) I am considering how I will use evaluation in the coming year. I'm not yet totally comfortable with my present evaluation process. I think I'd like more room on the form for recording observations, and I'd like to devise a system to keep whatever I'm writing on *very* handy for use in class.

Perhaps I will have a folder for each student and keep each class's folders together in a wire basket. This past year I paper-clipped each student's writing samples and other work together behind the IEP, but the volume became unwieldy.

I think I'll use the thirteen questions more extensively to follow the

Figure 16–9 *A Way to Use the Thirteen Questions, with a Coded System*

```
Name _____          \  Focus on this

                                       O  Discussed this

    _____

    INTERESTS

    General:



    Books:



    _____

    SELF-CONCEPT

    Is reading hard or easy for you?



    How are you doing with your reading now?



    _____

    ATTITUDE

    Do you think reading is important?_____  Why?



    Etc....
```

Figure 16–10 *Using Index Cards*

Date	Observations	Instructional Plans

---

students' attitudes. I'll use ruled lines to separate the different sections to make it clear for myself and use a coded system to point out areas to focus on, as shown in Figure 16–9.

I'll record on a separate form with lots of room to make anecdotal notes about informal reading that I listen to during the course of the year. I think I'll prepare lots of typescripts of stories so I'll have a wider choice when I ask someone to read.

I'll use five-by-eight index cards to record observations and interactions, making a vertical line off center to the right, as shown in Figure 16–10.

I'll keep the cards for each class together so that they're readily available to me during class times. As they get filled up, I'll staple them into the inside cover of each student's file, with the most recent one on top.

I will consider the entire portfolio the student's IEP. In the back of the file I'll staple a paper where I'll list the strategies we're working on together. I'll use a symbol for those that we both consider have been completed, and throughout the year we will review these together and discuss where the students are with the targeted strategies. These strategies can be drawn from any part of the portfolio. For instance, Jesús's may look like the one in Figure 16–11.

Figure 16–11 *Strategies for Jesús*

JESÚS 10/4/86	If you don't know a word, skip it, read on, and then come back to make a guess.
10/16/86	If you don't know a name when you're reading, make one up.

It feels good to step back, evaluate, and evolve my own system of evaluation, moving closer to being able to focus on significant interactions with learning in order to facilitate growth and provide useful information to everyone in our school.

"SO WHY DON'T I FEEL GOOD ABOUT MYSELF?"

Debra Goodman

"O-F-F. O-F-F. What's this O-F-F all over everything?" Steve muttered as he looked through the advertising pages spread around the table.

"That says 'off,' " Andy offered, as he pasted down the ads he had cut out. "You know. Fifty cents off. Twenty cents off."

"Fifty cents *off?*" Steve said. "Why not fifty cents *on?*"

"Or fifty cents *in*," said Andy.

I overheard this conversation in a kindergarten class one day. Although I was called a remedial reading teacher, I considered myself a reading specialist, helping students and teachers to revalue the reading process. Students' views of reading, their views of themselves as readers, and their teachers' views of both play big roles in their success in learning to read. It made sense to me to begin with our newest students, helping them to view themselves as successful readers before they could develop a view of themselves as losers in school.

In a program called "I Can Read" I met with the kindergartners in groups of six. I asked them to cut out "things you can read" and paste them on a piece of butcher's paper. After they completed their collage, I wrote their "readings" next to each picture. Each student also contributed one clipping to a class book entitled *We Can Read.*

It was a "teaching" activity, but I soon realized its tremendous evaluation potential. Some students associated labels with their generic meanings: "Crisco" was read as "grease" or "Crest" as "toothpaste." Others insisted on supplying brand names. "Coke" might be read as "Pepsi." Still others could read "peanut butter" as well as "Jif." All of the students were able to supply a message with their picture, but there were a few who did not know that print was the primary message carrier. Several students put printless pictures on their butcher's paper. Most announced, "That doesn't say anything. I just put it there for fun." But Alice "read" a picture of a strawberry: "That says 'strawberry.' "

While all of the students were tuned in to meanings, some were obviously tuned in to graphics as well. Steve noticed that many ads repeat the letters O-F-F. Andy knew that O-F-F represents "off," and explained in an advertising context—"fifty cents off." It was not apparent that either boy understood what "fifty cents off" means, although they did exhibit a good working knowledge of prepositions.

This is a good demonstration of the classroom evaluation process. Every activity is ripe for evaluation, especially as we grow more concerned with evaluation as a way of watching the learning process. The children's comments and actions can be observed by the teacher informally. They can be recorded, as I did, by simply writing down the student's "readings" of their pages. Progress can be "tested" later by having the students read their pages again at intervals.

I was also able to explain the beginning reading process to the kindergarten parents using their children's work as examples. It was obvious which students needed extra individual attention. And the class book became an evaluation tool that I later used to "test" other beginning readers.

THREE KEY QUESTIONS TEACHERS ASK

Contemporary American teachers ask three questions when they consider the evaluation of their students. First, "How do I know what help my students need and what progress my students are making?" Secondly, "How can I document (or help them to document) their abilities and their progress so that it is apparent to others, including parents, other teachers, administrators, and the students themselves?" Finally, "How do I satisfy the evaluation requirements imposed by administrators, school boards, and governmental bodies?"

As a federally funded reading specialist I had the distinction between these questions driven home to me during the first visit of a district supervisor to my whole language reading and writing center. My principal and colleagues were extremely pleased with my program after the first year. The district supervisor, totally unfamiliar with a whole language approach, judged me an unsatisfactory teacher. Unable to question the soundness of my actual teaching or its apparent results, he resorted to attacking my evaluation and record keeping.

Most reading specialists are expected to evaluate students on some sort of pre- and posttesting. They are expected to come up with specific objectives for each child. Individual progress is to be documented in some fashion. The entire prospect is overwhelming, particularly when we are expected to serve a large student population.

The reading specialist, however, is working with a student population that other staff members find a challenge to teach, if not totally "unteachable." Creative programs that provide success for these kids are usually welcomed with open arms. Growth is easily evident to parents and often other teachers. With a carefully documented evaluation system, the philosophical base of the program is difficult to question.

The trick is to develop an evaluation program that will answer the three evaluation questions at the same time. What will satisfy administrators, help me show student progress to the kids, to their parents, and to other teachers, and also provide me with useful information for my own work with the students?

So a fourth question or underlying assumption is, "What evaluation will support the whole language program that I know works well with my students?" It is important that our evaluation system fit our educational philosophy. Standardized tests tend to support a focus on skills and step-by-step learning. Test makers even provide computer-generated test-score interpretation sheets for parents that claim to tell parents what skills we should be teaching. The test interpretations, the test scores, and even test items can be in direct conflict with whole language evaluation and philosophy.

A very common item on basal reading mastery tests for beginners is a picture with several sentences beside it. The child is asked to select the sentence that "goes with" the picture. After a few months of being asked to make sense of what they were reading, my late starters tended to reconstruct *each* sentence so that it would make sense with the picture. This problem disappears for proficient readers. But how confusing for a beginner to be asked to read nonsense!

I needed evaluation that would reflect the benefits of holistic learning. I used recent research techniques such as reading miscue analysis, print awareness studies, and ethnographic observation and applied them, formally and informally, to in-class evaluation.

The evaluation program that I developed in a reading and writing center was threefold:

1. As a "pretest" I used a modified Reading Miscue Inventory and a book-handling–print-awareness task for beginning readers. I borrowed the Grid of Reading Strategies from *Reading Strategies: Focus on Comprehension* (Goodman and Burke, 1980) to develop a Profile of Reading Strategies that led naturally to whole language student objectives.
2. I documented many of my observations through a unit record-keeping system and anecdotal notes of individual conferences.
3. Students provided their own contributions to evaluation, including their written work and their own record keeping. This self-evaluation is an especially crucial aspect of revaluing in that it allows students to be informed by the evaluation process.

HOW CHILDREN HELPED ME DEVELOP MY EVALUATION

My evaluation methods were developed through six years of working with children labeled "problem readers." Developing these methods is an ongoing process constantly refined in response to the children I work with.

In evaluating many children I have also been able to see some general trends in the area of revaluing the process. Therefore I'd like to describe the evaluation through the children who have helped me evaluate my own methods.

THREE LATE BLOOMERS

In *Leo the Late Bloomer* Leo's mom admonishes Leo's dad, saying, "A watched bloomer doesn't bloom." Like Leo's dad, I'm still watching. But instead of anxiously awaiting signs of blooming, I watch the slower bloomers, the older beginners, to see what they can teach me about their learning.

Alice.   Alice (whom we just met in kindergarten) came to me again in first grade as a student who was really struggling with the reading program. During our initial evaluation I found that somewhere between kindergarten and first grade she had discovered print as a message carrier. She was able to "read" printed information on cereal boxes and advertisements. She also had a strong sense of story and could make predictions about story events, follow patterns in stories, retell stories, and make up her own stories. She was enthusiastic and energetic about school.

Most "readiness" measures wouldn't have revealed these strengths because Alice hadn't discovered how the alphabetic code of printed English works. She was not aware of how our spoken language is represented in written text. She "read" stories holistically and could not distinguish word boundaries or recognize words even after they'd been pointed out to her.

I was able to develop this profile of Alice's reading based on my own knowledge of early literacy learning. The book *Literacy before Schooling* (Ferreiro and Teberosky, 1982) describes the complex set of understandings children develop as they approach written language. While they have focused on the child's developing linguistic awareness, the work of Harste, Woodward, and Burke (1984) and Goodman and Altwerger (1981) has also explored the child's awareness of written language functions and holistic understandings of written language forms.

In my first meeting with a beginner we read a short book together and then a book of environmental print. I use the *We Can Read* book that I developed with the kindergartners since it is full of print that is familiar to students at my school. Most students are more successful with environmental print, but I use the book first because I sometimes discover that a student identified by a teacher as having a reading problem is able to read some of the book to me. (In that case my evaluation indicates that it is the teacher who needs to revalue.)

In an evaluation program that looks for what kids *can* do, it's possible for a beginner having problems to show many strengths:

• Does she see reading as a search for meaning, coming up with meaningful language as she "reads"?

- Does he recognize the function of a text and change reading language for different kinds of text (reading "Once upon a time" or "Buy Crest today")?
- Does she make predictions about what a text will be about and what might happen next?
- Does he pick up on language patterns that are repeated within a story?
- Does she know that print is a message carrier?
- Does he know that books are held right side up? That the story continues if you turn the page? That English print usually is written in horizontal lines? That you usually start reading on the left side?
- Does she enjoy hearing stories? Can she retell them?

Alice had many strengths that I could report to her teacher. She had certainly made progress since kindergarten. I could also advise Alice's teacher that phonics workbooks would be a waste of time for Alice, since she had not developed an understanding of the connection between written and oral language. She still needed more experience with reading and writing whole stories.

I formed a small group of first and second graders, taking them from their classes during the classroom reading period. If I was working with a whole language classroom teacher, I felt comfortable working in the classroom. It is extremely important that students like Alice be taken out of the preprimers so that they do not become confused about reading and discouraged about themselves. I could use my understanding of literacy development and my own evaluation of Alice to show Alice's teacher the futility of giving her a standardized textbook.

Christopher. Christopher was a very active first grader, the child of professionals. He and Alice were the only students recommended to me by a highly competent first-grade teacher who made few referrals to my program.

I began my initial evaluation by having Christopher read with me a little book called *Friends*. I had pulled together a series of increasingly complex books with good, predictable language. I made use of the old *Reading Unlimited* series because I wanted good but short pieces for my screening.

We talked about the title, *Friends*. When we turned to the first page, I asked Christopher if he could read it to me. He declined. I asked if he saw any words he recognized. I wondered particularly if he would remember the word *friends* from the title. He said, "No."

I read the sentence "Friends can be boys." Then I asked him to read the next page. After studying the picture, he supplied, "Friends can be girls." I asked if he could find the word *girls*. He found it by reading the sentence over and matching each word to the sentence that he knew. We worked our way through the book in this fashion.

After we read *Friends*, I took out *We Can Read*. Christopher was able to read many of the labels in the book. He read in a global way, ascribing a meaning to the entire sign or logo and not focusing on individual words on a page. However, he was able to answer the questions "How many words are on this page?" and "How many letters are on this page?"

In Christopher I found a reader with a strong sense of story. He was able to follow a pattern throughout the book. He used pictures and his own language background to recreate the story in storylike language. He did not appear to be using letter cues as a reading strategy and was probably not entirely alphabetic. (Indeed, his first-grade teacher said he didn't even know the alphabet.) Yet he had a concept of wordness and even of how words are represented on a page.

As the year progressed, Christopher applied himself enthusiastically to the various class activities. He was in a group of twelve first and second graders who met with me every morning. For the first half hour they had center time and selected from the listening post, the writing table, the book corner, or the unit table. The unit table provided activities extending the various units I had developed around literature, science, and social studies themes. Students worked independently, sometimes following illustrated instruction cards.

At least once a week each child came to the teaching post to meet with me. This gave me an opportunity to assist with journal writing and reading and to look over the students' record sheets. I provided a simple record-keeping system for students to keep track of their individual work. This gave students a sense of responsibility for their own learning (as well as practice with record keeping). I had a record-keeping package for each unit I did with the kids, with room for them to record unit activities and independent work. (See Figure 17–1.)

I also made a single sheet of teacher records for each child on which I recorded their progress on unit activities. (See Figure 17–2.) During the school year we would do at least one literature unit, science unit, and social studies unit.

Work-progress conferences helped students take ownership of their learning just as they were learning to feel ownership as readers and writers. During weekly conferences I kept anecdotal notes of my interactions with students as they were writing and reading. I also kept simple checklists to describe progress on unit activities, books students were reading, stories they published, or any other class activities. I had discovered in my first years of teaching that supervisors seemed satisfied if something was "taught" even if it wasn't learned. A checklist documented my "teaching" while helping me to keep track of class activities. I ran off a stack of checklists ruled horizontally so I could create my own vertical boxes depending on the length of notes I would need to make.

After the choice time students cleaned up and signed up for the next day's center by placing their names in slots on a chart. One child read to the class each day to start off group time. Group time included unit discussions and shared readings. A focus of my program for late beginners is to develop a language bank of stories that each child knows by heart. Slow starters have often not had the experience of being read

Figure 17–1 *Record-Keeping Package*

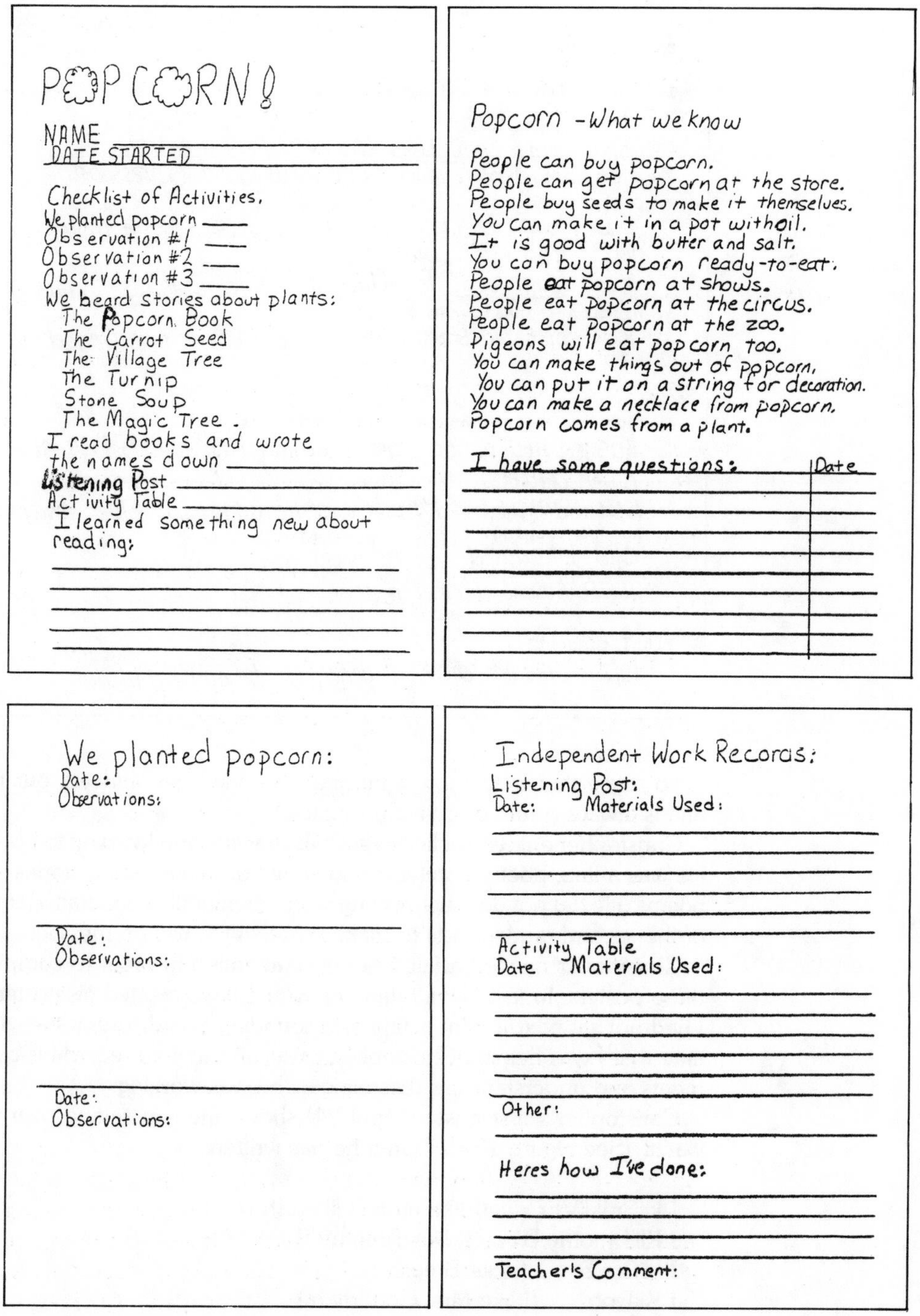

POPCORN!

NAME _____
DATE STARTED _____

Checklist of Activities.
We planted popcorn ____
Observation #1 ____
Observation #2 ____
Observation #3 ____
We heard stories about plants:
  The Popcorn Book
  The Carrot Seed
  The Village Tree
  The Turnip
  Stone Soup
  The Magic Tree.
I read books and wrote
the names down _____
Listening Post _____
Activity Table _____
I learned something new about
reading:
_____
_____
_____
_____

Popcorn – What we know

People can buy popcorn.
People can get popcorn at the store.
People buy seeds to make it themselves.
You can make it in a pot with oil.
It is good with butter and salt.
You can buy popcorn ready-to-eat.
People eat popcorn at shows.
People eat popcorn at the circus.
People eat popcorn at the zoo.
Pigeons will eat popcorn too.
You can make things out of popcorn.
You can put it on a string for decoration.
You can make a necklace from popcorn.
Popcorn comes from a plant.

I have some questions: | Date
_____ | ____
_____ | ____
_____ | ____
_____ | ____
_____ | ____
_____ | ____

We planted popcorn:
Date:
Observations:

Date:
Observations:

Date:
Observations:

Independent Work Records:
Listening Post:
Date: Materials Used:
_____
_____
_____
_____

Activity Table
Date   Materials Used:
_____
_____
_____
_____

Other:
_____

Heres how I've done:
_____
_____
_____

Teacher's Comment:

Figure 17-2 *Teacher Record*

Halloween: Teacher Records

Name: *Timothy*

Date(s): *10/18 —*

1. **Story listening and discussions:**
   10/24 The Trip
   *10/20 Read Bony-Legs to class. Has memorized
   much of it, and read with good expression.*
2. **Choral reading:**
   10/22 Round Is a Pancake — acting silly — asked to leave.
   10/23 Halloween countdown
   10/24 Countdown for fluency   11/2 Round Is — by memory
3. **Writing -- Halloween story:**
   10/24 Dictated story. Spent much of own time wandering.

4. **Centers -- Independent work:**
   *Has learned a lot from Listening Post, but is lost at
   other centers.
   10/30 Had to sit at table because he did not put folder away.*
5. **Record keeping:**
   *10/18 Introduced — needs assistance.
   10/20 Absent during review*

Final comment:
   10/26 Journal check: 1 page; wrote name and date.

---

to so much that they know a number of stories well. Indeed, our first unit is always a unit on nursery rhymes.

Christopher enjoyed activities such as drawing and listening to books. He was a fine, poetic storyteller and would dictate amazing stories and poems. He did not do much writing on his own until I encouraged some of the second-grade artists to make posters with written messages.

Christopher needed a fair amount of attention in order to complete these posters. In fact I don't think he would have created his posters if I had not sat next to him acting as a sounding board. But at the same time that I was helping Christopher, I was also able to record his comments and understand his reasoning as he was working.

Christopher's first poster (April 24) shows the sun setting over the water. (See Figure 17-3.) On it he has written:

I kliBrilkliVEr   (I like birds. I like fish.)
I KliTimothy.B   (I like Timothy B.)
I kliBra.B   (I like Brea B.)
I KliDoo   (I like Mrs. Goodman.)
   DMAN

Figure 17–3 *Christopher's First Poster*

Two pre-service teachers who were observing Christopher expressed concern over his "reversals" in the word *like*. I felt that Christopher did not have a perceptual problem. Instead he was showing a strategy of using graphics, as well as phonics, in his early writing. He was aware of the general appearance of the word *like*. I also predicted that he would write *like* conventionally by the end of the year.

I have noticed that children often use graphic strategies as they write. It's important to be aware of this. Some teachers actually encourage students to think about how words sound, because beginning writers do tend to invent phonetic spellings. Of course students should be encouraged to develop their own spelling strategies. But focusing on phonetic spellings ignores the fact that kids are readers and can use their memory of graphic patterns as well.

Christopher used several other strategies in this first piece. He used the initial sound *b* and *v* for *bird* and *fish*. After writing the first letter of each word, he felt that the word should be longer and "filled in" with letters from his own name. He got the names for his poster from classroom references (word cards) but did not copy directly. This resulted in some spelling variation and the placement of the periods after the first name instead of the last name.

Ferreiro and Teberosky (1982) talk about kids at a certain stage having a "minimal character" theory. This could explain Christopher's use of filler letters in the words *birds* and *fish*. I don't think this was the case, though. Christopher had no problem using one letter for the word *I*. I think Christopher simply knew that the other words have more than one letter. He may have been aware of three phonemes but not been able to represent these phonemes phonetically.

Although Christopher wrote "DOODMAN," he read this sentence, "I like Mrs. Goodman." He appeared undisturbed that *Mrs.* was not represented in his sentence. Perhaps he felt that one word was enough to represent one person.

In Christopher's second poster (May 10), he wrote, "I like Goodman. I like Christopher" (Figure 17–4).

Through his writing he has learned to spell *like* and *Goodman* conventionally, although he still leaves out *Mrs.* When Christopher finished his poster he said, "I forgot something I always draw on my best work." He then drew two balloons. As he drew the strings, he was struck by the similarity between the string and the letter *S*.

"You know what that is?" he asked. "A balloon. And you know why it has an *S* on it?" he continued. "That's my last name, S———." He then drew three more balloons. One had a J-shaped string for his middle name, and one had a C-shaped string for "Christopher." All the while he instructed me in a questioning style. He finished by putting an apostrophe next to the second balloon. "Know why that has a comma? It belongs to me! Comma *s*."

These two pictures show the fascinating mixture of knowledge and "stages" found in late beginners. Like a preschooler Christopher could still see letters as pictures; he used fillers for unknown words; and he seemed unconcerned about leaving unnecessary words out of a text. Like most first graders he was able to pick up initial sounds and was

Figure 17–4 *Christopher's Second Poster (Portion)*

beginning to spell some words conventionally. But he also showed sophistication in his use of graphics as well as phonics and in his use of word boundaries, upper- and lowercase letters, and punctuation.

On May 14 and 15 Christopher wrote a long story (Figure 17–5):

The Vair a gin on Kar Dri Kir ToPri Kar Knock ON Tve Kari
    Vistop, gophe I
Hrier to Yotoph on Phep Yoaou You You Doar Yoaou is Youario
    Krosr Phe Krosr is
came Phe r You Phe I Yto Yot toPri 205 gar pheri You Kauy.
    Yoe Yotopher.

(There was a girl named Kay who came to planet Check. She knocked on the gate.
    What do you want, the guard said. I
want to live on this planet. Yes you do. What is your
    name? My name is
Kay. Where are you from? I am from planet 205. Girls of planet Check should we let Kay in?
    Yes. The end.)

This story is actually a retelling of a story written by Christopher's older sister. As he worked on getting the meaning into print, he was concerned about many written language conventions. He erased the *g* in *girl* in the first line and moved it to the right so that word boundaries would be clear. He also expressed concern that his lines be straight as he was writing.

Figure 17–5 *Christopher's Story*

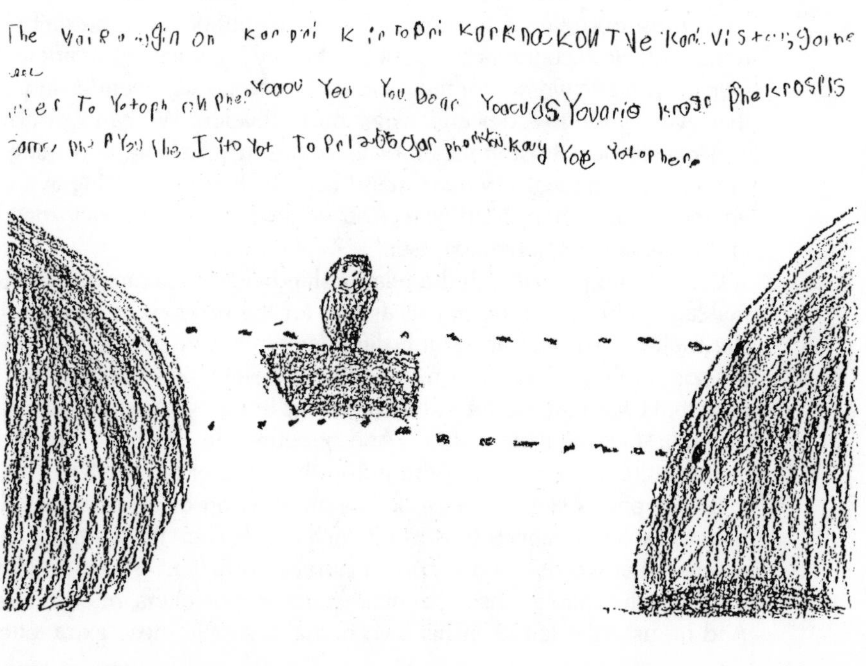

While writing, Christopher constantly reread his own text, often correcting his written text to fit his story. On line two he said, "What is . . ." and wrote "Yoaou you." Reading he said, "That ain't 'is,' that's 'can.' " He showed this tendency to fall into known words in using "came" for "Kay" in line three.

Christopher again used many writing strategies in this one sample. He used beginning letters for *girl, Kay, came, planet, gate*, and *guard*. He used letters from his name as fillers again, and sometimes for entire words. He used several known spellings—*a, on, to, you, is*, and *came*—sometimes substituting them for unknown words. He used me as a reluctant reference, and I did spell *knock* for him. He used himself as a reference, spelling *name* as "krosr" twice, and using "ToPri" from line one (which actually was "to planet") for *planet* in line three. In one case he used the letter *r* to represent the word *are*.

Christopher has one written word for every spoken word, except for two cases. " 'What do you want,' the guard said," is spelled "Vistop, gophe." "Girls of planet Check. Should we let Kay in?" is spelled "gar pheri You Kauy." Both of these cases are dialogue. Christopher placed a comma between "Vistop" and "gophe." He explained that he used it "to split up the sentences." It's possible that Christopher felt dialogue might be represented on the sentence level. I know (from observing) that "gophe" represents *guard*. Like *Mrs.*, the dialogue marker may have seemed unnecessary.

Christopher did not mark any other sentences in his story, but he did add a period after "Kauy" (Perhaps to separate the two speakers?). There is a great big period after "Yotopher" marking the end of the story. When Christopher finished his story he said, "This poster is history!" "Why?" "Because it's the best poster I ever made."

To most observers Christopher's work might appear to be scribbled nonsense. He recognizes his work as "history," a great landmark in his own growth as a writer. For me it shows the complexity of understanding that every young reader and writer must develop. We can't sit down and explain to Christopher all of the ways in which he is coming to understand language. We *can* stand back so that his learning is a celebration rather than a struggle. And we can support his own delight and flexibility as a language user.

Christopher played with the relationship between picture and written message in his use of his initials as tails for the balloons in his pictures. We make a big deal about the difference between picture and print. My son, at three, looked at me in total disbelief when I pointed to the print that I was reading in a Curious George book. "That's not George," he said, "George is not there." And of course he was right. The story is not in the picture or the print but in the mind of the reader.

Christopher's second piece shows an amazing blend of stages. He uses initial-letter sounds to start off each word. Then he seems to have a sense that words need a certain number of letters. Ferreiro (1982) discusses the child's sense of a minimal number of letters for each word. And he uses the letters in his own name to supply these extra letters.

He is apparently unconcerned about repeating the same letters in each word, though he does vary the patterns to some extent. He shows a concept of word boundaries that does not exist in the studies of four-year-old beginners. Yet in two places he represents whole sentences with one word. In spite of using four or five letters for most words, he also uses the letter *r* to represent the word *are*.

This one piece of writing, like many pieces of class work, could be analyzed for hours and become a major study. It does suggest the power of allowing a child to use all available resources and strategies. While entering into the world of alphabetic writing, Christopher decided on the monumental task of writing this story. It would have been impossibly tedious if he hadn't fallen back on previous writing strategies, returning to the alphabetic strategy when he could manage.

I want to stress that it is not the piece of writing but the fact that I was able to observe the creative process that makes Christopher's story a good evaluation tool. A sample of a child's work in process, interpreted by an informed teacher, is the most powerful evaluation tool I know. I showed Christopher's story to his mother and his teacher and explained to them the marvelous workings of this child's mind. They were both extremely impressed.

Children like Christopher are frequent members of my center classroom. They are kids who have a lot of knowledge and need more time and freedom to put it all together. A regular preprimer program will be extremely limiting and confusing to them and will probably lead them to become turned-off readers, like Jesse, whom I describe later.

Tom.   Tom had a different problem. He was in second grade but had not progressed from "level 2," the first level of the first-grade reader. He was a real problem to his teacher, who had trouble controlling him and had no idea where to begin in terms of teaching him to read.

Tom's profile looked different from Christopher's. While Tom was able to follow the pattern of pictures in *Friends*, he did not fall into the language pattern "Friends can be . . . ," as most kids do. He was unable to respond to questions about words and letters, pointing vaguely to the text. He understood that print was the message carrier but (like Alice) had no strategy (alphabetic or word placement) for locating specific words.

Tom did better on the environmental print in the *We Can Read* book. Most kids are familiar and comfortable with environmental print. One lab student from a background like Tom's read each logo as a TV commercial: "Buy Crest!" He'd done most of his reading from TV.

Tom's mother came into my room often. She was in need of a great deal of help herself and had a lot of difficulty handling a child like Tom. Tom appeared to have no background with stories and creative language forms other than TV commercials. Being kept at the preprimer level, which offers no stories, had not helped him, although he had not been poisoned with misconceptions about how written language was supposed to work, like many of the "Sesame Street" generation.

Tom's literacy development appeared to be well behind that of my son, Reuben, who at three had a large repertoire of holistically remembered stories. Yet Tom's progress would far surpass Reuben's that year.

My first goal was to help him develop the sort of language bank that most kids bring to school with them. Tom fell in love with the listening post and would sit there quietly every day of the week if I would allow him. He would not focus on anything else for the half-hour choice time but could listen to stories on tape for hours. He soon signed up to read to the class. His first "reading" was *Bonylegs* by Joanna Cole (1983), which is a longish folktale. He "read" with the expression and characterization that he had heard on the tape, and the class was really impressed.

As a teacher/learner I became fascinated with these story reconstructions. I knew that Tom couldn't recite the entire story from memory, yet he could produce it, almost verbatim, with the book as an aid. It was the combination of the pictures and the known language that made the book predictable to Tom. Tom's selection of stories was at the seven-year-old level. He was not interested in Dr. Seuss beginning books or Bill Martin's instant readers. His "beginning" texts were *Bonylegs* (1983), *The Three Billy Goats Gruff* (1987), and *The Gingerbread Man* (1987).

I followed Tom's progress through anecdotal notes of reading conferences. Sometime in January we were reading a pattern story called *The Lion's Tail* (1971). Tom's strategy at that time was to recreate the story in storylike language (good progress in half a year). He came to the sentence "I'll look for it" and read, "I'll find it for you."

He stopped suddenly and stared at the page. Then he read, "I'll look for it," and looked up at me. He said, "That says, 'I'll look for it.' " He too was recognizing a historic moment. He was a reader. It was interesting that he read the sentence as a whole, though he had used the graphic cues to correct his previous interpretation.

Tom did not suddenly switch to relying on the graphic cues as a reading strategy. As Christopher did in his writing, Tom incorporated his new reading strategy into his overall goal of making sense of what he was reading. If he was able to make sense with the aid of graphic cues, he used them. If not, he fell back on constructing the text from pictures, his own language and experience, and his experience with that book. "The neighbors thanked Clifford for saving the birds" became "The neighbors were so happy Clifford saved the birds." Tom spent the rest of the school year moving freely between these strategies and becoming a stronger and stronger reader.

My anecdotal notes recorded amazing progress in Tom's learning. I am sure that little of his progress would show up on a standardized test. He was still not a "proficient" reader by the end of second grade. Yet he had probably packed three years of learning into one year (the kind of progress that might be seen between three and six), and I'm sure his maturity was the determining factor.

Reflections. Ongoing evaluation of six-, seven-, and eight-year-old beginners indicates that it is a mistake to place them on a four- or five-year-old level. They may not have arrived at a workable alphabetic theory, but they have an extra several years of experience and understanding to draw on as they approach literacy activities. I have found that children seem to learn to read somewhere between the ages of four and eight. I have yet to discover a fourth grader who is an absolute nonreader.

Yet standardized measures inflexibly expect children to read words and word parts at six. Actual reading ability is ignored by readiness tests, while beginning reading strengths are ignored from first grade on. Most of my reading-center students do progress to the point where there is a change in their scores on standardized measures. Four of my first graders and five of my second graders were able to pass basal reading tests and return to their regular reading class "on grade level."

Students like Alice, Christopher, and Tom, however, did not show progress on standard measures in this one year. I was able to persuade Christopher's teacher to promote him to second grade on my promise that he would blossom as a second grader. Alice and Tom were retained. Alice did very well in her second year of first grade. I feel she might have done well as a second grader in a program that allows kids to grow in their own way.

Through in-depth, ongoing evaluation I was able to discover the strengths of these beginning readers. Brief anecdotal records and samples of their work allowed me to chronicle their progress as readers and writers. I could show parents and teachers that their students were strong learners, even if other measures could not. I had detailed records of my teaching for administrators and supervisors.

Most important, through evaluation I gained confidence in my own teaching. I have watched Alice, Christopher, and Tom learning. Like Leo's mother, I know that my Leos are bloomers. Because of my informal watching I can often predict how and when growth might occur. This helps me to trust the children and leave them the room to grow and learn in their own way and time.

THREE OLDER READERS

Beth. Beth's fourth-grade teacher came to me perplexed because Beth had twice failed the end-of-level test in the Ginn reader. He had put her through the skill book and workbook again after the first failure and didn't know what to do next. He thought I should work on her skills. Normally I wouldn't have worked with Beth since she was a "low-average" student and had not tested a year behind grade level (the base line for Chapter I students).

I had developed an informal Reading Miscue Inventory (Goodman, Watson, and Burke, 1987) with a series of short, predictable selections for students to read. I took them from The Scott Foresman *Reading Unlimited* series (1971), which allowed me to assign a "grade level" to a child's reading as well as to judge what strategies the child used. As in more formal miscue analysis, I had each story typed and copied, and prepared my own retelling guides to make scoring on the retellings easier.

Initially I followed the procedures of the Reading Miscue Inventory closely, tape-recording each session and carefully transcribing the miscues. (In order to save time with a large population, I do not use a tape recorder. I transcribe what I hear, understanding that I may miss a few things. If an RMI is going to be presented to staff or used to determine a child's progress or placement on the school level, it should definitely be tape-recorded.)

I use twenty miscues, which gives me an easy-to-figure 5 percent ratio per miscue. I use one of the newer coding formats, where meaning-level questions are answered for every sentence in the story, including sentences with no miscues. Since I don't usually tape-record the reader, I try to code the miscues immediately after the reading while my memory is fresh.

Beth was able to read both my third- and fourth-grade stories, although her focus was more on accuracy than on understanding. Indeed her graphophonic and grammatical skills were strong. In addition to doing the RMI, I went through the end-of-level test with her and talked to her about her answers. In some cases kids can be given test-taking strategies that eliminate the problem. But Beth was having some trouble reading the test items, particularly the vocabulary section, being unfamiliar with many of the concepts.

I reported to the teacher that she was having trouble with the reading series and that she seemed to have the greatest difficulty with concepts presented through reading vocabulary. A traditional approach would be to teach Beth "the words" on vocabulary work sheets. But she had failed twice to learn that way.

I opted for reading experience. For the next month Beth came down to the center every day while her class was having reading. She spent the time reading books of her own selection. I had a few conferences with her, but most of her time was spent reading. At the end of the month Beth passed the Ginn end-of-level test without difficulty.

This is a classic example of a reading problem created by the instructional program. Pushing kids through textbooks at a fast clip allows them no time to develop as competent readers. In Beth's case it shifted her focus from meaning to word accuracy. By looking closely at Beth's reading, and by using the test itself as an evaluation tool, I was able to convince the teacher that what Beth needed to revalue herself as a reader was experience with real reading.

In fact this case became a school model that allowed many teachers to relax and place the importance of the basal reader in a better perspective.

Billy. Billy, like Beth, did not have a background for the type of reading he was required to do. Billy was not reading a basal text, however. He was in a whole language classroom where a variety of texts and trade books were used. In seventh grade Billy was able to complete almost no class work. His teacher asked me to look at his reading. Billy was clearly a very weak student, but his profile was surprising to many people, including myself. He actually read stories fairly fluently. He had few miscues, and could retell a story with good understanding. In working with Billy's class assignments, however, I soon realized that Billy's problem was an extremely limited background in the concepts that were being discussed in class.

Since Billy was in a whole language classroom, I was able to work with him on class projects. For a time I spent an hour with him several times a week, going through the entire process of a written assignment. Each individual session was rich with material for evaluation and learning.

In each case, as Billy and I went through his reading assignments, the weakness in Billy's background came through. After seven years at school Billy had learned how to function in a traditional classroom. He knew how to answer questions at the end of a book. In a whole language classroom he was lost. He had no idea, for example, that a major social studies project should take priority over the weekly current events assignment.

He selected his current events article about the recent national election because it was the shortest one in the magazine, his goal being to finish the task quickly. I asked him to read the article out loud and to make a list of things he had found out. He repeated phrases from the piece without any understanding. After probing, I found out that Billy could not name a Michigan senator or congressman. He knew the names of our mayor and the president but could not name our governor or the vice president.

We stopped for a long discussion about our three branches of government. After about forty-five minutes Billy asked me, "What do they mean by seats, where they say, 'They won twelve seats'?" This was the first question he'd ever asked me and the first time he showed an interest in learning rather than in completing a task.

We went back to listing what he'd learned. I wrote down each thing that he said and questioned him about whether he understood what he was reciting. We referred to the article for additional clarification. When it was time to write, Billy hung back. "I'm not very good at putting things in my own words," he told me. I had Billy number our notes in order of importance, and we constructed a report. Then, I complimented him on using his own words so well. His puzzled look told me that he thought he was not allowed to repeat any of the words that the author used.

As I worked with Billy, I found that he did have knowledge and information to draw on. In taking notes for a report on Bunker Hill, he told me that the Americans hid behind stone fences and shrubs. This was not in the text we had read. He had picked up information from class discussions and his own background, but he didn't have a framework to organize his knowledge for someone else to see.

Like Tom's learning, Billy's could not be reflected by standard measures. It was difficult to see what he knew even in a whole language setting. Billy taught me and his seventh-grade teacher a great deal about how kids interpret assignments and how hard it can be to get at what kids actually know.

Billy's problem is not really a reading problem, although it is probably the most common problem I encounter in older students. Billy can't read when he doesn't have the background for understanding the material he is asked to read; This is true for all of us. Evaluation of students like Billy shows the need for exploring concepts in depth as part of literacy instruction.

Jesse.   Jesse typifies another common "reading problem." He was a very bright fourth grader who was convinced that he couldn't read. Jesse had very strong ideas about reading, central among them that guessing was bad and making mistakes even worse.

Jesse's RMI showed that he did indeed read. From the start he was extremely reluctant to go on if he did not "know" a word. He would cajole and whine when I insisted that he work it out himself. He even cried and had tantrums over the issue.

Jesse was in clear need of revaluing the reading process and how it works. When I worked with him, I placed another child between us so that Jesse would not be able to call on me readily for help. Jesse expressed his own theories well. Guessing, to him, was bad. I tried saying "making predictions" instead, but he couldn't buy it. He had to be accurate.

I decided to place reading in the more playful realm of games. I wrote a puzzle story using blank spaces and had Jesse and Mary read it together. They were well matched. Mary took more risks and did the reading. Jesse was better at predicting both unknown story words and guessing at my blank spaces. We developed a reading detective club and kept lists of what we were learning about reading.

I also used a retrospective miscue procedure with Jesse and Mary to extend what we could learn about reading. I had each child read a story into a tape recorder. We then went over the tape. I asked the kids to listen for miscues, and when we found them, we stopped the tape. We first asked the question "Does it make sense in the story?" If it did, we put a star by the miscue on our miscue list. If not, we talked about why the miscue had happened and made a check mark for good thinking.

Jesse resisted admitting that a miscue could be "good." He resisted being labeled a good thinker for making mistakes. One day he even said, "Everyone is telling me how good I'm doing, so why don't I feel good about myself?"

In each case, but in Jesse's most of all, I used my own evaluation strategies as teaching strategies. I knew from his RMI that Jesse had strengths as a reader, but the problem was convincing Jesse of that. Jesse had no problem with his background of concepts and knowledge. In fact his interests tended to propel him toward complex materials that he felt would be too difficult for him to read. But his view that reading must be accurate made becoming a reader an impossible task for him.

Reflections.   Ferreiro and Teberosky (1982) offhandedly suggest that once a child understands that written language is alphabetic, the rest is all mechanics. This is ironic, since we tend to focus kids on mechanics, particularly spelling, at a time when they're grappling with a philosophical understanding of the whole system.

Just as babies often seem to become talkers overnight, there does seem to be a breakthrough point when kids seem to make dramatic strides in reading and writing. I have also observed that, in whole language settings, there is a balancing-out of abilities. It is difficult by the end of second grade to pick out the kids who came into first grade already reading.

When I examine the reading of older students, I find that they seldom have a true reading problem. Most of their problems have to do with attitude (Jesse), experience (Billy), or the instructional program (Beth). All of the problems have to do with how they value reading and themselves as readers. Although experienced readers and writers are involved in fine-tuning language mechanics, we do not need to focus these students on the mechanics of reading. On the contrary, I have found that the mechanics are already well in place and the older reader who appears to be struggling with reading skills is probably struggling with a much more complex problem. This demonstrates the tremendous importance of a qualitative measure like the Reading Miscue Inventory to develop a revaluing program for older readers.

The RMI provides insight into the readers' strategies and into their own reading theories. It provides me with a starting place for talking with the classroom teacher. But astute observation of the students' work in class and even on standardized tests is also needed to help older readers.

THE PROFILE OF READING STRATEGIES

In *Reading Strategies: Focus on Comprehension*, Goodman and Burke (1980) have developed a grid of strategies. I borrowed the outline of their grid to develop a profile of reading strategies used by a single reader. (See Figure 17–6.) This profile is used to assist me in interpreting the Reading Miscue Inventory and print-awareness tasks that I have described. It also satisfies the requirement that there be learning objectives for each of my students.

I have developed a series of questions that I ask myself as I reflect on my evaluation of a student. (See Figure 17–7.) These questions are listed in the strategies grid outline. Not every question applies to every reader. In each box of the grid I describe the strengths that the student shows in that area. Then I may describe a problem that I see as well. It's important to point out that not all strategies are equally useful. For example, focusing on phonetic relationships is not especially useful if a focus on meaning is not present.

Based on the profile of reading strategies, I develop four or five objectives for the year. The objectives usually identify these areas: developing a focus on reading for meaning, developing an awareness of language patterns, developing effective strategies for self-correction in order to gain meaning, helping the student to discuss his or her growing understanding of literature and literacy, and addressing any specific difficulty a child may have.

Figure 17–8 shows a sample of a completed profile.

Figure 17–6 *Profile of Reading Strategies (Based on Goodman and Burke 1980)*

Name_____   Date_____

	SEMANTIC	SYNTACTIC	GRAPHOPHONIC
P R E D I C T I N G			
C O N F I R M I N G			

I N T E G R A T I N G	Objectives
	1._____
	_____
	2._____
	_____
	3._____
	_____
	4._____
	_____
	5._____
	_____

Figure 17–7 *Questions for "Profile of Reading Strategies" Form*

Name _____   Date _____

	SEMANTIC	SYNTACTIC	GRAPHOPHONIC
P R E D I C T I N G	1. Focus on meaning: How effective is the student using the reading task for gathering meaning? (RMI) 2. Understands uses of print: Does the student understand the various functions and purposes print holds in his or her life? (Observation and conference) 3. Uses sequencing and order or story pattern. (RMI – reading and retelling) 4. Specific areas of strength or weakness. (RMI – Observation)	1. Sounds like language: Does the reader read with the syntactic flow of meaningful Language? (RMI – reading) 2. Syntactic acceptability: Does the student use understanding of syntax in reading? (RMI – syntax) 3. List specific areas of strength and weakness. (RMI and observation)	1. Describe the use of graphophonic cues: – Not used – Overused – Used efficiently (RMI – Graphics in relation to meaning) 2. List specific strength and weakness. (RMI and observation)

	Correction strategy: Does the reader tend to correct?		
	For meaning	For grammatical function	For graphophonics
	Is the reader making effective use of correction strategies? To what extent? (RMI – story)		

	SEMANTIC	SYNTACTIC	GRAPHOPHONIC
C O N F I R M I N G	5a. Reader rereads to gain meaning b. Reader reads ahead to gain meaning. (RMI – Observation) 6. Reader shows increased understanding of story as it develops. (RMI – Transcript) 7. Specific areas of strength and weakness. (RMI – Observation)	4. Repeated substitutions: To what extent is reader successful in gaining meaning after repeated attempts on a word or phrase? (RMI – Profile) 5. Punctuation: How effectively does the reader use punctuation? (Story, RMI, observation of writing) 6. List any specific strategies to be developed. (RMI – observation)	3. What strategies does the reader use as reflected by insertions, non-words, omissions, synonyms, etc? (RMI) 4. How effective are the reader's strategies for unfamiliar words? What is the degree of balance in use of graphophonic cues as compared to syntactic and semantic cues? (RMI – Observation) 5. List any specific strategies to be developed. (RMI – Observation)

I N T E G R A T I N G	8. Story conception: Does the reader show understanding of the story? (Retelling) 9. Is the reader able to use resources to read for information? (Observation) 10. Is the reader showing an understanding of characters and story setting? Plot development? Theme development? (Retelling) 11. Does the reader use meanings from reading in other settings? (Observation) 12. Does the reader relate different texts and text types? (Observation) 13. Does the reader make inferences and develop a viewpoint? (Observation)	**Objectives** 1. Focus on meaning/use of print: The first objectives should be reading for meaning and print awareness. 2. Sound of language: The next objective should be awareness that written language follows language patterns. 3. Strategies for correcting and confirming: Focus is on effective strategies for gaining meaning from print 4. Integrating meaning: Focus is on ability to infer, generalize, and express understanding of printed texts. 5. Specific difficulties: Focus is on any specific concepts or strategies that may need development or expansion.

209

Figure 17-8 *Sample of Completed "Profile of Reading Strategies" Form*

Name _Susan_   Date _10/16/87_

	SEMANTIC	SYNTACTIC	GRAPHOPHONIC
P R E D I C T I N G	Minimal focus on making sense. Knows print carries message. Knows balloons carry dialogue. Predicts dialogue and boy's questions. Substitutes conceptually related nouns: room/house.	Knows book. Knows left to right. Knows sentence starters: This is / The. Attempts to form questions: What? Tries to maintain story sense—cohesive ties. Uses grammatically accept-able nouns and non-words.	Makes strong use of graphophonics: beginning, middle, ending, and vowels. Examples: town/t.. end street/sees bad/box that, the/this, there the
C O N F I R M I N G	Does not attempt to regress to correct. Self-corrects across text: tries "the," returns to "there"; tries diff. words for "street," "door." Uses pictures. Looks up at teacher. Needs to build self-confidence.	Changes words across text, retains grammatical function.	Makes use of graphics pictures. Not able to recreate story.
I N T E G R A T I N G	Can give a retelling. Not reading enough. Enjoys hearing stories and discussing them.	Objectives 1. _Focus on story meaning. Build confidence in use of semantics and meaning._ 2. _Support her use of language patterns and increase use of own language ability in reading._ 3. _Develop independent reading strategies to encourage self-correction strategies._ 4. _Build story sense; encourage story telling and retellings._ 5. _Improve opportunities for listening to focus on story sense._	

EVALUATING LARGE GROUPS:
THINKING ON A SCHOOL LEVEL

In my building, a group of Chapter I students was selected by stan-
dardized test scores. About two hundred students were identified, and
I was expected to select the students I would work with over the year.
Consequently my evaluation was sometimes part of this screening process.

I work in an inner-city school with large classes and a required basal
reader. There are many students who could benefit from my Reading
and Writing Center. Some Chapter I teachers in Detroit actually attempt
to work with all the Chapter I students, seeing them in groups of twelve
once or twice a week.

I find that students having difficulty need very consistent, continuous
activities and should be seen daily. I work with the younger students
in groups, taking them during reading instruction time, and tend to focus
my efforts on grades one through three. This seems heartless, but it has
long-term results. Younger students are not as far behind, they have
not usually given up on literacy learning, and they can often be helped
to catch up with the rest of their class. These younger students are then
not as likely to need help in middle grades.

I work with older students one on one, using their own class assignments if possible. This means accepting fewer students at the upper
levels. I also plan workshops and special activities for large groups of
students, such as the kindergarten program I have described.

Individualized evaluation takes time and does not work well for two
hundred students. I ask teachers to help me out by recommending the
two or three students in their class who need the most assistance. I give
specific criteria: Which students appear to be unable to function in the
classroom program? Which are behind and might benefit from some
extra attention? In this way I am usually ready to start the evaluation
process with a small group of students.

Some teachers, however, insist on listing seven or eight students for
me to evaluate. Since my stories are "grade-leveled," it's easy for me
to determine whether a student is in real need. For beginners I always
start with the book activity. First graders will survive the classroom
program if they are able to read a pattern story with some prompting,
can find individual words after a sentence has been read to them, and
can recognize a word on the next page. ("You said the word is *girl*?
Where does it say *girl* on this page?") First graders who recognize many
words are probably not in great need of my program. Second graders
are likely to identify a few words, however, and still not be getting sense
from texts.

Because the evaluation process is tedious, I start my first- and second-
grade group as soon as I have evaluated the first and second grade,
and so on. Eventually I get to the upper grades, and my program is in
full swing.

Occasionally I have been required to evaluate ten or fifteen students
in one class. In this case I use a cloze-miscue procedure. I type up my
complete stories with two cloze sections. The first ten blank spaces start
in about the third paragraph, and the second ten blank spaces come

toward the end of the story. These twenty answers can be coded like miscues except on the categories of sound and graphics. Correction can even be coded if you give students pencils without erasers.

With this procedure I use a written retelling, asking several open-ended questions. After each student completes the task, I read through the retelling and ask additional questions if needed. This procedure was developed by Margaret Lindberg and is described in her doctoral dissertation (1977).

SOME CONCLUDING REFLECTIONS

The evaluation process in my reading and writing center has helped me to demonstrate what I am teaching in my program to administrators, parents, and teachers. It has assisted me in designing a program and finding materials suited to each student. It has certainly helped students assess their own strengths and their own learning and feel a sense of ownership of their reading and writing.

But it has been most valuable as a learning process, helping me to see the essential goals of any reading program, particularly a program for readers in trouble. A good program must allow learners to use all of the language resources available to them. A good program must provide a great deal of opportunity for real reading and writing. A good program must focus on content and help children develop concepts and background for reading and writing. A good program must help students see that all learning is a process of trial and error. And a good program must help children feel good about themselves as learners and as language users.

LOOKING AT INVENTED SPELLING:
A KIDWATCHER'S GUIDE TO
SPELLING,
PART 1

Sandra Wilde

Anyone who has been to elementary school in North America is likely to remember spending a *lot* of time on spelling. Who can forget activities such as writing words five times, putting words in sentences, and breaking words into syllables, not to mention spelling bees and the endless weekly testing? Today's whole language teachers have for the most part abandoned the daily spelling lesson; recent research on children's invented spelling and on the writing process has enabled teachers to feel comfortable in returning ownership of the process of learning to spell to children themselves. Allowing children to use their own spelling as they write both frees them as writers and gives them the opportunity to form their own hypotheses about how spelling works. Using textbook lists of prescribed words has given way to helping children discover how to spell the words they choose to use in their writing. Teachers also realize that the time formerly spent each day on spelling lessons can be better used not only for writing, which provides an arena for using spelling, but also for wide reading, which exposes children to a far broader variety of words than they see in a spelling book.

Teachers, however, may find themselves wondering if eliminating organized spelling instruction means having no method of evaluating spelling. Fortunately current spelling research suggests that growth in spelling can be evaluated in ways that are not only less tedious but more informative and meaningful than the old twenty-word-test-on-Friday method. There are four major principles to a new research-based model of spelling evaluation.

213

FOUR MAJOR PRINCIPLES

1. SPELLING IS EVALUATED ON THE BASIS OF NATURAL WRITING RATHER THAN TESTS.

We learn to spell so that when we write a story, a letter, a poem, or a report, we'll be able to communicate our meaning. If we want to see how well children can use spelling as a tool for communicating meaning as they write, we ought to look at their stories, letters, poems, and reports, where they use the words *they* have chosen to express what *they* want to say. This is bound to be more relevant to the real goal of spelling than seeing how they spell a teacher-dictated list of long-vowel words.

2. SPELLING IS EVALUATED ANALYTICALLY RATHER THAN AS MERELY RIGHT OR WRONG.

Let's look at some writing samples here. Elaine, a Native American third grader, wrote the following story in January. As you read it, be aware of your reactions to her spelling. (Her punctuation has been conventionalized to aid the reader.)

> One day I was skying in Arizona, me and my frineds. And then thay startd to laf. Me to. And we went Home. Then we had a pley and it was clad. Then we went to sleep. We went back to the arizona skying ples, then we went to two, then we went soonme.

> (One day I was skiing in Arizona, me and my friends. And then they started to laugh. Me too. And we went home. Then we had a party and it was cold. Then we went to sleep. We went back to the Arizona skiing place, then we went to town, then we went swimming.)

The next writing sample is from April of Elaine's fourth-grade year. See if you notice any changes in the types of invented spellings she produced.

> **The day some of are class dance to the aerobics**
> One day we dance to the aerobics. And we are going to dance for the paraets for mothers day. We march and clap are heans to. We clap, jump, turn. 14 kids come in at lunch. It takes are hole recses.

> **(The Day Some of Our Class Danced to the Aerobics**
> (One day we danced to the aerobics. And we are going to dance for the parents for Mother's Day. We march and clap our hands too. We clap, jump, turn. 14 kids come in at lunch. It takes our whole recess.)

Although these two texts have about the same proportion of invented spellings (roughly 20 percent of all words used), the second one is clearly easier to read, which is probably due at least in part to the quality of invented spellings in it. PLEY in the first text is hardly an obvious spelling for *party*, while ARE in the second text is, in Elaine's dialect, a homophone for *our* and thus a reasonable spelling for it. With practice teachers can learn to see these qualitative differences between invented spellings and to appreciate the growth that occurs on the way to controlling the system of conventional (correct) spelling. Traditional evaluation has looked at spelling as being either right or wrong, with no middle ground, and with no appreciation of the thought processes that might produce an invented spelling. (Did anyone ever get extra credit on a spelling test for creativity?)

3. SPELLING IS LOOKED AT IN TERMS OF CHILDREN'S STRATEGIES RATHER THAN IN ISOLATION.

Observing children as they write helps us to discover aspects of their knowledge of and approach to spelling that we could never know about from just looking at their written text. For instance, Elaine spelled *aerobics* correctly in her fourth-grade story because she had an aerobic-dance book to refer to, and she wrote PARAETS for *parents* not because she didn't know it had an *n* but because she miscopied it from the dictionary.

All that traditional spelling tests could tell us when we looked at them were the kinds of spellings that children could produce on their own, silently, with only a blank piece of paper in front of them. Seeing how children go about spelling when they are surrounded by other people, reference books, their own earlier written work, and other resources helps us evaluate the authentic task that is our ultimate interest: spelling in the context of writing.

4. THE TEACHER EVALUTATES SPELLING AS AN INFORMED PROFESSIONAL RATHER THAN AS A MECHANICAL TEST SCORER.

A holistic, kidwatcher's approach to evaluating spelling requires knowledge on the teacher's part: knowledge of the linguistic structure of written English, knowledge of developmental patterns in children's spelling, knowledge of children's personalities and of common spelling strategies. This knowledge base helps teachers not only to evaluate spelling but also to decide what kind of instruction would be relevant and when to step back and let growth proceed on its own. Such knowledgeable teachers can also help parents see growth in children's spelling and help them understand how it develops. By contrast a traditional spelling test could be processed completely by machine.

FROM DISCOVERY TO MATURITY: ANALYZING INVENTED SPELLINGS

This chapter provides some ideas about understanding and evaluating children's invented spellings; the following chapter then helps us to see spelling in the broader context of children's strategies and thinking processes and suggests some ideas for curriculum and instruction.

When we see invented spellings such as CHRIE for *try* and MABEY for *maybe* we intuitively recognize a difference between them. The second one "looks" better, seems to represent the sound of the word better, and is a closer match to the conventional spelling. Is there any way to characterize, perhaps even to quantify, these differences? I grappled with this problem when I looked at the invented spellings of three children whose spelling proficiency varied widely. In attempting to describe how these children differed, I came up with a series of eight questions that can be asked about an invented spelling in order to gain a sense of how sophisticated or mature it is. In order to understand the focus of these questions, we must first take a short detour into an explanation of how the English spelling system works and how it evolved.

THE NATURE OF ENGLISH SPELLING

The spelling system of English has often been criticized for not being logical, since it doesn't represent each sound by a single letter in the same way every time. A spelling such as *cat* seems sensible to most people but one such as *wrought* doesn't. Actually English spelling is more logical than it looks at first glance, but on several levels rather than one simple one.

The most obvious pattern in English spelling is the relationship between sounds (phonemes) and letters (graphemes). This is because written English is an alphabetic system, unlike, for instance, Arabic numerals (1, 2, 3) or Chinese, in which symbols represent meaning directly rather than sounds. However, since English uses more than thirty-five phonemes (depending on dialect) but only twenty-six letters, correspondence between phonemes and graphemes can't be one to one but must be more complex. Some phonemes, such as /t/ and other consonants, are spelled fairly regularly, while others, particularly vowels, have a variety of common spellings. For instance, the same vowel sound is spelled differently in *beet*, *heat*, and *Pete*; one has to know the word to know which way to spell the vowel.

If we had a simple alphabetic system, knowing the pronunciation of a word would enable us to predict its spelling with greater accuracy, through a small set of consistent rules telling how each phoneme is spelled. Over twenty years ago some researchers tried to make up a set of rules that would do this for 17,009 English words (Hanna, Hanna, Hodges, and Rudorf, 1966). Unfortunately, even 203 often complicated rules (such as, in my rephrasing, "Spell long I as *igh* if it comes before a /t/ sound and is in the middle of a syllable") produced spellings that were correct only 49.9 percent of the time and spellings with no more than one error 86.3 percent of the time.

The reason why 203 rules were necessary is that spellings of particular sounds are influenced by factors such as position in the word and surrounding letters. These are some of the features that make English spelling seem illogical, but they are actually more regular than we might think. Here are some examples:

Location in the word. The word *judge* starts and ends with the same sound, but we don't spell it *juj*. *J* (or even *je*) doesn't normally occur at the end of English words.

Adjacent sounds. The words *keep, cap*, and *quip* start with the same sound but different letters. The letter *c* is the usual spelling for this sound, but *k* or *q* is used before certain vowels.

Markers. Some phonemes have to be spelled with more than one letter, since we have more sounds than letters; this phenomenon affects vowel spellings especially. Marker letters don't carry any sound themselves but give information about phonemes represented by other letters. Thus a final *e* distinguishes between the vowels in *hat* and *hate*, and the extra consonant letter *p* tells us how to pronounce the first vowel in *supper* (as opposed to *super*).

Graphemic or visual patterns. Some English spelling rules are quite arbitrary in that they don't affect pronunciation. They are really rules about letter patterns rather than the relationships between sounds and letters. For instance, English words do not usually end with a single *f* or *z* (*stiff, buzz*) or in *u* or *v* (*glue, have*).

Even with all these factors taken into consideration, the 203 spelling rules did not always predict correctly. One reason is that in some cases the meaning of a word gives necessary information about its spelling that we could not know from its sound alone. For instance, the endings of *packed, played*, and *pounded* are spelled the same, even though they are pronounced differently, as a signal that the words are all past-tense verbs. Some words, known as homophones, are spelled differently even though they are pronounced the same (e.g., *meet* and *meat*); the spelling lets us know which meaning is intended.

How did our spelling system end up being so complicated? Much of its complexity has historical roots; spelling changes more slowly than speech, so that "we represent in the spelling of many words their sound as it was five or six centuries ago. It is for this reason that English spelling is sometimes said to be not phonetic but etymological" (Vallins, 1965, p. 11). Examples of this are the silent letters beginning words such as *gnat, knot*, and *wrong*, which were once pronounced. Also, some words that seem to have irregular spellings do so because of their foreign origin; examples are the *c* in *cello* and the *gn* in *poignant*.

Rather than bemoan the complexity of English spelling, we might be well advised to appreciate it. For instance, just think of the wonderful versatility of the silent final *e*. In a word such as *age* it tells us how to pronounce both the *g* and the *a*. The final *e* can also serve as a graphic marker to prevent words from ending in *u* or *v* (*give*); avoid a two-letter content word, not usually seen in English (*foe*); help indicate which syllable is stressed (*Corvette*, as opposed to *comet*); and indicate that the word is not a plural form (*please* as opposed to *pleas*) (P. T. Smith, 1980). Since the spelling system is complex, it's not learned overnight. (But then neither is oral language!) Looking at children's spellings knowledgeably can help us to see children coming to terms with that complexity.

EIGHT QUESTIONS

When we look at a child's invented spelling, the main question we want to answer for ourselves is "Where did this spelling come from?" We want to know why it took the form that it did in order to grasp what kinds of knowledge the child was using. Correct spellings don't tell us much about children's understanding of the spelling system, since they could be produced in a variety of ways. If a child writes COMING, he or she may or may not know the rule for dropping *e* before an affix, since the word could have been learned as a unit; but if it's spelled COMEING, we know that the rule is at best not fully internalized. In the same way that miscues provide, in Ken Goodman's words, a window on the reading process, invented spellings provide a window on the spelling process. This series of eight questions is intended to help us look through that window more knowledgeably. They are arranged in a rough hierarchy to suggest a progression from the least to the most sophisticated kinds of spellings; after discussing all eight questions, we'll consider the meaning of that hierarchical order. To provide some examples of spellings for discussion, I've included three stories, one from each of the children mentioned earlier whose spelling patterns I tried to characterize. These stories (see Figure 18–1) were all written in the second half of fourth grade; they do, however, contain spelling patterns that occur across the elementary school years.

QUESTION 1. IS THE SPELLING AN UNUSUAL ONE?

Sometimes we look at spellings and just can't figure out where they came from. Two examples of this are PLICEA (police) and HAPLDOL (hospital) from Elaine's story. Although parts of them make sense (they start with the correct consonant, they're about the right length, and they include most or all of the expected consonant letters), we certainly can't see a sequential attempt to spell each sound in the word the way we can in a spelling such as AMBELENS (ambulance).

In some ways these unusual spellings are reminiscent of the writing of very young children who use "letter strings" to represent a message globally before they have begun to relate letters to sounds as they write; these are therefore not very sophisticated or mature spellings. Since such spellings look somewhat bizarre, they're sometimes taken as a sign of a learning disability, but such a conclusion is premature. In Elaine's case these unusual spellings were deliberate invented spellings; she would write a spelling that she knew was wrong because it was the quickest way to get on with her story. When she tried to produce a correct spelling, even if what she came up with wasn't the conventional spelling, it would be a more logical one than these unusual ones. If a child produces unusual spellings more than occasionally, it's crucial to

Figure 18–1 *Stories by Three Children*

Note: Invented spellings are boldfaced, and translated when they first
appear. Punctuation has been conventionalized to make the text more
readable.

ELAINE

One day the sun came up. Me and Monica were going to **twon**
[town]. Then the sun was up, and it was **bring** [brighting] in **are** [our]
eyes. Then we **con't** [couldn't] see and we **almots** [almost] went **of**
[off] the **rode** [road]. Then we **stered** [started] to cry, but we **crreted**
[crashed]. Then the **plicea** [police] came, and the **ambelens**
[ambulance], and we got in the **hapldol** [hospital], so that's **hold**
[how] it all **hapend** [happened].

GORDON

THE DAY THE INDIAN GOT POWER FROM GOD
There was once a boy named Little **Nife** [Knife]. Little **Nife** was brave
and fast but he was not strong. One day Little **Nifes Farther** [Knife's
father] said, "Little **Nife**, come with me. We are going hunting. You
can help me **cary** [carry] the deer." Little **Nife** got **sacred** [scared]
when his **farther** said that he can **cary** the deer with him. Little **Nife**
said, "**Farther**, I am not strong." "Little **Nife**," said his **farther**, "**Dont
werey** [don't worry]. When you pick up that deer, God **well** [will] give
you power." When Little **Nife** picked up the deer, God gave him
powers. Little **Nife** was so happy he **caryed** [carried] the deer all by
his slfe [himself]. He said, "From now on, I am going to **cary** the
animals we catch for you." When Little **Nife** got home, his **mouther**
[mother] said, "Little **Nife**, go get some more wood for the fire." And
he **bring** [brought] lots of wood for the fire.

DANA

THE WILLIAM TELL STORY
The movie was about a great man. Well, one day William was fixing a
bow and arrow for his **sons** [son's] birthday, when a father came to
talk to William about a meeting. He said, "Can you come to a meeting
tonight?" William said, "No, because **its** [it's] my **sons** birthday." So
the father left. Then William went back to work. When his son was on
his way to **William** [William's] for lunch, he met some men. They
were mean men, **especciley** [especially] the one in the wagon. The
boy was brave **enouhg** [enough] to tell them off. Then they were
going to eat the goat. But they didn't want the goat so they threw the
goat down. The boy got the goat and ran to William. He told him all
about it. They went because it was getting dark. When they got home,
they all celebrated his birthday and on the same night **helled** [held]
the meeting. One of them was a **trator** [traitor]. So he told **there**
[their] master. After he had **herd** [heard], he said, "Stand up a **poll**
[pole] with my hat on it." When they did, everybody had to bow to it,
except William didn't. When they caught him, they made him shoot an
apple **of** [off] his **sons** head. When he did, he **treatned** [threatened]
the king. The guards were going to kill them when the townspeople
killed them. After that they celebrated his son's birthday.

observe and talk to him or her and find out what strategy or process the spellings represent.

QUESTION 2. DOES THE SPELLING REPRESENT
CONSONANTS NONCONVENTIONALLY?

English consonants are far more regular than vowels in their spelling. Not surprisingly, Charles Read (1975) found that even preschoolers spell them appropriately most of the time. When they don't, there's usually a good reason. Let's look at some examples from the three stories:

Pronunciation. Sometimes the way consonants are spelled is different from the way they're pronounced. Silent letters (NIFE/Knife) are an obvious example. The knowledgeable teacher must consider the way the *child* pronounces the word; the missing *t* in STERED (started) and *d* in CON'T (couldn't) were likely to have been reduced or silent in Elaine's pronunciation. (The *l* in *couldn't* is, of course, silent in all dialects.) The use of *t* rather than *th* in TREATNED (threatened) may also reflect pronunciation. Children's pronunciation may differ from the teacher's because of regional or cultural dialect (these three children are Native Americans) or merely because it represents child and not adult language; the important point is that all young spellers use letter patterns to represent the sounds of their own speech (and eventually move on to more varied spelling strategies).

Alternative representations. A few consonant sounds are trickier to spell than others because they have more than one common spelling. The *s* in AMBELENS (ambulance) is certainly understandable; the letter *c* is actually an unnecessary one in our alphabet, since the sounds it represents can always be spelled with either *s* or *k*. Children therefore sometimes replace *c* with *s* or *k*, or vice versa; the same thing occurs with *g* and *j*.

Double consonants. We can't tell from listening to a word whether it has a double consonant or not; this is one of those markers discussed earlier that is tied to rules about vowel pronunciation. Developing spellers understandably tend not to use double consonants; as they get older, this pattern persists: OF (off); CARY (carry); HAPEND (happened). But they also begin to use double consonants both when they're needed and sometimes when they aren't: HELLED (held); ESPECCILEY (especially). This is a sign of spelling growth because it shows awareness of a feature that is visual rather than directly phonetic.

QUESTION 3. DOES THE SPELLING REPRESENT VOWELS
NONCONVENTIONALLY?

Vowels may be the most complex part of the English spelling system. The same vowel sound can be spelled in various ways (*pane, pain*) and a single spelling can represent different sounds (*food, good*). It is therefore common for invented spellings at all ages to show exploration of vowel spelling patterns.

Letter-name spellings. Very young children typically spell a vowel according to the name of the letter that sounds most like it. This produces some surprises in the case of short vowels, since they are not always closest phonetically to the name of the letter usually used to spell them. Rounded vowels, which usually include *o* in their spelling, are often spelled with just an *o*, or with *ow*, by young children. Vowels followed by *r* are often spelled with just an *r* and no vowel; in a word such as *car* or *her* we hear an *r* sound but not a separate vowel. The following table shows typical vowel spellings found in young children that teachers can recognize as part of a natural developmental process. (The examples are taken from Read, 1971; his lengthy discussion there of vowel spelling is of great interest.)

Long Vowels	Short Vowels	Rounded Vowels	R-Vowels
DA/day	FALL/fell	SOWN/soon	GRL/girl
FEL/feel	FES/fish	OL/all	STRT/start
LIK/like	GIT/got	GOWT/goat	
	LIV/love		

Variable vowel spellings. As children mature, the relatively easy short vowel spellings tend to become regularized, but other vowels remain difficult because their spelling is so variable and often unpredictable. Not only is a phoneme such as long *o* usually spelled with more than one letter, they are not even the same letters every time. Even if children have moved beyond a letter-name strategy for long vowels, they might not always choose the right option. Thus in the case of long *o* Elaine produced *o–e* when *oa* would have been appropriate (RODE/road), while Dana used just an *o* instead of *o–e* (POLL/pole). Both of their spellings were, of course, real words as well; they used perfectly good spellings but of the wrong word! Vowels followed by *r* are even less predictable, but Gordon's spelling WEREY (worry) and Dana's HERD (heard) are very logical attempts, possible analogies to *were* and *her*.

Unstressed vowels. Unstressed vowels are extremely difficult to spell. An unstressed or reduced vowel is one with the schwa sound (/ə/), as in the first syllable of *about*, and may be spelled with any vowel letter, depending on the word. The *only* way to spell a reduced vowel correctly is to know the word, since they all sound the same. It is therefore not surprising that young spellers often choose the wrong letter, as in the second and third vowels of AMBELENS (ambulance). Even a spelling such as Gordon's WELL (will) may reflect this pattern, since function words are often unstressed in connected speech. When an unstressed vowel occurs before the consonants *l, m, n,* or *r*, it may be omitted entirely since all one hears is the consonant (TREATNED/threatened).

QUESTION 4. DOES THE SPELLING USE SUFFIXES
NONCONVENTIONALLY?

Learning to use suffixes appropriately involves two steps: first, realizing
that a suffix represents a generalized meaning and tends to be spelled
the same regardless of pronunciation; and second, learning the rules
for changes in some root words when attaching suffixes. Young writers
often spell suffixes phonetically (HAPEND/happened) or in other ways
that don't reflect an abstract understanding of the suffix (ESPECCILEY/
especially). Interestingly, they may also overgeneralize; some English
past-tense forms, usually those in which the root word changes inter-
nally, don't end with -*ed*, yet children may spell them that way (Dana's
HELLED/held). Even once the suffix has been generalized, children still
very commonly spell inflected words as root word plus suffix, without
making obligatory changes in the former (CARYED/carried). Teachers
can see growth in this area as indicating an increasing ability to represent
abstract information in spelling.

QUESTION 5. IS THE INVENTED SPELLING A PERMUTATION
OF THE INTENDED WORD?

What is a permutation? It's a spelling that has all the right letters but in
the wrong order. The examples seen in our three stories here are TWON
(town), ALMOTS (almost), HIS SLFE (hisself, in Gordon's dialect), and
ENOUHG (enough). Permutations are relatively common in invented
spelling; in a collection of over two thousand invented spellings by six
children (including these three), about 8 percent were permutations
(Wilde, 1986). I believe that they are a fairly advanced, mature kind of
invented spelling, since they reflect considerable visual exposure to and
memory of words; they are well beyond the sounding-out stage represented by a spelling such as ENUF (enough). The child has to have
seen *enough* in print to be able to spell it ENOUHG. These permutations
may represent a transitional stage between phonetically focused and
conventional spelling; the writer almost has the word right but isn't quite
there. They are also reminiscent of the changes in letter order that are
so common in touch-typing; they may be "slips of the pen" related to
mechanical processes, "typos" of the pencil caused by rapid writing.
(These spellings, like adult typos, may be relatively easy to correct
through proofreading.) An increase in permutations may signal a de-
crease in less sophisticated spellings; teachers should see permutations
as a sign of growth, strength, and maturity in young writers.

QUESTION 6. DOES THE INVENTED SPELLING DIFFER
FROM THE CONVENTIONAL ONE BY ONLY A SINGLE LETTER?

Many invented spellings are near misses; if one letter had been added,
dropped, or changed, the spelling would have been the conventional
one. Examples from these three children include OF (off), CARY (carry),
and TRATOR (traitor) (letter missing); MOUTHER (extra letter); and

WELL (will) and POLL (pole) (letter changed). As always, the child's dialect must be taken into account; when Gordon wrote, "he bring lots of wood," he was likely to have been spelling not *brought* but *brang*, and would therefore have been off by only one letter. Like permutations, these spellings reflect a good deal of knowledge about the word involved and can therefore be seen as fairly high level.

QUESTION 7. IS THE INVENTED SPELLING A REAL WORD?

Many invented spellings are real words; in fact, in the study of two thousand invented spellings 32.2 percent were real words (Wilde, 1986). Why is this the case? Some of these real-word spellings are homophones of or close in sound to the intended word (RODE/road, FARTHER/father), some are another form of the same word (SONS/son's, BRING/brang), but others are less closely related (HOLD/how). Spelling often involves a feedback and self-correction loop whereby a spelling may be changed if it doesn't "look right." Perhaps if an invented spelling is a real word, it is more likely to look right and therefore be passed over for correction. Real-word invented spellings are high-level ones because the writer is, of course, spelling a real word. Adults often produce invented spellings that either are real words or contain parts of real words, since mature spellers often spell by analogy to other words. My favorite example is from a woman who, in an essay about herself as a writer, said she had been placed in "excellerated" classes all through school. This seems even better than the usual spelling, since "excellerated" classes are indeed for those who excel!

QUESTION 8. ARE THE INVENTED AND CONVENTIONAL
SPELLINGS PUNCTUATED DIFFERENTLY?

The examples here involve either apostrophes or word boundaries. Apostrophes are a surprisingly tricky feature of English spelling. Although the rules for using them are fairly straightforward, they're often either left out or inserted where they don't belong. (I see this on menus and signs constantly!) Words with apostrophes are really a special case of homophones, since *sons, son's,* and *sons'* are pronounced identically. Even children who are good spellers may not have figured out how to use them. Or they may use them based on their own idiosyncratic rules. Gordon often wrote *but* with an apostrophe (BU'T). When asked why he replied, "It's like 'don't,' sort of bad news!" Word boundaries can also be considered a punctuation feature of some invented spellings; children may write one word as two (HIS SLFE/himself) or vice versa. In all these cases involving punctuation the invented and conventional spellings differ in only a minor way.

USING THE EIGHT QUESTIONS

How can these eight questions help us understand what is going on in an individual child's spelling? Let's take a look at profiles for Elaine,

Table 18–1 *Invented Spelling Codings for Three Stories*

Elaine		Gordon		Dana	
Spelling	Code(s)	Spelling	Code(s)	Spelling	Code(s)
TWON/town	5	NIFE/Knife	2, 6	SONS/son's	7, 8
BRING/brighting	2, 3, 7	NIFES/Knife's	2, 6, 8	ITS/it's	7, 8
ARE/our	3, 7	FARTHER/father	2, 6, 7	WILLIAM/William's	6, 7, 8
CON'T/couldn't	2, 3	CARY/carry	2, 6	ESPECCILEY/ especially	2, 3, 4
ALMOTS/almost	5	SACRED/scared	5, 7		
OF/off	2, 6, 7	DONT/don't	8	ENOUHG/enough	5
RODE/road	3, 7	WEREY/worry	2, 3	HELLED/held	2, 4
STERED/started	2, 3	WELL/will	3, 6, 7	TRATOR/traitor	3, 6
CRRSTED/crashed	2, 3	CARYED/carried	2, 4	THERE/their	3, 7
PLICEA/police	1	HIS SLFE/himself (hisself)	5, 8	HERD/heard	3, 6, 7
				POLL/pole	2, 3, 6, 7

Key: 1. Unusual? 2. Consonants? 3. Vowels? 4. Suffix? 5. Permutation? 6. Single letter? 7. Real word? 8. Punctuation?

Gordon, and Dana. Table 18–1 shows the first ten invented spellings from each of their stories coded for the eight questions; Table 18–2 summarizes the totals for each question.

If a spelling was considered unusual, there was no attempt to classify it further because, for instance, there was no way to tell which letters were intended to represent some of the consonant and vowel phonemes. If a word was classified as a permutation, it wasn't coded under the vowel or consonant categories, the reasoning being that a spelling such as ALMOTS (almost) probably didn't represent a misjudging of the final consonant cluster in the same way that CARY (carry) involved a lack of awareness of the double consonant. Many of my categorizations were of necessity judgment calls, as many of yours will be, but increasing experience with invented spelling helps us draw conclusions about chil-

Table 18–2 *Comparison of Three Spellers*

	Elaine	Gordon	Dana
1. Unusual?	1	0	0
2. Consonants?	5	6	3
3. Vowels?	6	2	5
4. Suffix?	0	1	2
5. Permutation?	2	2	1
6. Single letter?	1	5	4
7. Real word?	4	3	6
8. Punctuation?	0	3	3

Numbers indicate how many words (from a sample of 10 per story) received a "yes" answer to each question.

dren's spellings from an increasing knowledge base. For instance, why did I classify HAPLDOL (hospital) as unusual but not CRRSTED (crashed)? In the case of the latter, I could see plausible relationships between Elaine's graphemes and the phonemes of the word, knowing that children sometimes omit vowels in the presence of *r*, and that Elaine may have pronounced the word "crashted."

Let's look now at some principles for analyzing invented spellings using tables such as these.

1. ANALYSIS OF INVENTED SPELLING MUST TAKE PLACE IN THE CONTEXT OF *ALL* SPELLING.

Invented spellings made up only 21 percent of Elaine's story, 16 percent of Gordon's, and 6 percent of Dana's. (All other words were spelled conventionally.) Thus, although Elaine had problems with vowels in six out of her first ten invented spellings, plus one unusual spelling, this doesn't mean that she had a severe vowel problem, since 85 percent of the words in her story used vowels appropriately. Similarly, Dana had punctuation problems in three of ten invented spellings, but all occurrences of these in the story made up only 2 percent of the text. To evaluate spelling we have to consider both quantity (the rate of invented spelling) and quality (the patterns found in individual spellings).

2. ANALYSIS SHOWS THAT MANY INVENTED SPELLINGS HAVE MORE THAN ONE CAUSE.

Sometimes invented spellings are caused by incomplete internalization of two or more separate spelling principles. We can see this in NIFES (Knife's), which Gordon spelled more or less phonetically, without including either the initial silent consonant letter or the apostrophe. This spelling also illustrates the importance of looking at the level of linguistic knowledge involved rather than surface-level patterns. There are two omitted features in Gordon's spelling, but they have very different meanings; if the *i* and *e* had been omitted, that would have indicated something different still (a less mature, consonant-only spelling strategy).

In other cases multiple causes illustrate spelling strength. A spelling such as POLL (pole) is nonconventional, but the fact that it is a real word and a homophone indicates that both the vowel and consonant are spelled in ways that reflect knowledge of language.

3. ANALYSIS OF INVENTED SPELLING IS MOST USEFUL AS A QUALITATIVE AND HEURISTIC TOOL RATHER THAN A QUANTITATIVE ONE.

It's very important to remember that, although Table 18–2 shows numbers of invented spellings corresponding to numbered questions, it's not a numerical scale. The questions are arranged in a rough hierarchy, but their numbers don't represent "quantities" of spelling ability that can be tabulated and turned into spelling scores. The major purpose of the questions is to get the teacher to look at an invented spelling and think about what it reflects about the child's knowledge of spelling, providing the teacher in turn with the appropriate knowledge base to support the child's growth and to communicate with parents.

4. ANALYSIS OF INVENTED SPELLING CAN, IF USED CAREFULLY, INDICATE GROWTH IN SPELLING ABILITY.

There are two signs of growth in spelling, which may or may not go in tandem. One is an increase in the proportion of words spelled conventionally; the other is a change in the type of invented spellings. Both are important. Gordon went from using invented spellings for one out of five words in third grade to one out of ten in fourth grade, and produced similar kinds of spellings in both years. His invented spellings reflected a good variety of patterns and strategies, and growth for him apparently consisted largely of spelling many more words successfully. Elaine actually spelled a little less conventionally in fourth grade than in third, but the quality of her invented spellings improved greatly. Analysis of a random sample showed that she used far fewer unusual spellings in fourth grade, more plausible kinds of vowel spellings, and many more spellings that were off by only one letter than she had done in third grade (Wilde, 1986). Both children therefore grew as spellers, but in quite different ways. Dana, interestingly, showed little improvement either quantitatively or qualitatively. Why? He was so good to start with! His invented spellings were so infrequent (one out of twenty words) and of such high quality that there was less room to improve. His spelling vocabulary, of course, has continued to expand.

5. ANALYSIS OF INVENTED SPELLING CAN EASILY BE INCORPORATED INTO AN OVERALL EVALUATION PLAN.

The most important use of analytical spelling evaluation is an informal one. As we develop an eye for invented spelling and an appreciation for what it involves, we find ourselves instinctively assessing spellings as we see them in children's writing: "Isn't that neat? Last week she wrote LAF for *laugh*, but this week she wrote LUAGH. She's moved to a much stronger visual sense of the word."

Teachers can also, however, do more formal analysis and record keeping, particularly in a situation where spelling assessment is expected or required. Once a month or so the teacher can take student writing samples and list the first ten (or more) invented spellings and analyze them using the eight questions. (It can also be useful to tabulate the percentage of invented spellings in a story.) Although this takes some time, it is bound to be less than the time spent administering, scoring, and keeping records of weekly spelling tests. More important, it's time well spent for the teacher, because we are using our minds and learning about children's spelling as we do it.

UNDERSTANDING SPELLING STRATEGIES: A KIDWATCHER'S GUIDE TO SPELLING, PART 2

Sandra Wilde

One day fourth grader Gordon got out a dictionary to look for the word *scared*; he spotted *sacred* instead and began to write it down. When I asked how he knew it was the right word, he read the definition, his face lighting up as he said, "See! It says right here, 'They play scary [sic] music in church!' " Someone who read his story without having seen him use the dictionary would probably assume he'd just reversed the letters on his own. By observing children as they write and talking with them about their spelling, it's possible to discover a good deal about their intentions and strategies. Through doing so teachers can learn far more than they could from just looking at finished products. They can find out what children think about spelling and how they actually go about getting a particular spelling on paper.

I talked regularly about spelling with two children, Gordon and Elaine (see Chapter 18), during their third- and fourth-grade years; I also watched them write about once a week. My observations suggested to me that children use a variety of strategies that govern their production of the written word. My observations will, I hope, suggest to teachers patterns to look for in their students' approaches to spelling.

In the case of these two children I observed five major spelling strategies; I have named the strategies, but Gordon's and Elaine's words describe them:

1. Placeholder spelling strategy: "I just wrote it any way."
2. Human-resource strategy: "How do you spell *people*?"
3. Textual resource strategy: "I need the dictionary."
4. Generation, monitoring, and revision strategy: "*Say* is s-a-y, huh?"
5. Ownership strategy: "I know how to spell *rodeo*."

I've put them in hierarchical order; the higher-level strategies reflect an increasing reliance on one's own resources as a speller. They don't necessarily produce more conventional spelling (asking one's teacher how to spell every unknown word is the best strategy if perfection is the goal), but they involve greater independence as a speller and provide more opportunities for internalization of the spelling system. Higher level also doesn't necessarily imply better; children are capable of different strategies at different stages in their development. Outside resources are a valuable avenue of learning about spelling and, as we shall see, even the lowest-level strategy can be growth enhancing, as it was for Elaine.

PLACEHOLDER SPELLING

During third grade Elaine was a perfectionistic speller. She felt it was important to spell words conventionally and often annoyed seatmates by repeatedly asking them how to spell words. Later she became less concerned with correctness and was more willing to use invented spellings. Many of those spellings were the unusual ones we've already seen. When asked how she produced her unusual spellings, she typically responded, "I just wrote it any way," meaning that she wasn't trying to spell the word right but simply wanted to get something down on paper. These spellings usually contained just enough information for her to tell what the word was (with the help of context) when she reread her story. The term I've used here is "placeholder" spellings; they represent words globally rather than alphabetically. These could also be called deliberate invented spellings, that is, *choosing* to produce a misspelling. As a spelling strategy it's low level because it represents an abandonment of the goal of conventional spelling; it is often very valuable, however, as a writing strategy because it lets the writer temporarily lay spelling aside in order to concentrate more fully on the expression of ideas.

For Elaine the ability to drop back to this low-level spelling strategy was an important step in her growth as a writer. Spelling was difficult enough for her that if she tried to produce perfect spelling, she could write only very slowly and with frequent help from others; being able to relinquish her perfectionism about spelling allowed her to write much more quickly and to focus more on content.

She appeared, at least some of the time, to prefer placeholder spelling to trying to invent more accurate spellings, which would have been a slower process. She would sometimes switch to placeholder spelling while writing a story if she got tired of concentrating on spelling. For instance, her spellings became more unusual in the second half of the story she wrote about a car accident (see Figure 18–1); she used a dictionary earlier in the story but then stopped doing that and just wrote.

Since placeholder spellings aren't an attempt to spell the word as well as possible, it's important not to take them as a full representation of the child's ability. In Elaine's case the placeholder strategy masked her true spelling ability—what she could do if she gave spelling her best effort. One day Elaine was finishing a story in which she had spelled most words with no outside help and with reasonable success. When she got to the final word of the story, *shirt*, she asked me how to spell it, but I told her to try it herself. Annoyed and tired, Elaine wrote SHOSS, then admitted that she "just wrote it any way." She then decided to revise it, changing the spelling to SHRT. Even with her best effort the vowel in *shirt* was difficult for her, but the second spelling gave a far truer picture of her spelling ability than the first one did; in other words, Elaine's spelling performance was not always a true reflection of her competence. She presumably could have produced higher-level invented spellings (or conventional spellings) in place of many of her unusual ones if she had chosen to take the time to do so, but it probably would have been at the cost of distracting her from the content of her writing.

How can teachers know if children are using placeholder spellings? Watch and ask. Observe how children spell when they're writing rapidly, involved in a story and not wanting to slow down enough to think through a spelling. When you see an unusual spelling, ask the child why she or he spelled it that way. (Use neutral wording: "How did you decide how to spell that?" rather than the more judgmental "Why did you spell it *that* way?") Placeholder spelling is especially useful for children who feel frustrated because they want to say far more than they can spell easily; if they aren't already using this strategy, you may want to suggest it to them.

HUMAN RESOURCES

Young writers who don't know the spelling of many of the words that they want to use and who hope to produce conventional spellings if possible have two choices: appealing to outside authority or relying on their own resources. A student who sets a high priority on producing conventional spelling or a low value on his or her abilities is likely to look to external sources for help with spelling. Asking someone else is the easiest, most available source of spelling information, and both Elaine and Gordon did this frequently. Elaine often did it out of insecurity, assuming that other children would be more likely to know spellings that she didn't and being unwilling to trust her own powers of invention. Gordon just enjoyed talking with his classmates and would help others with spelling as often as he asked for help himself.

Observing a small group of children writing together and consulting each other on spelling can be an enlightening experience. Since children, unlike the teacher, are still actively involved in learning about the spelling of words, they often need to negotiate spellings through a collaborative process. For instance, one time Gordon tried to write *treat*, came up with TEAT, and then asked for help. One child in his small group suggested that he first write the word *tree*, while another told Gordon he could just add an *r* to what he already had, which was the option he chose.

Kidwatching of such small-group interaction can help us understand both conventional and invented spellings. We know that Gordon spelled *treat* conventionally in that story because of his friend's input; if he had followed the other child's advice, he would have ended up with the invented spelling TREET. Elaine one day started to look for *people* in the dictionary but stopped when a friend wrote PEPOLE on a scrap of paper for her; when this spelling appeared in her story, it was still an invented spelling but not Elaine's!

The teacher is also, of course, a source of spelling information. Back before teachers discovered the value of encouraging children to use their own spellings rather than trying to spell every word perfectly, the teacher's role during classroom writing times was often primarily one of spelling provider. Although there's certainly a place for giving a child a spelling from time to time, particularly when a word has a very uncommon spelling, overdependence on the teacher should be discouraged. Our ultimate goal is to create ease in writing and independence in spelling; both of these are enhanced by refusing to allow the writing process to be interrupted by a compulsive quest for perfect spelling.

TEXTUAL RESOURCES

Using textual resources (a variety of written material) for help in producing spellings takes more independence and initiative than asking someone else how to spell a word since it means deciding not only where to look but whether the right word has been found. Both Gordon and Elaine used many different kinds of textual resources in their drive to spell as conventionally as possible. Any kind of written material found in a classroom will probably be used by children to help them spell, as these examples show.

Wall charts. Elaine and Gordon's third-grade teacher made word lists, charts, and posters related to thematic units, which were a valuable spelling resource. Their fourth-grade teacher had a series of charts on the wall that showed common words in alphabetical order; these were used a great deal. Elaine sometimes had trouble remembering the difference between lowercase *b* and *d*, which she would resolve by looking at an alphabet chart (intended for handwriting practice) while saying or thinking "*a-b-c-d.*"

Dictionaries. Watching Elaine and Gordon use dictionaries to find words revealed a good deal of interesting information about how children interact with this rich, complex resource:

- Children use different dictionaries for different purposes. Gordon would go first to a simple Dr. Seuss picture dictionary for concrete words such as *chair* or *round* but to a bigger one for more abstract words such as *gang* or *surrounded*. He showed an understanding of which word would be in which dictionary.
- Dictionary use isn't always efficient. Both Elaine and Gordon tended to use a very slow dictionary search strategy: determining the initial letter, then reading or scanning all words beginning with that letter. Sometimes the search was successful, while sometimes they would choose the wrong word or skip right over the correct one. When

Elaine's teacher helped her to generate the probable first three letters of a spelling *before* turning to the dictionary, her efficiency improved a great deal.

- Dictionaries offer multiple means of confirming spellings. Usually the children knew they had found the right word in the dictionary by reading it. Elaine would sometimes break the word into parts, a confirmation strategy that didn't always work correctly: looking for her coined word "brighting" (i.e. "shining brightly") for her car crash story, she found *bring* and said it was right because "it has a *br-* and an *-ing*." Definitions can also be used to confirm a spelling, though again not always correctly, as in Gordon's use of *sacred* for *scared*.
- Dictionaries can be a source of serendipitous incidental learning. Gordon loved to browse in the dictionary. One day while looking for *tired* he spotted a picture of the solar system and paused there, reading aloud all the planets' names. Another day while looking for *bundle* he found a picture of a bassoon and ran to show it to his teacher since the class had been studying musical instruments. Browsing through words and pictures often used up a good deal of his time with the dictionary; in a few cases friends of his would find the word he needed in another dictionary and tell him the spelling while he was still discovering completely unrelated words.

Other resources. Donald Graves (personal communication) speaks of young writers "living off the land": I certainly saw Gordon and Elaine do this with spelling resources. Gordon got *Saturday* from a calendar, named a parrot after a card from a board game ("Draw Two"), and got the spelling of *parrot* from my field notes, where I'd just written, "Gordon asks me how to spell *parrot*"! Elaine often looked back to the first appearance of a word in her story to help herself write it again. In one story her second spellings of three words were copied from earlier usages in the text: *safe* was spelled conventionally twice, HSPHTOOL (hospital) occurred twice, and ENTESC (auntie's) was followed by ANETSC (auntie) on the next page, which was a miscopying rather than a reinvention.

Again, watching children write can illuminate both conventional and nonconventional spellings. A word may be spelled appropriately because a textual resource was used, and an apparent invented spelling may be either a miscopying of the right word, an accurate copying of the wrong word, or a miscopying of the wrong word. Watching children use textual resources also helps us appreciate the ingenuity and variety of their strategies and helps us see where a little judicious one-to-one support could be helpful (e.g. on the use of guide words in the dictionary).

GENERATION, MONITORING, AND REVISION

Both Elaine and Gordon produced many of their spellings by a process in which they first generated a possible spelling, using several levels of knowledge about language, and then in many cases monitored what they produced, revising and correcting if they thought it necessary. This strategy, unlike those described so far, involves both an attempt to produce a conventional spelling and a willingness to do it primarily on one's own (although the revision stage sometimes calls for recourse to outside resources).

Elaine sometimes generated more than one possible spelling of a word in order to see which one sounded or looked right. For instance, trying once to spell *then*, she asked a classmate, said both "*t-h-e-n*" and "*t-h-e-r-e*" aloud, and then wrote both of those spellings before choosing the former one. Since she wasn't a highly proficient speller, her corrections weren't always improvements, as when she changed the second *o* to *v* in COROLFAROV (carnival). The important point is that she had generated the spelling on her own and then attempted to make it better on her own. As she became a better speller, her revisions became more likely to produce at least more logical spellings, if not conventional ones. Her comments revealed that when she revised a word, she often thought of her first spelling of it as the result of a momentary lapse; she would say, "I know how to spell [the word]" or "I forgot my *e* up here." Another time, when I pointed out that she'd written "ot" (to) earlier in a story, she found it funny, presumably because she recognized it as a slip of the pen. She sometimes also overcorrected, as when she wrote the first four letters of *rodeo* conventionally, erased it, asked how to spell it, said "*r-o-d-e . . .*," and realized she'd been right in the first place.

Gordon was comfortable with inventing spellings when he couldn't find them in a textual resource (e.g., failing to find *always* on a wall chart, he generated it independently as ALLWAYS, presumably constructing it like a compound).

When a textual resource is unproductive, one can either drop back to greater dependency by asking someone for the spelling or move to greater independence by inventing it; Gordon did both at different times. Gordon also revised many of his spellings, though sometimes he chose not to, particularly when he wanted to get on with his writing. In such cases he took only the first step of the two-part revision process: he recognized that the original spelling wasn't satisfactory but then decided not to change it. For instance, one day he asked if DONW (down) was spelled right, implying that it didn't look right to him, but then decided to leave it. Later in the same story he made one revision of HELLDS (hills), erasing the *d*, questioned whether it was right, but decided not to change it further. Another day he wrote GREES, then said, "Is that how you spell *grass*? Oh, I'm just going to leave it." Later, while rereading his text, he successfully corrected it. These examples illustrate that the correction stage of a spelling revision may follow the recognition stage immediately, later, or not at all, and may be followed by a second revision cycle with the same word.

As with Elaine's, Gordon's revisions didn't always lead to the conventional spelling, though some unconventional spellings were improved even if not perfected on revision, such as changing BRNEING (burning) and GOTS (ghost) to BRUNING and GOST.

Gordon once spent a good deal of time revising a single word. Trying to spell the word *because*, he looked (without finding it) at three textual resources, said, "I think I know how to spell it," and wrote BCESU. Unsatisfied with that, he erased the last two letters and walked around the room, asking three people how to spell the word, and finally got a satisfactory answer. His need to socialize temporarily slaked, he returned to his seat and changed the spelling to BECUASE. Still feeling it didn't look right, he said aloud, "*Because* doesn't have an *o* in it, does it?" and got four or five classmates involved in a debate over that issue before making his final revision to BECAUSE. This was a case where the basic process of generation, monitoring, and revision was supplemented by recourse to human and textual resources.

The teacher observing this process tends to become very aware of the breadth of knowledge that children can draw on as they spell. They may sound out words, try different letter sequences aloud, write a root word and then an affix, think about the two parts of a compound, wonder aloud about which of a pair of homophones is the right one, use analogies to other words, and/or see if a word looks right. Such observation can help us to be less worried about how children will ever master the complexities of English spelling, since we can see them exploring that complexity daily in a spirit of great intellectual involvement.

OWNERSHIP

The ultimate spelling strategy is ownership: knowing how to spell a word and knowing that one knows. This could also be referred to as spelling confidence. Elaine's spelling confidence wasn't very strong early in third grade; if she couldn't find someone to tell her how to spell a word, she would sometimes change what she was writing in order to use a word she thought she could spell. She gradually moved toward more independence, deciding to use textual resources and realizing it was all right to use invented spellings if she chose (although there were still times when she tried to spell every word conventionally). Although even early on there were many words that she realized she knew how to spell, their number increased, and she would sometimes even begin to look in the dictionary and then say, "I know how to spell that," and close the dictionary, realizing that she didn't need the textual resource after all. By the end of fourth grade she was even observed volunteering information to other children about how to spell words, having moved from relying heavily on human resources to becoming one herself.

Gordon also often revealed his sense of ownership of spelling. In an early third-grade story he wrote a word with the help of a textual resource, then looked back at an earlier, self-generated spelling of the same word and said, "I was right!" He realized that spelling knowledge of particular words can come and go; when he was having trouble spelling a word one day, he commented, "I forgot how to spell *just*! I used to know." Only occasionally did he consider changing what he wanted to say because of spelling insecurity, as when, unsure of how to spell *used to be*, he considered abandoning "The mountains used to be volcanoes" for "The mountains were volcanoes a long time ago but they aren't now." Gordon was clearly proud of his spelling knowledge; his confidence was reflected in his self-assured explanations of some features of his spellings (even if they seemed like non sequiturs to the listener): for instance, *didn't* has an apostrophe because "it means you didn't do it."

Since most of the conventionally spelled words produced by Gordon and Elaine, particularly high-frequency ones such as *the* and *and*, were produced automatically (i.e. without a conscious focus on spelling), it is probably fair to say that beginning at a relatively early age ownership is the most common spelling strategy. Watching children write can help us appreciate how many words they *do* know how to spell, words they can write without having to stop and think about them. Perhaps the process of becoming an adult speller is one of developing that kind of confident ownership of more and more words, with the less efficient strategies always available to fall back on.

HOW TO OBSERVE SPELLING STRATEGIES

These are the main spelling strategies I observed two children using as they wrote; other teachers may find others. This kind of observation need not be complicated or time consuming. As children in your classroom write, you can sit down with them, as individuals or in small groups, and watch all the varied and wonderful processes they go through as they explore the English spelling system. Taking notes can help you keep tabs on what strategies are common aspects of your classroom climate and can be a very useful way of monitoring the progress of a child who is having trouble with spelling (as with Elaine's growth from overreliance on human resources to increasing self-generation of spelling).

You can also ask children about their strategies. Some sample questions:

- What do you do when you think you don't know how to spell a word?
- Who would you ask for help with spelling? Why?
- How do you look for a word in the dictionary?
- Where else could you find a spelling? How would you know where to look?
- How do you know if a spelling is right?
- What makes you decide to change a spelling?
- What does it mean to say you know how to spell a word?

This kind of observation and interaction related to spelling is informative, enjoyable, and satisfying. It's a great intellectual pleasure to watch children's behavior in all its richness and then gradually come to see the patterns in that behavior, the mental processes that are manifested and acted out in it. This kind of high-level, sophisticated evaluation is at the heart of what it means to be a teacher. It's wonderful to find and build on strength where less-informed observers see only weakness.

FROM EVALUATION TO CURRICULUM

I won't attempt here to give a complete picture of a curriculum that enhances spelling growth, but I do want to suggest some logical follow-ups to the kinds of evaluation presented here.

1. HELP CHILDREN EXPAND THEIR RANGE OF SPELLING STRATEGIES.

As we have seen, learning to spell is a complex process. The more strategies children have for dealing with spelling, the better they will be able to learn about that complexity. This begins with an awareness of the concept of invented spelling itself; children need to realize that first-draft spellings need not be as accurate as final-draft ones, and that using their own spellings not only lets them write more fluently but also gives them a chance to figure out spelling principles for themselves.

You can also make children aware of the strategies I've described Gordon and Elaine using. For instance, you can talk informally with your class about all the sources of written words in the classroom that they can use for spelling resources. The goal in doing so isn't to push children on to higher-level strategies but to expand the range of strategies available to them, with the choice of the appropriate one for any given moment being left up to the child. (For some children at some times placeholder spelling is a very helpful strategy.) Encouraging wide strategy use also means providing an appropriate classroom climate where a range of dictionaries and other reference materials is readily available and where peer interaction about spelling is welcomed.

2. USE BOTH INDIVIDUAL AND GROUP INSTRUCTION.

Since children vary a great deal in their understanding of spelling, instruction that is individualized and takes place at critical moments is probably of the greatest benefit. A child who consistently uses spellings such as CHASEING and CARRYED is probably ready to learn the rules for changing root words when suffixes are added, while such a lesson would go right over the head of a child who uses many spellings such as SAIDY (saying) and MARDIT (married). A more general kind of lesson, such as one about dictionary search strategies, is likely to be relevant to groups of children if not the whole class. Brief "minilessons" (Calkins, 1986) are probably the best avenue for this.

3. CONSIDER TEACHING LINGUISTICS AS A CONTENT AREA.

The English language is a fascinating object of study. Particularly for students in the intermediate grades and above, a thematic unit on language could be an enjoyable topic of learning that is also bound to have positive effects on spelling. Such a unit could explore questions such as the prevalence of both Germanic and Romance language words in English, the source of loan words in our vocabulary, changes in spelling over time, and the etymology of silent letters. (Tompkins and Yaden 1986 give many specific suggestions for such a unit.)

4. REALIZE THAT SPELLING IS MORE LEARNED THAN TAUGHT.

The emphasis in learning spelling should be more on curriculum in a general sense than on instruction, because we learn to spell far more words than we could ever be taught. Children need to read widely, since they usually need to see a word to know how to spell it, and they need to write extensively, since they need to try out their spelling hypotheses as they need them if they are going to grow and develop.

Picking up spellings from seeing them and writing them is probably quite easy. Do you remember Elaine's spelling CORVLFAROV (carnival)? A week later she spelled the word conventionally, without needing to ask anyone or use a reference book, and stopping to think only briefly. When I asked her how she had suddenly become able to spell *carnival*, she said offhandedly, "I saw Cheryl write it yesterday and I remembered." I imagine that her experience of reading the word on a classmate's paper, combined with a general interest in spelling, produced an "Aha!" experience: "So *that's* how you spell *carnival*!" We need to allow children the time, space, and opportunity to make such discoveries daily. The traditional spelling curriculum, with its exercises, drills, and tests, has often been children's favorite school subject, perhaps because it is so clearly defined, perhaps because it feels so much like "playing school." But when children are free to explore spelling as part of the context of writing, and when teachers are freed from what a nineteenth-century study called "the futility of the spelling grind" (Rice, 1897), perhaps we can all learn not only to like spelling but to recognize it as a creative linguistic and intellectual process. Ultimately spelling should feel not like playing school but like part of life.

"THEY'LL GROW INTO 'EM":
EVALUATION, SELF-EVALUATION,
AND SELF-ESTEEM IN SPECIAL
EDUCATION

Paul Crowley

It was an unusually quiet third period. John was absent, Ellen was in the library, Robert was finishing a journal entry, and Scott was reading silently. Scott looked up from his book and asked if I had seen the television show the previous night concerning dyslexia. I told him that I hadn't and asked him to tell me about it; Robert continued writing.

"It was about people who have dyslexia," Scott said. "You know, people who read things backwards. I have that." Without missing a beat Robert looked up from his paper and added, "I have that too." In mock horror I backed away and exclaimed, "I hope it isn't contagious!" Scott and Robert rolled their eyes, knowing that I wasn't going to leave this one alone. I drew *p, d, q,* and *b* on the board and asked them to tell me what the letters were. They were able to do so without hesitation. I wrote *was* and *saw* on the board and asked them if these words looked the same. They didn't. I wrote a sentence on the board and asked them to read it. They began at the left and read to the right. I asked for some evidence of the dyslexia that they "have" and how the malady manifests itself. Obviously neither was able to explain a phenomenon that they were not experiencing. Early in their lives their pediatricians had told their parents that they had dyslexia, although neither boy knew how this disease had been diagnosed.

Although they believed that they had dyslexia, Scott and Robert were actively involved in the business of reading, writing, and learning.

"Active involvement" in our classroom means that language is not treated as a skill to master in school and later apply to real-life situations. Rather, language serves as a tool for learning to meet self-directed purposes in authentic situations. Scott and Robert used language to inform, to learn, to have fun, to express opinions, to inquire, to argue

—to meet countless personal and curricular functions. They communicated with themselves and with me in their journals, responded to books in literature discussion groups, read for their own purposes during sustained silent reading time, corresponded with their elementary school learning partners and college pen pals, related what they were learning in school to the community and the world by using the newspaper, shared their stories in writing, and explored their curricula in learning logs.

Two years in a whole language classroom that encouraged risk taking and built on strengths helped them become comfortable with engagement in purposeful language use in and out of the classroom. The labels that had been expedient for other people in the past remained as extra baggage. How we look at kids influences how they see themselves. We must, therefore, help them see themselves in realistic and positive ways.

VALUING LEARNERS' ATTEMPTS

When we evaluate, we look for the best and value the attempts learners make. Evaluation, in whatever form, must communicate direction and choice. Whether a student takes the challenge today is not so much the issue but rather that the option is available, the invitation extended. Supporting learners in their attempts to move beyond the comfortable and the careful, to take risks, and to learn from mistakes promotes self-confidence and self-valuing. Choice provides learners with the options available for making meaning, and evaluation should be a natural extension of the activities.

Evaluation in our classroom takes many forms, including the following.

SELF-EVALUATION

Formal self-evaluation is used for projects that students design and carry out. They submit proposals to me for approval or feedback for revision. Included in these proposals is a plan of action (subject to change as the project progresses), a form for self-evaluation, and a form for peer and teacher evaluation. Each self-evaluation form focuses primarily on personal involvement and effort. Product quality is considered, but effort and engagement are valued above all else.

If a student brings a piece of writing and asks me what I think, I redirect the question to the student, emphasizing that the first critic is the author. By doing so, I encourage self-evaluation in informal situations. After the student comments on the piece, I ask how I can help. Rather than expecting me to praise or criticize, I want students to use me as a resource to help solve problems that they identify.

Evaluation should help learners develop realistic intrinsic self-evaluation strategies. When students are asked to carry out tasks for which they see little or no value, external rewards—points, stars, checkmarks, or letter grades—are needed. Kids are not fooled by "Good job" when it is heard repeatedly for everything from a well-formed *k* to a creative solution to a problem. Hollow praise offered in the name of "positive reinforcement" does not promote self-evaluation. When students are actively involved in planning, executing, and evaluating their own learning, they have the opportunity to become self-directed, independent learners.

PEER EVALUATION

Students know more about one another's lives than the teacher. In a supportive learning environment peers can offer valuable feedback and help set directions for further learning. Peer evaluation can be informal, such as conferring about a written piece, as well as more formal, such as making written responses to presentations. Peer evaluation must always be positive, but this doesn't mean that kids can't suggest improvements. The teacher serves as a model for peer evaluation. In this setting, students become collaborators along with the teacher.

KEEPING A TEACHING JOURNAL

When something that students say or do strikes me as clever, interesting, or puzzling, I record it in my journal. Just as I invite students to use journals to explore and reflect on ideas, my journal is a place to record and reflect on my teaching and my students' progress. Entries include interesting anecdotes about students, insights from a literature discussion, or a question I have about the motivation for a student's behavior.

Keeping a journal on student progress allows me to think through questions and to celebrate achievement. When parents are invited into the classroom, my journal is an important source of accurate information that can be easily understood. Rather than being presented with a barrage of test scores, percentile ranks, or mastered objectives, parents are given a clear picture of everyday experiences in our classroom.

The following are excerpts from my journal:

10/4   Fourth period: Matt—reading a note from one of Mary Evans's kids [first-grade pen pals]: "He spells better than I do. I had to look on his letter to see how to spell *friend.*"

10/6   Third period: Beth asked if she could have a written conversation with Lacey.

10/25   Fourth period: John wrote a letter for the whole hour after editing his piece; I did the final editing. His spelling is probably 60–70% standard.

11/1   Second period: Read from *To Kill a Mockingbird*—they loved it; they're interested in the Depression economy.

It is not always necessary to look back at the entries in my journal to learn from them; the act of writing itself invites learning and reflecting. I highlight certain entries that are particularly interesting so that I can easily find them at a later time for end-of-the-year reports and for parent conferences.

HONEST REACTIONS FROM REAL AUDIENCES

Whenever possible we share projects, written pieces, and ideas with others outside the classroom. My students work with elementary school students and often return to the classroom with language stories of their own. Toni told of the first grader who asked her what college she went to. Robin marveled that a second grader was having the same problems in math that she had. I received a call from a teacher that she was impressed with Gregg. When the second-grade boy he was writing a story with asked him how to spell a word, Gregg encouraged him to spell it as best he could and go on. Gregg told the boy that expressing his thoughts was what was important and they'd worry about spelling later if they needed to. Gregg was a reticent writer himself, often unwilling to take risks with written language. By helping another student, though, he was able to see the value in the strategies I encouraged him to use in his own writing.

Our school has an academic festival each year in which students take paper-and-pencil tests in various subjects. My students have rarely participated and never won. In place of this competition we develop projects involving writing, reading, and art and display these for the faculty. Attached to each project are comment sheets asking for feedback from the teachers. The comments are always supportive and the suggestions helpful. Students compete with themselves and receive honest responses to their efforts.

Student work is also displayed in the classroom. Written pieces are put on the bulletin board, responses to books are posted near the bookshelf, drawings find their way into any open space. These shared creations often lead to written communication between students from different periods. Alan's directions on how to repair a car that were posted on the wall were challenged by another student. I suggested he attach a note. Alan noticed the note, read it, and began responding to it the next day before the bell rang without anyone telling him it was there.

Students had the opportunity to meet their college pen pals from the methods of teaching reading class (around one hundred students) and shared their poetry, stories, and favorite authors in front of the entire group. The comments, questions, notes, delighted smiles, and thunderous applause were honest and joyful evaluation.

Real responses from real audiences are the evaluation of everyday life. Part of the performance of any task is the result: Who, besides myself, will evaluate what I do and why? In schools students should be partners in their own evaluation and should be engaged in real, purposeful situations in which they can see the value of what they do.

GRADING

Grading is a political issue, not a pedagogical one. A curriculum driven by grades must be seriously questioned, because if students are rewarded or punished by a single, reduced measure of their abilities, their energies are misdirected. Grading leads to competition and draws at-

241
*"They'll Grow into
'Em": Evaluation,
Self-Evaluation, and
Self-Esteem in
Special Education*

tention away from the real purposes of learning. No attempt to standardize grading is successful because people (teachers, students, parents) are not standardized. How can we compare a successful student who doesn't need to put much effort into a class to get an A with a student who has trouble in school and struggles each day to stay afloat?

My principal told me that I had to grade, so I asked the next logical question: How? I was told I could grade in any way that I wanted, so I told the students that they would be graded like graduate students. I grade them on their involvement as learners—that is, the effort they put forth in setting their own goals, carrying out their plans, and supporting other students in their efforts. An A is expected, because regardless of how students compare to others, they are compared only to themselves. A B means that they have not taken enough independent control of their learning, and a C means that they do very little without direction.

After the first quarter Gregg came storming into the room waving his grade card and demanded an explanation for the grade I gave him. "I gave you a B," I told him, "because you have missed too many days. Based on what you do when you are here, you deserve an A, but being a serious learner includes the responsibility of getting yourself to school." Gregg understood. "How are your other grades?" I asked. "Oh, O.K." When he showed me his grade card he had two F's, three D's and two B's (our class and gym). The only grade that he was concerned with was the one that reflected his efforts as a learner. Gregg was used to getting low grades when they reflected only test scores and points amassed in daily assignments.

UNDO THE DAMAGE

Chris. Chris reluctantly plodded through the interest inventory my students complete at the beginning of their seventh-grade year (Watson and Crowley, 1988). He slumped on the paper, put his head on the table, and took forty minutes to complete six of the twenty items. A number of times he asked how to spell certain words, and I directed his attention to the last sentence of the directions: "Don't worry about spelling." But Chris *did* worry about spelling and became frustrated when words were not spelled for him.

Chris finally turned in his paper. I had some difficulty reading one of his answers: "Jrumnchprd" (an *s* had been erased and replaced with the *c*). After looking over Chris's response for a moment, I reread the question on the inventory: "Tell me something about your pets, if you have any." I looked up at Chris and asked him to tell me about his German shepherd. We chatted a bit about his dog, and then I told him how impressed I was with his spelling. Chris gave me a puzzled look. I wrote "Jrumnchprd" on the board and explained to the class how much Chris knew about the sounds and symbols of English. I pointed out that he had erased an *s* and replaced it with a *c*, showing that he is aware that there are alternate ways of representing sounds and that he is experimenting with them.

Only by understanding how written language works could I share this information. I have read the research on spelling and have collected samples of student work in my own informal classroom research. Without an understanding of logical, developmental spelling, Chris's sophistication would have gone unnoticed, or worse, his positive efforts would have been criticized.

After offering realistic praise for what I considered a wonderful example of invented spelling, Chris responded, "Nobody's ever said anything nice about my spelling before." In his eight years in school no one had ever been positive about his spelling! It is not surprising that he is concerned with correctness and frustrated by his inability to attain it.

Chris knew that his spelling was nonstandard, but I helped him see the linguistic sophistication of his attempt and, most important, his ability to communicate meaningfully through written language. Initially Chris was not impressed by his performance on the inventory. It was typical of his previous experiences with writing: he knew he had spelled a lot of words wrong. In this instance, though, I valued his performance. Rather than evaluating Chris's writing on a standard of perfection, I evaluated it based on what we know about language growth and development.

For evaluation to be substantive and meaningful, students' efforts must be compared to what the research tells us. Too often, though, students are compared to one another or the norms of publishers and test makers. I evaluate my students based on what I know and believe about all learners—these learners in particular—and my research-based theory.

When Chris is allowed to use his background experiences and his linguistic resources, he begins to look like other learners. He has no learning disability. Chris had been evaluated on a deficit model of learning and was found to be deficient. He had become disengaged from real reading and writing and was focused on isolated bits of language; he previously had been in a program in which isolated skills were drilled until mastery had been reached before the student could proceed to the next skill. Chris had learned to devalue his abilities.

The first step in helping Chris revalue himself as a learner involved finding out what Chris knows and in what areas he is an expert. The curriculum started with these strengths. Chris read, wrote, and talked about things that he knew about and was comfortable with. He served as a consultant if dogs or dirt bikes were the topic. Chris also needed to collaborate with other students who knew more about the world of a seventh grader than I. Efforts were always respected, and honest attempts at involvement in the processes of reading, writing, and learning were valued. After being helped to revalue his efforts and abilities, Chris was back on the road to evaluating himself realistically, based on real language and learning principles that focus on growth.

When teachers begin with what kids are doing right, everyone learns. This does not mean that we hide our heads in the sand and ignore concerns or weaknesses. Rather, we see individual differences as natural and expected, and we develop and refine theories by confronting and

243
*"They'll Grow into
'Em": Evaluation,
Self-Evaluation, and
Self-Esteem in
Special Education*

analyzing anomalies based on a view of language and learning that gives credit to kids.

Tanya. Tanya had been in special classes since first grade. At one time or another, she had been given all the most popular labels, often more than one at a time. It was reported that she had no attention span and was behaviorally disordered owing to her emotional disturbance. Her I.Q. test results indicated borderline mental retardation at one time and a learning disability at another. Tanya had a hard time in school. When she was invited to join in social situations with other seventh graders, she became frustrated, which often led to tears and anger. She wanted to take the seat behind the file cabinet and do "seat work" (worksheets). My life and the lives of the other students would have been considerably more peaceful had we acquiesced. What Tanya really needed, though, was to deal with real life inside and outside the classroom.

We were clipping newspaper articles dealing with problems in the community, country, and world and were generating solutions. Tanya chose an article about a local hospital that had lost a large portion of the funding that was keeping it open. She couldn't read the article independently, so I read it to her. The solutions proposed by experts that were quoted in the article suggested alternative funding sources. After listening to me read the article, Tanya wrote that she thought they should close off part of the hospital to save on utility bills. None of us had considered this alternative (nor had any of the experts in the article), and we all agreed that Tanya's solution to the problem was very sensible.

When we use labels to categorize people, the individual is reduced to the stereotypes associated with that particular label; institutionalized name-calling does nothing but muddy our view of the real person behind the label. This applies to high-status labels (such as "gifted") as well as low-status labels (such as "mentally handicapped"). In the process of trying to live up or down to their labels, learners often lose self-confidence and self-esteem.

Individualization has always been an important characteristic of special education. Unfortunately, individualization is often interpreted as "isolation": "Get your manila folder, go to your spot, and complete your seat work."

Perhaps "personalization" better describes what goes on in the whole language classroom, where individual differences are expected and respected. We are individuals within social groups. Student involvement with others on personally valuable activities in the classroom, school, and community is essential in helping them become contributing members.

LEARNERS VALUE THEMSELVES

Evaluation is not just in the eyes of the beholder. Scott, Robert, Chris, and Tanya taught me that when we focus our magnifying glass on children and evaluate what we perceive to be going on, we are also holding up a mirror for them to view themselves. When we evaluate what learners do, we are not only assessing their abilities; we are placing a value on these abilities. Whether we place them in the fifth stanine, the eightieth percentile, the bluebird group, the gifted and talented class, or label them "learning disabled," the students have their own perceptions about what these value judgments mean, accurate or not.

Scott, Robert, and Chris had been labeled "learning disabled" for much of their school careers. Each started junior high with similar negative attitudes about his language and learning. Each, in his own way and in his own time, learned to value himself as an able learner. As a seventh grader Scott hated to write, hated to read, and hated school, and he demonstrated his feelings daily. One time Scott was challenged by another student to write a story about China. Although Scott had failed World Cultures in the first quarter, he took the challenge and wrote a four-page report on the food, housing, recreation, and history of China. He wanted to revise and edit his piece to share with his parents and his World Cultures teacher. The final product was also displayed on the wall for the remainder of the year as a celebration and as a good example of strong writing. From that day, because of the challenge of another student, Scott became involved. With some students this change is gradual and can go unnoticed, but there is no doubt that this was the *day* when Scott became a real student; that is, he saw that school was a place where he can show what he knows and a place where he can learn things that he wants to know.

Robert did not see value in the school curriculum. Although he had more school success than Scott, he did not see much purpose in reading literature and studying about paramecia. His interests centered on his job; he worked after school each day and on weekends fixing cars. The curriculum in our class started with his interests and needs. The materials I provided answered the questions Robert was asking. He filled out tax forms, read car books, and consulted the want ads. He also began to look at literature differently. He realized that he was allowed to hate certain books and choose others. He found that authors wrote books about things he was interested in. He made journal entries and wrote stories about cars. When school served his purposes and met his needs, Robert began to open up to new areas of interest.

Scott and Robert had abandoned the learned helplessness and dislike of school that are common to severely labeled students; they had learned to revalue their abilities and expand their interests. Still, the burden of the earlier remained; devaluation makes a strong impact.

Chris had received little support for his efforts, and he had learned to quit trying. Tanya was happy to be told what to do and be left alone. Students who have misguided views of language and learning and a negative view of their abilities must have the opportunity to revalue themselves through positive, successful experiences with language.

It is important to help learners understand their own learning and language so that they can develop meaningful strategies that support them in their individual endeavors. They can evaluate their own language and language learning and understand what is working for them and why. My final evaluation of the school year taps what the informants, the students, are aware of in terms of their own language and learning.

245
*"They'll Grow into
'Em": Evaluation,
Self-Evaluation, and
Self-Esteem in
Special Education*

The following questions are from the "final exam" each of my students takes at the end of the year. This kind of evaluation reflects what is valued in our classroom.

WHEN YOU'RE WRITING AND SOMEONE ASKS HOW TO SPELL A WORD, MR. CROWLEY SAYS TO SPELL IT THE BEST YOU CAN AND GO ON. WHY?

SCOTT: You need to get your thoughts down on paper first and then go over it and correct.

ROBERT: Because when people don't know how to spell the word out, that person can sound it out and spell it like it sounds.

CHRIS: Because you learn better when it is your mind thinking.

HOW CAN YOU TELL IF A PERSON IS A GOOD WRITER?

SCOTT: If there is lots of descriptive writing and they have a good plot and just can make their mind wander.

ROBERT: If you can tell what he/she is writing about and they explain themselves.

CHRIS: A person that can put their ideas on paper.

Many of my students consider standard spelling a prerequisite to writing. Frequently (and ironically), what linguists have identified as functional, logical spelling is used to distinguish students as "learning disabled." Many students enter my class in seventh grade convinced that they cannot write unless each word they are unsure of is spelled for them. Interrupting their thought processes (composing) to focus on surface features (spelling) is a backward, dysfunctional strategy that must be reversed if writing is to be clear, coherent, and interesting. By writing and reading, kids learn to spell. I always explain to new students why I tell them to spell a word as best they can and go on—so that they can get their thoughts on paper and have the opportunity to hypothesize symbol-sound relationships in the context of composing.

WHEN YOU'RE READING AND YOU COME TO SOMETHING THAT GIVES YOU TROUBLE, WHAT DO YOU DO?

SCOTT: Skip it and read on if then it doesn't make sense then try sounding it out.

ROBERT: Skip it and go on and you will figure it out later if it is a name call it something else.

CHRIS: Skip it and go on. If you skip it and go on you will know what it is talking about.

Students labeled "learning disabled" often have a misguided view of reading. Just as they often see writing as correct spelling or neat handwriting, they often see reading as an exact (miscue-free) process. This misguided notion is learned. Direct phonics teaching is the instructional method of choice in the traditional special education paradigm, and the students I see who have the most trouble with reading are those who are forever barking at print—trying, in vain, to replicate the text by focusing on symbol-sound cues to the exclusion of other cues such as meaning and grammar. They need to see reading as a process of making meaning and moving along in the text, a willingness to take linguistic risks (such as skipping unfamiliar words) and trusting writers to help them make sense by writing authentic texts.

WHY IS RISK TAKING IMPORTANT IN LEARNING?

SCOTT: You can't sit and cry over one thing. Guess and go on and learn the next.

ROBERT: Because you have to take a chance at everything you do to see if it is right or wrong.

CHRIS: Because you learn by your mistakes.

Failure inhibits performance. By seventh grade, students who are in special education have had their share of school failure in attempting to do things the other students do. It is rarely the skills of these learners that is causing the problem. Rather, it is the tasks that they are expected to complete and the penalities associated with failure. They must be allowed to fall on their faces and have it be all right. Success is possible only if the learner is allowed to try out new things and learn from mistakes. A curriculum that revolves around right and wrong answers guarantees that some students will fail. The most important thing I can teach my students is that learning involves risk taking and it's all right if things don't always turn out the way we want as long as the effort is made. If they learn this, the rest is easy.

It is clear that Scott, Robert, and Chris have developed realistic attitudes about language and language learning. They identify reading and writing strategies that keep them going in the process of making meaning by concerning themselves with meaning, not perfection. Their willingness to take risks in their learning allows them the freedom to explore, discover, and grow.

CONCLUSION

We can learn from Cassie's father in Mildred Taylor's *Roll of Thunder, Hear My Cry* (1976). After returning home with *The Count of Monte Christo, The Three Musketeers,* and *Aesop's Fables* for his young children, he recounts, "Man said to me, they right hard reading for children, but I told him he didn't know my babies. They can't read 'em now, I said, they'll grow into 'em." (p. 116). Like Cassie's father, I know my students are developing naturally with support and help from me and from other students. This supportive social learning helps move students through what Vygotsky (1978) calls the "zone of proximal development." The teacher or other students can help learners do things that they are at present unable to accomplish on their own. With this support, however, they will be more likely to carry out the task independently the next time.

If students aren't doing what we might hope or expect, we need not lower our expectations, but we need to examine our expectations. Cassie's father understood that children are not static; they will learn to do things beyond their current reach when these are valued and valuable. Kids need to know what they can do now with language and learning, and that it's O.K. to try those things that are difficult now because, with a little help, "they'll grow into 'em."

SPECIAL EDUCATION AND WHOLE LANGUAGE: FROM AN EVALUATOR'S VIEWPOINT

Phyllis Brazee / Susan W. Haynes

As often happens, fate and good fortune brought the authors together several years ago. Susan was returning to graduate school, taking courses in special education to update her 1969 master's degree and certification in that area. She was looking for a whole language reading course to support previously unvoiced beliefs about language learning. Our initial dialogue has grown into collaborative efforts to explore philosophical issues affecting the underlying framework of special education.

Having been involved in whole language instruction for many years, and having had the opportunity to work with many special educators in her graduate course in remedial reading (the only reading or language arts requirement for special educators in both states where she has taught this course), Phyllis had grown extremely uncomfortable with the evaluation, labeling, and instructional procedures recommended, or in most cases prescribed, for special educators in the areas of reading and language arts. As Susan took additional courses in special education, she came to share Phyllis's concerns.

As a group of education specialists sit around a table to share their diagnostic findings about a particular student during a special education evaluation meeting, it becomes painfully obvious that each specialist's beliefs about diagnosis, evaluation, and instruction drive the decisions that need to be made concerning which diagnostic instruments to choose, what the results mean, and which instructional suggestions will be made. At the heart of this philosophical struggle sits the student. Around the country at many special education evaluation meetings the fate of that student at school, and perhaps throughout life, rests with the ultimate compromise decision of that evaluation meeting. It is our contention that many students have been misdiagnosed, mislabeled, and given an inaccurate and often damaging instructional program because the results of that meeting rest on an invalid theory of literacy, literacy learning, and literacy evaluation.

WHOLE LANGUAGE ANALYSIS OF ONE DIAGNOSTIC TOOL OFTEN USED BY SPECIAL EDUCATORS— FROM A UNIVERSITY PROFESSOR'S VIEW (PHYLLIS)

Over ten years of working with special educators and their evaluation tools, I had come to the conclusion early on that many or most of those tools violate basic whole language principles. One such instrument is the WRAT (Wide-Range Achievement Test), which has been used for decades as a quick measure of an individual's achievement in academic skills including reading and spelling. The 1984 version states:

> Reading: recognizing and naming letters and pronouncing words out of context. Spelling: copying marks resembling letters, writing the name, and writing single words to dictation.

These descriptions of the tasks accurately reflect what students are asked to do in each subtest. They also clearly reveal the test makers' definition of reading and spelling. This definition is further amplified in the 1984 manual:

> The purpose of the *WRAT-R* is to measure the codes which are needed to learn the basic skills of reading, spelling, and arithmetic. . . . It can be a valuable tool in the determination of learning ability or learning disability. The *WRAT-R* was intentionally designed to eliminate, as totally as possible, the effects of comprehension.
>
> When dealing with the area of learning disabilities, especially in reading, it is essential to determine whether the problem is due to an inability to learn the codes which are necessary to acquire the skill or whether the problem is due to an inability to derive meaning from the codes.
>
> Since the *WRAT-R* scores are free from the contaminating effects of comprehension, it is thereby possible to compare *WRAT-R* standard scores with comprehension standard scores from other tests such as the Wechsler scales. One can then determine precisely where the individual is having difficulty and can then prescribe those remedial/educational programs which will target treatment for the specific defect. *It is a grave mistake to emphasize comprehension if the person lacks the coding skills to learn the mechanics of reading.* It is an equally grave mistake to emphasize reading mechanics with an already good reader whose problem is an inability to comprehend or get meaning. The *WRAT-R*, if properly used, will prevent teaching errors of this kind. (Italics added.)

Clearly, the WRAT-R test is firmly rooted in a skills-in-isolation construct of reading and writing. The manual emphatically states that the reading test was designed purposely to be "free from the contaminating effects of comprehension." Education specialists at pupil-evaluation meetings must understand this philosophical construct when given diagnostic findings and interpretations from the WRAT-R. If specialists hold a different construct of reading and writing processes (i.e. a view that readers and writers construct meaning from print), then they must be able to state clearly their philosophy to the users of the WRAT-R and explain why the results of the WRAT-R test will, in most cases, *conflict* with information gathered by using meaning-centered evaluation processes. If the WRAT-R has been given and is a focal point of the evaluation, then all specialists need to be able to take the quantitative data from the WRAT-R and reinterpret it from a whole language perspective.

One key defense against the Reading Subtest of the WRAT-R is Ken Goodman's study (1965), in which he examined the oral reading of first, second, and third graders as they read words in isolation in lists and those same words embedded in stories. The results indicated that children at all three grade levels read considerably more words in context than they did in isolation. His final conclusion was:

> The children in this study found it harder to recognize words than to read them in stories. Eventually I believe we must abandon our concentration on words in teaching [and testing] reading and develop a theory of reading and a methodology which puts the focus where it belongs: on language.   (p. 643)

A CASE IN POINT

Dan was brought to me at the University of Maine Reading/Writing Center by his mother after he had undergone extensive testing by a private corporation that could not adequately deduce Dan's reading and writing "problems." This testing revealed that Dan, according to the WISC, had an I.Q. of 120. As an eighth grader, though, who had been placed by teachers in the "slow" group since third grade, Dan had a self-concept as a reader and writer that was extremely low. He certainly was not functioning in school settings as a student of above-average intelligence, and his mother was extremely worried about Dan's placement in high school. In order to demonstrate my theory that the WRAT-R mislabels students in both reading and spelling, I administered the WRAT-R to Dan; his scores, according to the manual, confirmed that he was a "poor" reader and speller. His reading grade equivalent was 6E (end of sixth grade), and his spelling grade equivalent was 5B (beginning of fifth grade).

Qualitative analysis.   I carefully recorded all of Dan's errors in the reading subtest in order to examine what Dan's strategies were when he encountered a list of words in isolation. The manual just asks the examiner to indicate whether the word was correctly pronounced or not. I knew that this data would reveal important information, so I ignored these directions in the manual. The following is a list of mispronounced words with the test words underneath:

Dan:	three	through	eliminent	imagine
text:	tree	toughen	eliminate	image
Dan:	biography	uninimus	salad	mosic
text:	bibliography	unanimous	scald	mosaic
Dan:	deceive	begin	desolent	
text:	decisive	benign	desolate	

Examination of eleven "errors" indicates that, without access to syntactic and semantic cues for prediction and confirmation, Dan used a great deal of graphophonic information to pronounce the words. In seven of the eleven cases Dan substituted a real word that was graphically very similar to the test word. He is *not* a disabled reader, as the WRAT-R test evaluation indicates. Instead, he is doing the best he can given a nonmeaningful task.

When Dan was asked to read one narrative and one expository passage aloud for miscue and retelling analysis using an adapted form of the Reading Miscue Inventory (Goodman, Watson, and Burke, 1987), he showed overwhelming evidence of the ability to use all three cueing systems (graphophonic, syntactic, and semantic) efficiently and effectively. According to the Dale-Chall readability formula, the narrative passage was at the eighth-grade reading level and the expository passage was at the tenth. At an evaluation meeting, then, an education specialist using the WRAT-R and believing in its results could "confirm" that Dan was reading three years below grade level. Another education specialist, however, with an entirely different view of the reading process, using a different form of evidence, could state that Dan was highly capable of reading material at and above grade level. Who is to be believed?

Spelling analysis. At the same evaluation meeting the WRAT-R would confirm that Dan is also a poor speller, spelling three years below grade level. An examination of his actual spelling errors, however, again reveals some extremely important data:

Dan:	matrial	preasus	physican
text:	material	precious	physician
Dan:	fashin	elogical	curtius
text:	fashion	illogical	courteous
Dan:	beleave	quanity	position
text:	believe	quantity	possession
Dan:	equiptment	excutive	lucitaty
text:	equipment	executive	lucidity
Dan:	majoraty	necesity	ezadurate
text:	majority	necessity	exaggerate

Dan:	litterature	oppertunity	revrence
text:	literature	opportunity	reverence
Dan:	anzinity	measume	concance
text:	anxiety	museum	conscience

In every instance Dan's spelling is only one or a few letters away from being conventional. To use only a right-wrong paradigm for analyzing his spelling ability totally ignores Dan's knowledge of English spelling processes. Dan relies almost exclusively on his well-cemented knowledge of the set of graphophonic relationships (phonic rules) he has absorbed over the years. He spells the way he says the word: *ezadurate*. Careful analysis of each of Dan's produced words compared to the expected test word also reveals that Dan has control over initial and final units of words and has morphological knowledge, as shown by his producing such forms as -ment, -ial, -ological, -ty, -ion, -ure, -ity, -ate.

I asked Dan to write about himself for me during our diagnostic session. He produced a first-draft text forty-nine words long. Every word was spelled conventionally except for *eighth*, which he spelled "eigth." This performance raises the question in my mind that Dan, and many others like him, might be a more conventional speller in continuous text writing than in a words-in-isolation task such as that on the WRAT-R. This would relate directly to Goodman's findings in reading. All of this information *must* be shared at Dan's evaluation meeting. Education specialists who hold a whole language perspective of the reading and writing processes must be prepared to question the results of tests such as the WRAT-R and offer contradictory data gleaned from continuous text reading and writing situations.

FROM A WHOLE LANGUAGE SPECIAL EDUCATOR'S PERSPECTIVE (SUSAN)

Special education over the past twenty years has been involved with a variety of issues and has shifted focus within them. In 1969, when I received my master's degree in teaching emotionally disturbed children, training concentrated on developmental issues. Curriculum study involved adapting standard methods to meet both educational and psychological needs of the disturbed child. The main issue of the day seemed to be how one interpreted the teacher-therapist model. My first three years as a professional focused on a therapeutic-developmental approach, first as a nursery school teacher, then as a play therapist in a children's hospital.

I reentered the field of special education more than ten years later, when my youngest son reached school age. I intended to update my qualifications in both elementary education and special education. My first awareness of the enormous changes within my former field came through a study of the special education evaluation process, an outgrowth of PL 94-142 (the federal law requiring free appropriate education for all identified handicapped children). Special education has become legitimized, organized, and concertedly accountable. While I do not deny the importance of access to education guaranteed by the accountability of the pupil-evaluation process, a major issue seemed to me to be the framework within which assessment procedures and program planning under the Individual Education Plan (IEP) were carried out. As a professional operating within a developmental, holistic philosophy of learning (increasingly supported by the whole language studies in which I was engaged), I became disturbed by what seemed to be a focus on a deficiency model in relation to original documentation of a handicap, ongoing assessments of learning difficulties, and related remediation.

I was faced with the dilemma, as well as the opportunity, of translating my orientation to teaching and learning within the pupil-evaluation process. I accepted a position in a high school special education department to teach English classes. From the beginning of the year I developed the English curriculum by planning meaningful, purposeful language arts activities geared to the perceived needs of my students. The classes were as varied as the groups in each, and activities were further varied among individuals within those groups. At all times I both invited and encouraged the students to take ownership of literacy processes, interwoven within each class's theme. My group of sophomore girls, for example, was interested in adolescent problems. One student wrote stories, songs, and poems about her own traumatic experiences. She also developed a resource file of information about drugs, alcohol, and sexual abuse. The class used her resource file as a source of information for our "Dear Sidney" newsletter, which invited the student body to write to us about their problems. The novels we read together, *Island Keeper* and *Snowbound* by Harry Mazer (1986), *A Place Called Ugly* by Avi (1981), and *Sweet Illusions* by Walter Dean Myers (1986), all dealt with personal growth through coping with adolescent problems. Some students in a number of my classes, however, were reluctant to take the ownership I encouraged. The greatest barrier for them seemed to be a fear of failure in the face of an overwhelming sense of personal inadequacy. My major goal was to develop a shared sense of trust among us as a community of learners.

Bimonthly pupil evaluation meetings required me to translate our interactions into accountable Individual Education Plans. Beginning with the learning goal of personally purposeful utilization of literacy processes, I did not find it difficult to develop a whole language Individual Education Plan.

A further challenge came when I was asked to coordinate a three-year assessment update on one of my students. This required using formal tests to assess her educational progress as well as her current learning status in relation to her identified handicap. Here is a summary of the evaluation within the perspective of a whole language orientation, as well as some background on my student.

SHARON

Sharon is a sixteen-year-old sophomore. Her documented handicapping condition is language. When she entered kindergarten at age five,

Sharon was assessed as having little receptive and no expressive language. Sharon's language handicap was perceived to be related to her illiterate, poverty-stricken home environment, in which language was poorly modeled by developmentally delayed parents and siblings. Ongoing assessments throughout elementary as well as high school showed weaknesses in verbal tasks in relation to performance, with receptive language skills at a much higher level than expressive. Sharon's discrepancies in these areas as well as her documented competencies indicated at least low-normal intelligence.

In English class at the beginning of the year Sharon rarely shared in our discussions and did not wish to read orally during shared reading. She often glowed with understanding, however, when others read, and she participated actively in a writers' workshop, creating her own stories. I evaluated her progress in both oral and written expression in consultation with Trisha Rhodes, our speech and language clinician, who was evolving toward a whole language perspective in her field. We collaborated in her three-year assessment, evaluating the results from a whole language perspective.

The following formal standardized tests were administered to Sharon:

- WISC-R (Wechsler Intelligence Scale for Children)
- Gates MacGinitie (reading)
- Key math
- Morrison-McCall (spelling)
- Clinical Evaluation of Language Function (CELF) (complete battery)
- Weis Comprehensive Articulation Test
- Test of Nonverbal Intelligence
- *Peabody Picture Vocabulary Test*—Revised

The following whole language evaluations were used:

- Adapted miscue analysis
- Developmental analysis of spelling strategies
- Analysis of Sharon's writing
- Reflections of informal observations

Language testing.   The speech and language tests and the WISC-R revealed a consistent finding—that Sharon appears to be operating in the low-average intelligence range for performance and language processing but the mentally handicapped range for verbal expression of language. Her scores point out that Sharon is far more intellectually capable than her expressive abilities would lead one to believe. Trisha noted that the tests revealed that Sharon has difficulty producing various sounds, and that she omits or distorts sounds. Her syntax shows unconventional usage of noun-verb agreement, verb tense, pronouns, articles, and negation. Trisha remarked that within her field a typical intervention in relation to these findings would involve starting with isolated drill on sounds or syntax, leading up to their use in spontaneous expression. In the past, she commented, while Sharon could replicate these skills in workbook or isolated oral exercises, she was consistently not carrying them over into her spontaneous speech.

Analysis of writing.   When Trisha and I analyzed Sharon's writing, which included two short stories, we discovered solid competencies. The syntax of her written language is far more appropriate than that of her oral language, spontaneous or tested. From an examination of both her written and oral language we realized that Sharon uses somewhat telegraphic language—that is, her language contains enough information to convey meaning but often omits articles and other function words. We both noted, however, that Sharon seems to be filling in more words in both writing and speaking all the time.

Sharon's stories, despite their incomplete sentences, contain all the elements of story grammar. For example, her first story, "Halloween" (Figure 21–1), includes the following:

- Setting: Halloween night, the woods.
- Initiating event: Wolfman chases Dawn and her brothers.
- Internal response: They wake up—it was a dream.
- Goal: To conquer their fear.
- Attempt: Dawn reassures her brothers, "Nothing out there."
- Outcome: "She loves her brothers a lot."

Figure 21–1   *Sharon's First Story*

Once upon a time this girl went out on Halloween night. Something came out of the wood This girls name is Dawn. Dawn thinks nothing is out on Halloween night. when she took out her brothers. Then something chases her and her Brother The thing chasing them is a wolfman. She and her brothers turn around. Wolfman scares them out they sleep. They thought wolfman was in the room before Halloween night. Next day is Holloween. Dawn says to her brother, "no more dream about wolfman today." Her brothers say to her, "we won't go out with you to night, because we think wolfman out there." Dawn tells her Brothers, "nothing is out there and one more thing." her brothers say, "what?" Dawn says to her Brothers, "wild animals are out there at night, not in day time." she mean it she loves her brothers a lot.

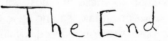

A second story by Sharon, "About Drugs," has clearer cause and effect and two subplots. Sharon's interest in writing and pride in her accomplishments seem to be powerfully motivating forces for language growth.

Analysis of reading. I assessed Sharon's reading development through the Gates MacGinitie test and an adapted miscue analysis. When she was tested by the Gates MacGinitie in September 1985, Sharon's vocabulary reflected a grade level of 3.1 while her comprehension reflected a grade level of 3.3. In December 1986, as a part of her three-year evaluation, Sharon's scores were vocabulary 3.2 and comprehension 4.3. Comprehension, according to this measurement, soared beyond isolated vocabulary ability. More important, however, her miscue analysis, a holistic and comprehensive look at reading strategies and comprehension, revealed significant abilities: an integrated use of the three cueing systems, ability to summarize the main ideas, and the ability to support summaries with details. She read to me from *Snowbound*, a book we had begun in class. Her miscues all maintained the author's meaning or were self-corrected. In general they reflected the same syntactical idiosyncrasies found in both her oral and written expression. Sharon appeared to be translating text into her own idiolect, revealing even further that she really is a reader with access to all three cueing systems. When asked what she liked about the book, she mentioned both characters because they fought like she did with her brother. Also she liked the snow, which she has always been fond of. Her responses indicate that she is actively constructing meaning upon the text through an integration of the story with her personal background. Open-ended questions that encourage this integration give information about comprehension beyond the text-bound questions of the Gates MacGinitie.

Analysis of spelling. My analysis of Sharon's spelling involved a whole language perspective imposed on the Morrison-McCall test similar to the qualitative analysis Phyllis had done of the WRAT-R. Sharon's grade equivalent for this test in September 1985 was 3.3; in December 1986, for her three-year evaluation, it was 3.4. If one looks at the following examples, however, tremendous growth in her representation of sounds can be noted:

Word	1985	1986
must	ma	mars
cast	ca	skist
able	app	aboil
dash	da	dese
stood	sa	stid
district	da	dacet
difference	s	different
assure	u	asore

In 1985 she often represented only the first part of the word ("ca" for *cast*) or one sound ("s" for *difference*) for words she did not know. In 1986 she attempted to represent the entire word using her perception of sound-letter correspondence. A whole language developmental look at her words tells us so much more than a quantitative score about her actual spelling abilities. Sharon's writing also reveals strengths in spelling. She knows the conventional spelling of many basic words (nothing, brothers, around, there, boyfriend, and money). In fact, in her stories Sharon spells most of her words conventionally.

IMPLICATIONS

Trisha and I discussed the implications of these findings in relation to planning Sharon's English and speech and language IEPs. We felt that coordination of the two programs was crucial if we were to maximize her language instruction. Our program goals began with our intention to support Sharon's meaningful utilization of all the language processes (reading, writing, listening, speaking). Our real accountability to Sharon's growth in learning lay, we felt, within this perspective. The activities we planned are meant to enhance Sharon's sense of purpose in learning. By concentrating on her diagnosed "deficiencies," we felt we would be undermining her own self-motivated, meaningful language growth. We will continue to encourage her own writing, read books with her that relate to her personal background and interests, and support her independent reading. We will also engage in informal conversations and discussions with Sharon, valuing her spontaneous expression.

Sharon, I have noticed lately, is not only responding more fully to my questions but is also initiating more conversations. As she reveals more of her ideas and feelings, she shares more of her warm and caring personality. Her risk taking is worthy of much celebration.

Many of my other students are also showing significant signs of risk taking. David, a sophomore, once told me that if I asked him to write, he would take himself to the principal's office. Recently, however, he finished his first story, entitled "That's When Super Glue Came IN." The class let him know how much we all liked it, particularly his splendid wit, which shone through. He seemed so pleased as he called out at the end of class, "See you tomorrow!" not realizing that it was Friday.

Megan, I was told at the beginning of the year, was slow and needed to be motivated. "I like reading now," she said recently. She enjoys the books we read as a class as well as the books she personally selects and shares with a peer assistant. While she often expresses her thoughts slowly, she has contributed some fine insights to our literature discussions. She seems more and more comfortable with writing these days and is very proud of her first published book of personal experiences, "Megan's Stories."

In valuing the integrity of where these students are, I hope to hold on to a perspective that transforms a potential deficiency orientation. Every interaction we have could be measured, I feel, by how it enhances or diminishes this valuing. This measurement is my ultimate accountability.

WHAT WHOLE LANGUAGE EDUCATORS CAN DO
IN PUPIL-EVALUATION MEETINGS
IN DEFENSE OF THE STUDENT

The following are some things whole language educators can do during pupil-evaluation meetings:

1. Know the diagnostic tools used by the special educator and the other district specialists inside and out. Know the exact tasks—what students are *really* expected to do despite the test task label. Know from a whole language theoretical point of view what is limiting about each test task, and be able, competently but tactfully, to point out these limitations.

2. Know how to present data, from an ongoing whole language perspective, that will most likely conflict with data gathered from traditional diagnostic tools. Often the presentation of this data will be as much an educational session for the experts around the table as it is a presentation of knowledge about the particular student. Using real-life data analyzed from a whole language perspective can be an extremely powerful tool for opening avenues of healthy educational discussion. Be prepared to follow up such a session with one or two well-chosen articles that further build your case. Perhaps follow this up with an annotated bibligraphy of references that amplify the ideas in the article.

3. Keep in close contact with parents. Many parents were taught under a skills-in-isolation basal-driven approach. They need help understanding the implications of whole language evaluation and instruction, and specifically how and why it is bound to conflict with other data. In a pupil-evaluation meeting parents are often extremely vulnerable and easily intimidated by the barrage of pronouncements by a roomful of experts. They often have no basis for understanding the reports of each expert, especially if the report focuses on deficiencies. Parents must go to such meetings armed with a clear understanding of the processes (such as reading and writing) that will be discussed.

4. Special education master's degrees often include only one course in reading and no courses in writing. Many special educators have not had the opportunity to learn about whole language philosophy and its implications for diagnosis and instruction. Many, however, are ready for such new information because what they were taught to do for literacy evaluation and instruction has not had the impact on individual students that they had hoped for. These people need immediate access to "books that can make a difference." Whole language reading specialists should write into their individual budget enough money to purchase several copies of books to lend out to special education teachers and also to parents, as well as enough

money to duplicate relevant articles throughout the year. Ideally, small groups of educators would form informal study groups to trade reactions to such books and articles. If this does not occur, however, consumers of these texts need person-to-person follow-up to have a chance to expand, rework, and question their responses to these texts.

As all educators grow in their understanding of students' language strengths, honoring and extending these abilities, they will encourage significant growth far beyond the measurements reflected in formal, standardized testing.

reflections

WHOLE LANGUAGE, WHOLE TEACHING, WHOLE BEING: THE NEED FOR REFLECTION IN THE TEACHING PROCESS

Geane R. Hanson

For me there have always been connections. Somewhere out there amid the educational theory, child development theory, and what goes on in school instruction lies a unifying element we have largely overlooked in our theory and practice. Where can we look for such an element? Perhaps it lies in that aesthetic aspect of learning we have ignored for so many years in classroom practice. Rosenblatt (1982) asks, "Is there not evidence of the importance of the affective, the imaginative, the fantasizing activities even for the development of cognitive abilities and creativity in all modes of human endeavor?" (p. 274). Perhaps, then, this unifying element lies in that basic sense of what it is to be human not only intellectually but also as sentient beings. If we have overlooked this aspect of our own nature, it follows that we have not had the vision to reflect such knowledge and awareness in our classrooms. Therefore we have forced ourselves more and more into superficial instructional programs. Too often we assess students, and are assessed as teachers, on the basis of what is apparent on the surface. Slowly we have become separated from our intuition, spontaneity, creativity—the whole experience of what it really is to be a teacher, an enabler of other learners. I am suggesting that it is this very self-awareness that ultimately underlies our ability to empower ourselves and our students.

There is no one magical answer, contrary to what many educational publishers would have us think. But there are *solutions*. These rest in looking at where we have been, what we have come to know, and where we can go by empowering ourselves and our students as able meaning makers. A growing body of research is forming to favor such awareness, expansion, and growth.

263

In the research whole language is one strong focus that empowers both teacher and student. The potential of whole language to bring this about derives from its assertion that meaning and purpose are the primary features of language. Whole language is not separate from real living language practice. Likewise, a whole language teacher does not stand apart from the beliefs or philosophical underpinnings of a successful whole language program. "Whole Language is first of all a lens for viewing, a framework that insists that beliefs shape practice" (Altwerger, Edelsky, and Flores, 1987, p. 148). It demands that teachers' beliefs and attitudes be examined as much as, if not more than, their classroom practices.

I believe that this need for evaluation and reflection on the underlying belief structures and attitudes we have about ourselves, our students, and even the world around us is what empowers teachers and students. Unfortunately, in our quest for easy answers and prefab programs we risk draining the life force at the heart of whole language, turning it into another set of "teacher-proof" materials, and allowing that Invisible Wizard from the Land of Educational Oz to prevail once again. It's time to pull back the curtain and reveal where the real power lies.

PARENTS' ROLE

From the beginning parents naturally empower their children. Bruner (1983) notes the impact of mothers on the developing communication systems of their babies. He refers to this as the Gricean cycle, in which the mother interprets her child's intentions and fulfills both sides of the communication. Parents' attitudes play an enormous role in children's development. As Harkness sees it:

> The patterns of mothers' speech to their children may be partly determined by their attitude about how children develop and the extent of their own role in this development. (1976, p. 110)

These attitudes and the power with which they interact with an infant's language development can be seen also in Shirley Brice Heath's study (1983) of Tracton and Roadville and the difference between these communities' views of infants. Attitudes are a powerful determinant of what we see and come to know in development. In the truest sense of reality, then, we do see what we know and not know what we see, as Piaget indicated (Goodman, 1987, p. 100).

As Wells (1986) has noted, children are meaning makers and naturally come to know appropriate communication with all the nuances of their culture through their experience in communicating. A child's brain is aware and constantly learning, we are reminded by Frank Smith (1981). Child learning is pervasive; just as they may learn they can't, so they may learn they can (Goodman, 1982).

Parents powerfully enable their children by naturally responding to them, given their own beliefs and attitudes about what they can do. By school age, children have emerged from their own unique cultural her-

265

*Whole Language,
Whole Teaching,
Whole Being: The
Need for Reflection in
the Teaching Process*

itage as capable learners able to participate in their continuing growth. Awareness of this process will make parents and teachers better enablers of children.

TEACHERS' ROLE

As a child enters school, teachers' attitudes and beliefs play a central role in the child's developing life as well. Rosenthal and Jacobson (1968) began the research in the area of teachers' attitudes and how they affect student performance (Rosenthal, 1973). They found reason to believe that what teachers think about a child's capabilities affects what that child comes to achieve.

The attitudes teachers have about their own experience are also important. A teacher who loves books will see that children have experience with books, if only by scheduling more frequent trips to the school library (Rye, 1983). And teachers who love books will see that a school provides rich, meaningful books, and that children's time with books is respected. Teachers, then, can gain great insight into why they do what they do by reflecting on their own attitudes toward teaching and learning.

WHOLE TEACHERS

The appropriate focus may be to look at what we can observe, given the natural context of the classroom. When we look at teachers who enable children to learn and discover themselves, some interesting ideas emerge. A study by Okech (1987) indicates that successful teaching is related to teachers' attitudes about themselves. Okech found a positive correlation between self-concept and effective teaching. The types of people teachers are and the way they feel about themselves are in direct correlation with the effectiveness of their teaching and the students' openness and ability to learn.

Manning and Payne also found that the teachers who exhibited a positive self-perception elicited positive classroom interactions, such as "accepting feelings and ideas, praise, and total student talk" (1987, p. 146). The centrality of these interactions in a whole language classroom cannot be underestimated. And Manning and Payne's work indicates that these are the result of how teachers perceive themselves. Students with low self-esteem tend to have higher anxiety (e.g. math; Powers, Douglas, Choroszy, and Cool, 1986). Therefore, the way both teachers and students perceive themselves is of utmost significance to effectiveness in the classroom environment. Teachers who cannot enable themselves will not be effective at enabling students. Similarly, students who cannot enable themselves through a positive self-perception will not be effective in their ability to learn and communicate what they have learned.

Teachers who examine their attitudes can develop more appropriate attitudes enabling themselves and becoming better enablers of students. The role of teacher becomes infinitely more dynamic, and the teacher can be viewed as a learner as well.

STUDENTS' ROLE

It is difficult, if not nearly impossible, to find stimulation and meaning in the context of the classroom if students do not have a sense of personal power and confidence to reach beyond themselves. The stimulation to learn may present itself outside the learners, but the motivation toward productive expansion of their schemas, or mental structures of the world, comes from inside.

> Originality means personal interest in the question, personal initiative in turning over the suggestions furnished by others and sincerity in following them out to a tested conclusion. (Dewey, 1978, p. 336).

Ultimately it is the child's choice (Rye, 1983). This kind of learning is just not able to go full circle when basic issues of self-worth are left unresolved.

In *Reading, Writing, and Rage* Underleider talks about Tony, who was labeled dyslexic. When Tony was empowered through partnership in his own learning, he

> responded to methods that gave him success and he used the confidence he gained to dare to learn things formerly associated with failure. Most important, he began to feel that he could learn and developed the motivation to try. (1985, p. xvii)

Once Tony believed he could be successful and experienced himself as successful, his self-concept as a learner changed. As noted by Combs, this issue of self-concept in the learning process cannot be underestimated:

> People behave in terms of their self-concept. What a person believes about himself affects everything he does, even what he sees and hears—and hence, is of tremendous significance in determining how effectively he will be able to deal with the world in which he lives. (1971, p. 353)

When I walked into a classroom and asked first graders about reading, their responses were most revealing. Many of them had negative attitudes about reading because they didn't think they could read and believed that reading is hard. Their attitude toward the whole idea of reading was one of defeat. The classroom I am referring to was a remedial first-grade class, which made me wonder how many children were there simply because they had been alienated in their first formal experience of reading and decided that they couldn't do it. How many students are labeled learning disordered in elementary school because their first experiences with learning gave them a negative attitude toward themselves as learners? How many learned that they couldn't read before they were given the opportunity to discover they could? When we empower teachers, the likelihood of this experience for children declines. It is when we empower programs and materials, things that

267
Whole Language,
Whole Teaching,
Whole Being: The
Need for Reflection in
the Teaching Process

are neither whole nor integrated, that this kind of miscarriage occurs in child learning. Only empowered teachers make for empowered learners.

Just as "reading is a personal act" (Altwerger, Edelsky, Flores 1987, p. 150), teaching can also be seen as a personal act. When viewed in a perspective like that from which we perceive language in the whole language philosophy, much of what makes a good teacher effective is seen to center on an indivisible whole comprising our notions of being, thinking, and perceiving. Teachers, then, are learners too. Our brains are actively engaging the reality in which we live. By placing ourselves in bondage to "teacher-proof" materials and fragmented bits of information in basal-reader manuals, we put in disarray the natural and basic sense of wholeness that we experience in our reality. We must not, then, focus on the surface at the expense of the underlying meanings.

When we look at what we have been doing in the classroom versus what the research about language and language learning is telling us about child development, it is no great surprise that our view of teachers reflects the same narrowness as our view of children. Just as we have not empowered children, so we have not empowered ourselves as teachers. Instead we have empowered the programs, curriculum guides, and teachers' manuals common to many classrooms today. Yet, as Frank Smith notes, "There is no evidence that any child ever learned to read because of a program" or that any teacher ever learned to teach by following a program (1981, p. 639).

"Our educational system may be effective in teaching us answers" (Lester and Onore, 1986, p. 699), but it doesn't give us meaning. In many classrooms today "answers" are the main focus. Teachers are most often expected to teach according to a program and then evaluate according to the students' success in relation to it. Therefore, for teachers to be evaluated as successful with these programs, they must ignore what they know about kids and how they learn, which produces neither empowerment nor a strong professional or personal self-confidence. At the root of this practice is the belief that teachers don't know what they are doing and that teaching should be left in the hands of the Invisible Wizard.

Smith sees programs as making teachers look "ineffectual" and teachers making programs "look good." As he reveals,

> The assumption [is] that the program will be more sensitive and intelligent than the teacher, that instructional decisions will be better made in advance by individuals who do not know and cannot see the child who is supposed to be learning from the program.   (1981, pp. 641, 636)

Wells also rejects the notion of "experts" who don't know the classroom, and their "bypassing" teachers with their "teacher-proof" materials:

> Teaching can no longer be seen as the imparting of information to relatively passive recipients and then checking to see that they can correctly reproduce it.   (1986, pp. 220, 221)

To extend this idea, neither can we view teachers as passive translators of information from invisible experts, who must be monitored by administrators.

So how can we prevent teachers from becoming an endangered species in an age of diminished freedom to teach and increased accountability? (Smith, 1981, p. 640).

ADMINISTRATORS' ROLE

We need to go farther up the ladder and look at administrators and their part in this process. John Goodlad found that

> rising feelings of potency in teachers clearly were threatening to principals' feelings of self-worth. They needed their peer principals badly; their meetings took on added importance. Those inadequate teachers now are becoming too adequate. (1977, p. 102)

Has our program-oriented heritage given both principals and teachers such a need for stratification that there is a threat in the inadequate becoming adequate and the slow becoming efficient? Will our effectiveness be questioned if we don't meet our quota of failures? Has our "teacher-proofing" taken us so far out of the human realm that we function more in the interest of calculated failure than growth and empowerment? In reference to New Zealand schools and their openness to whole language ideas, Goodman writes, "Their administrators have faith in kids as learners" (1987, p. 11).

We need that spirit of cooperation in American schools. In their study on organizing teachers and administrators into collegial support groups, Johnson and Johnson found many factors that resulted from a cooperative structure. There were gains in "achievement, positive interpersonal relationships, social support, and self-esteem" (1987, p. 30). They also noted that cooperation tended to promote less competition. It is obvious that these findings indicate a new approach that needs to be taken in the educational framework to maximize our potential as teachers and administrators. Many whole language teachers are finding support groups beneficial, and groups such as TAWL (Teachers Applying Whole Language) in Tucson, Arizona, have been growing in numbers. Schools would do well to incorporate this kind of collaborative structure into the educational system at large, for it provides teachers with a means of constantly self-reflecting and growing through interaction with peers.

TEACHER TRAINING

In transferring the responsibility of teaching back to its rightful inheritors, universities must also reevaluate their teacher-training programs. "The way most teachers are trained . . . leads them to be dependent upon

269
*Whole Language,
Whole Teaching,
Whole Being: The
Need for Reflection in
the Teaching Process*

programs" (Smith, 1981, p. 641). They are led to make assumptions regarding themselves and their students based on program guidelines. Okech (1987) noted in his study of teacher attitudes that often feelings of competence in teaching subject matter relates to teacher success. Unfortunately, in the classroom we put competency assessments into "teacher-proof" packages, placing them outside the realm of the teacher's control. How, then, can teachers experience feelings of control and competence? Since it is teachers who teach and not programs, we must reevaluate where we are telling beginning teachers to look for answers and become sensitive to their individual development in the context of their own learning, just as they will be expected to be sensitive in the context of their classrooms.

Although subject-area training is important, it is not the successful determinant, according to Okech. Teachers' self-perceptions and attitudes about themselves are also significant in determining classroom effectiveness.

> The type of person the teacher is and teacher's effectiveness in dealing with children on a personal and group basis are generally, at least in practice, more basic determinants of teacher success than is knowledge of the course or ability to follow a lesson plan. (1987, p. 33)

Kids respond most effectively to what is real and whole in their world, in keeping with our knowledge of child development, and not with what is supposedly significant according to course outlines. They don't separate who the teacher is from what the teacher knows. Okech's research seems to indicate that who the teacher is may, in significant ways, determine a child's potential to know. As John Dewey has written:

> With the young, the influence of the teachers' personality is intimately fused with that of the subject; the child does not separate nor even distinguish the two. (1978, pp. 218, 219)

Therefore, in organizing teacher-training programs we must take seriously the importance of this personal awareness and reflection to the process of becoming a sound teacher. Okech notes:

> Such findings may suggest that attention be given to the personality adjustment in the training of teachers. This implication is pointed out because, typically, teacher training institutions heavily assess the quality of their teachers based on the mastery of subject matter. Little stress is given to the training of teachers in relation to such factors as responsiveness to student interests and motivation in order to convey the content to students. If individuals are to be successful teachers, they must be concerned with their feelings and attitudes of self which influence effective teaching. (1987, p. 33)

The teacher and the teacher's self-concept have too often been "neglected" (Newman and Abrahamson, 1981, p. 58).

The research presented here supports the idea that "positive strong personal dimensions of teachers beget positive classroom results" (Manning and Payne, 1987, p. 146). Yet it is difficult to shed light on what these personality characteristics are exactly in teachers and how they can be fostered. Dewey cautioned us over seventy years ago that

> teachers—and this holds especially of the stronger and better teachers—tend to rely upon their personal strong points to hold a child to his work, and thereby to substitute their personal influence for that of subject matter as a motive to study.   (1978, p. 219)

With the current research that informs whole language we can now focus on both the personal qualities of the teacher and the curriculum, helping pre-service teachers to see the importance of self-reflection. One enables the other. Perhaps we are now ready to go back in time and bring Dewey's progressive education forward as it becomes more relevant and possible in light of whole language.

WHOLENESS

"Whole Language teachers accept responsibility but with it they expect power—authority to be the key decision maker in their classrooms" (Goodman, 1987, p. 11). As Goodman notes, many teachers who are "fed up with being told what to do" are motivated toward whole language (p. 11). These are teachers who want to empower kids and know that they must empower themselves as well, a process facilitated by the idea of "teacher as learner." Lester and Onore (1986) suggest that teachers are engaging in learning when they examine their beliefs and question their assumptions. This act of reflection is central to revealing a sense of power as learners to both teachers and students alike: "We can't change what we are unaware even exists" (p. 699). Searching inevitably sets us free, for we can no longer be victims of unexamined beliefs and assumptions.

As active participants in the learning process we come to realize that learning does not follow a step-by-step, bottom-up pattern, and that our partnership in learning with our students is the key to growth and reflection that motivates the process (Lester and Onore, 1986). As Lester and Onore further note, teachers who look for answers also find more questions, and thus the cycle is virtually endless, a living demonstration of the true educational process.

As observant and reflective teachers learn alongside their students, what better place to facilitate their own research than the context of their own classrooms? Ultimately this is where the heart of all accountability lies. As we provide opportunities for kids to learn in a holistic manner, we must see our opportunities to learn in a similar fashion and demystify the idea that only research in the laboratory, an unreal setting, is valid justification for what we think and practice as teachers. The idea

271
*Whole Language,
Whole Teaching,
Whole Being: The
Need for Reflection in
the Teaching Process*

of teachers as researchers is a powerful one; as Rich quotes one teacher-researcher, "I am grasping a giant window ledge and peeking over the gigantic window sill." I agree with this teacher and with Rich that "the view is a promising one for both teacher education and educational research" (1983, p. 894).

Through looking at ourselves as teacher-researchers we allow ourselves to look at our own construction of knowledge and build on our understanding of what we do in our classrooms. We become empowered. We focus on the aspects of what we are doing that are most important to us, get to know our children well, and learn along with them. In this sense we gain a "tremendous sense of discovery" (McConaghy, 1986, p. 727).

Empowerment gives us the perspective to be continually aware of the whole of what we are viewing in the midst of the parts. Our experience is not fragmented into bits and pieces of abstract information from a teacher's manual. We are able to approach what we do with the same integration and awareness of the whole meaningful context of our lives and consequently provide this for our children.

Many years ago John Dewey said we "learn by doing." Today McConaghy discovers Dewey's concept for herself:

> I was now beginning to see the difference between knowledge
> acquired from other people's experience and knowledge that I
> had gained in a very personal and intimate way—knowledge that
> I now felt I owned. I was also learning that the roots of personal
> knowledge lie in doing.   (1986, p. 728)

It is important here to recognize that many teachers, without formally referring to themselves as teacher-researchers, are involved in similar activities every day. Like McConaghy, they plan their lessons in ways that allow them to learn about their students and themselves. They rely on their intuitive sense of what they know as teachers to guide them. As Newman states, "Our beliefs about learning and teaching are largely tacit. We operate a good deal of the time from an intuitive sense of what is going on" (1987, p. 727). These teachers rely on their sense of wholeness.

What the idea of teacher-researcher allows us to do is to empower our "intuitive sense," which we have been utilizing with reflection and awareness. This gives us tangible reasons to support why we do what we do. This knowledge and insight can, in turn, be shared with other teachers, administrators, parents, and students, allowing us to "make public our professional beliefs, goals, and hopes" and give our profession new roots (Newman and Abrahamson, 1981, p. 58).

You might say, "This is all well and good but a bit idealistic. There are limits to what people know and what they are capable of learning. You make it sound like anybody can do anything!" Voilà! I am proposing we start by assuming that, yes, by and large we can do anything we believe we can do. There is no point in creating imaginary obstacles for ourselves when we're dealing with real-life problems. What we believe about ourselves, the children we teach, and the teachers we administer has a powerful effect on what we see and what comes to be. Rather than see reality and children's intelligence as fixed, we must come to believe that "you and I are not the victims of child intelligence; we are in the business of creating it" (Combs, 1971, p. 350). Limits do exist, but let them show themselves in the natural course of events rather than trying to find and impose them ahead of time. Empowering teachers and kids enables them to feel good about themselves and what they are doing as multifaceted human beings and learners. A responsibility to the future awaits, and whole language gives us the elements with which to form a new understanding that is whole, real, and relevant.

In my opinion whole language teachers truly look into their beliefs surrounding children and learning and are masters at empowering students with a strong sense of self-worth early in their experience with school. They assume that the children are capable of communicating orally within the social context and come to school with a wealth of knowledge and experience.

Kids are not in school to orbit around what the school thinks; rather, school is there to be sensitive to and ultimately orbit around what children know and are capable of continuing to know. It is our responsibility to construct a receptive environment based on what we know as teacher-researchers and to track behind our students, interpreting and expanding as the learning evolves. In a speech before the Tucson TAWL in 1987, Mary Ellen Giacobbe said:

> We have two obligations as teachers: to like what we do and to know what we are doing. One feeds the other. As we like what we do, we learn more about it and come to like it more. The more we like it, the more we learn; the more we learn, the more we know what we are doing; [and] the more we like it.

BEING AS IT IS

Educational practice has at times reflected society's insensitivity to human nature. New light dawns on the horizon. The initial source of this light is developing a positive and purposeful sensitivity to ourselves and what we do—not only for our students' learning but for the ways in which this touches our families, our communities, and, most important, our sense of what it is to be alive, unique, and human.

AFTERWORD:
LAURA'S LEGACY

Carol Avery

May 8, 1987

We celebrate Mother's Day in our first-grade classroom this Friday afternoon. The children perform a play for their mothers entitled "The Big Race," the story of the tortoise and the hare. Laura is the "turtle" who wins the race.

A few minutes later Laura reads aloud the book she has authored about her mother. The group laughs as she reads about learning to count with her cousins when she was three years old. Laura writes: "I was learning six. Then my Mom came in and asked what we were doing. I said, 'I'm learning sex!' " Laura's mother was delighted. The reading continues with a hilarious account of a family squabble between Mom and Dad over a broken plate. Laura concludes the anecdote, "So then I just went in and watched TV." Laura looks at me and smiles as she pauses, waiting for her audience to quiet before she goes on. I wink at her; I know she is thinking, "Wait till they hear the next part. It's the funniest of all." She reads about a llama spitting in Mom's eye on a visit to the zoo. Laura's way with words has brought delight to everyone. I remember a week earlier when Laura and I sat to type her draft and she said, "This is the best part. I put it last so that everyone will feel happy at the end."

May 9, 1987

Saturday night, around 11:45 P.M., a light bulb ignites fabric in a closet outside Laura's bedroom. Laura wakes. She cannot get through the flames, and by the time firefighters reach her it is too late. Laura dies. No one else is injured.

May 11, 1987

The children and I gather on our Sharing Rug in the classroom on Monday morning. I have no plans. We start to talk. There are endless interruptions until Michael says, "Mrs. Avery, can we shut the door so people stop bothering us?" So Michael shuts the door. "Are you going to read us the newspapers?" they ask. "Is that what you'd like?" "Yes," comes the unanimous response. The children huddle close; a dozen knees nuzzle against me. I read aloud the four-paragraph story on the front page of the *Sunday News* that accompanies a picture of our Laura sprawled on the lawn of her home with firefighters working over her. I read the longer story in Monday morning's paper that carries Laura's school picture. We cry. We talk and cry some more. And then we read

273

Laura's books—writings which Laura determined were her best throughout the year and which were "published" to become part of our classroom library. These books are stories of Laura and her family, stories with titles such as "My Dad Had a Birthday" and "When My Grandmother Came to My House." Laura's voice comes through loud and clear with its sense of humor and enthusiasm. We laugh and enjoy her words. "Laura was a good writer," they say. "She always makes us laugh when we read her stories." Then Dustin says, "You know, it feels like Laura is right here with us, right now. We just can't see her."

A short time later we begin our writing workshop. Every child chooses to write about Laura this day. Some write about the fire, some write memories of Laura as a friend. I write with them. After forty-five minutes it is time to go to art, and there are cries of disappointment at having to stop. We will come back to the writing. There will be plenty of time. The last five weeks of school will be filled with memories of Laura as we work through our loss together. The children will decide to leave her desk in its place in the room because "it's not in our way, and anyway, this is still Laura's room even if she's not really here anymore." Laura's mother and little brother will come in to see us. On the last day they will bring us garden roses that Laura would have brought. Laura will always be a part of us, and none of us will ever be the same.

In the days immediately following Laura's death and in the weeks since then certain thoughts have been rattling around in my head: I'm so glad that I teach the way I do. I'm so glad I really knew Laura. I know that I can never again teach in a way that is not focused on children. I can never again put a textbook or a "program" between me and the children. I'm glad I knew Laura so well. I'm glad all of us knew her so well. I'm glad the classroom context allowed her to read real books, to write about real events and experiences in her life, to share herself with us and to become part of us and we of her. I'm grateful for a classroom community that nurtured us all throughout the year and especially when Laura was gone. Laura left a legacy. Part of that legacy is the six little published books and the five-inch-thick stack of paper that is her writing from our daily writing workshops. When we read her words, we hear again her voice and her laughter.

REFERENCES

TEACHER RESOURCES

Altwerger, B.; C. Edelsky; and B. Flores. "Whole Language: What's New?" *The Reading Teacher* 41 (1987): 144–54.

Archambault, R. D., ed. *John Dewey on Education*. Chicago: University of Chicago Press, 1964.

Atwell, N. *In the Middle: Writing, Reading, and Learning with Adolescents*. Portsmouth, NH: Boynton/Cook, 1987.

———. "Writing and Reading from the Inside Out." In *Breaking Ground: Teachers Relate Reading and Writing in the Elementary School*. Ed. by J. Hansen, T. Newkirk, and D. Graves. Portsmouth, NH: Heinemann, 1985.

Baratta-Lorton, M. *Mathematics Their Way*. Menlo Park, CA: Addison-Wesley, 1976.

Berthoff, A. E. *The Making of Meaning: Metaphors, Models, and Maxims for Writing Teachers*. Portsmouth, NH: Boynton/Cook, 1981.

Britton, J. "Language and the Nature of Learning: An Individual Perspective." In *The Seventy-Sixth Yearbook of the National Society for the Study of Education*. Chicago: University of Chicago Press, 1977.

Brophy, J. E. "Research on the Self-Fulfilling Prophecy and Teacher Expectations." *Journal of Educational Psychology* 75 (1983): 631–61.

Brown, R. "Evaluation and Learning." In *The Teaching of Writing: Eighty-Fifth Yearbook of the National Society for the Study of Education, Part II*. Ed. by R. Petrosky & D. Bartholomae. Chicago: University of Chicago Press, 1986.

Bruner, J. S. "The Role of Dialogue in Language Learning." In *The Child's Conception of Language*. Ed. by R. Jarvella and W. Levelt. Berlin: Springer-Verlag, 1978.

———. *Child's Talk: Learning to Use Language*. New York: W. W. Norton, 1983.

Calkins, L. M. *The Art of Teaching Writing*. Portsmouth, NH: Heinemann, 1986.

Clay, M. "The Reading Behavior of Five-Year Old Children." *New Zealand Journal of Educational Studies* 2 (1966): 11–31.

———. *What Did I Write?* Auckland: Heinemann, 1975.

Coles, R. E. "Personalized Reading Programs." In *English Teachers at Work: Ideas and Strategies from Five Countries*. Ed. by S. N. Tchudi. Portsmouth, NH: Boynton/Cook, 1986.

Combs, A. W. "New Concepts of Human Potentials: New Challenge for Teachers." *Childhood Education* 47 (1971): 349–55.

Dewey, J. "How We Think." In *John Dewey: The Middle Works, 1899–1924*. Ed. by J. A. Boydstom. Vol. 6, 1910–1911. Carbondale: Southern Illinois University Press, 1978.

Donaldson, M. *Children's Minds*. New York: W. W. Norton, 1978.

Dreikers, R., and V. Soltz. *Children, the Challenge*. New York: Hawthorne Books, 1964.

Duran, R. *Latino Language and Communicative Behavior*. Norwood, NJ: Ablex, 1981.

Edelsky, C. "Living in the Author's World: Analyzing the Author's Craft." *The California Reader* 21:3 (1988).

———. *Writing in a Bilingual Program: Habia Una Vez*. Norwood, NJ: Ablex, 1986.

Edelsky, C., and K. Smith. "Is That Writing—Or Are Those Marks Just a Figment of Your Curriculum?" *Language Arts* 58:3 (1984): 55–59.

Eisner, E. W. "Educational Connoisseurship and Criticism: Their Form and Functions in Educational Evaluation." *Journal of Aesthetic Education* 10 (1976): 135–50.

Ferreiro, E., and A. Teberosky. *Literacy before Schooling*. Portsmouth, NH: Heinemann, 1982.

Freeman, D.; Y. Freeman; and R. D. Gonzalez. "Success for LEP Students." *TESOL Quarterly* 21 (1987): 361–72.

Giacobbe, M. E. "Helping Children Become More Responsible for Their Writing." *Live Wire* (1984): 7–9.

Goodlad, J. "An Ecological Approach to Change in Elementary-School Settings." *Elementary School Journal* 78 (1977): 95–105.

Goodman, K. "A Linguistic Study of Cues and Miscues in Reading," *Elementary English* 42:6 (October 1965): 639–43.

———. "Revaluing Readers and Reading." *Topics in Learning and Learning Disabilities* 1 (1982): 87–93.

———. *What's Whole in Whole Language?* Richmond Hill, Ontario: Scholastic TAB, 1986. (Distributed in the U.S. by Heinemann.)

———. "Who Can Be a Whole Language Teacher?" *Teachers Networking* 1 (1987): 10–11.

Goodman, K.; E. B. Smith; R. Meredith; and Y. Goodman. *Language and Thinking in School: A Whole Language Curriculum*. New York: Richard C. Owen, 1987.

Goodman, Y., and B. Altwerger. "Print Awareness in Preschool Children: A Study of the Development of Literacy in Preschool Children." Occasional Paper no. 4. Tucson: Program in Language and Literacy, University of Arizona, 1981.

Goodman, Y., and C. Burke. *Reading Strategies: Focus on Comprehension*. New York: Richard C. Owen, 1980.

Goodman, Y.; D. Watson; and C. Burke. *Reading Miscue Inventory: Alternative Procedures*. New York: Richard C. Owen, 1987.

Graves, D. H. *Writing: Teachers and Children at Work*. Portsmouth, NH: Heinemann, 1983.

Halliday, M. A. K. "Three Aspects of Children's Language Development: Learning Language, Learning Through Language, and Learning about Language." In *Impact of Language Research on Curriculum.* Ed. by G. Pinnell and M. M. Haussler. Newark, DE: International Reading Association, 1988.

Hanna, P. R.; J. S. Hanna; R. E. Hodges; and E. H. Rudorf, Jr. "Phoneme-Grapheme Correspondenses as Cues to Spelling Improvement." *ERIC Document Reproduction Service No. ED 128 835.* Washington, DC: US Office of Education, 1966.

Harkness, S. "Mother's Language." In *Baby Talk and Infant Speech.* Ed. by W. Raffler-Engel and Y. Lebrun. Amsterdam: Swets and Zeitlinger, 1976.

Harste, J.; V. A. Woodward; and C. Burke. *Language Stories and Literacy Lessons.* Portsmouth, NH: Heinemann, 1984.

Heath, S. B. *Ways with Words: Language, Life, and Work in Communities and Classrooms.* New York: Cambridge University Press, 1983.

Jaggar, A. "On Observing the Language Learner: Introduction and Overview." In *Observing the Language Learner.* Ed. by A. Jaggar and M. T. Smith-Burke. Newark, DE, and Urbana, IL: International Reading Association and National Council of Teachers of English, 1985.

Johnson, D. W., and R. T. Johnson. "Research Shows the Benefits of Adult Cooperation." *Educational Leadership* 45 (1987): 27–30.

Kagan, S. "Cooperative Learning and Sociocultural Factors in Schooling." In *Beyond Language: Social and Cultural Factors in Schooling Language Minority Students.* Los Angeles: Evaluation, Dissemination, and Assessment Center, 1986.

Kasten, W. "The Behaviors Accompanying the Writing Process in Selected Third and Fourth Grade Native American Children." PhD. diss., University of Arizona, 1984.

Kitagawa, M. M., and C. Kitagawa. *Making Connections with Writing: An Expressive Writing Model in Japanese Schools.* Portsmouth, NH: Heinemann, 1987.

Lester, N. B., and C. S. Onore. "From Teacher-Teacher to Teacher-Learner: Making the Grade." *Language Arts* 63 (1986): 724–28.

Lindberg, M. "A Descriptive Analysis of the Relationship Between Selected 'Pre-linguistic,' Linguistic, and Psycholinguistic Measures of Readability." PhD diss., Wayne State University, 1977.

McConaghy, J. "On Becoming Teacher Experts: Research as a Way of Knowing." *Language Arts* 63 (1986): 724–28.

Macdonald, J. B. "An Evaluation of Evaluation." *The Urban Review* 7 (1974): 3–14.

Macrorie, K. *Twenty Teachers.* New York: Oxford University Press, 1984.

Manning, B. H., and B. D. Payne. "Student Teacher Classroom Interactions and Self-Perception of Personality." *Journal of Instructional Psychology* 14 (1987): 140–47.

Marek, A.; D. Howard; et al. "The Kidwatcher's Guide: A Whole Language Guide to Evaluation." Occasional Paper no. 9: Tucson Program in Language and Literacy. Tucson: University of Arizona, 1984.

Marek, A. T. "Retrospective Miscue Analysis as an Instructional Strategy with Adult Readers." Ph.D. diss., University of Arizona, 1987.

Murray, D. *A Writer Teaches Writing.* 2d ed. Boston: Houghton Mifflin, 1984.

Newman, J. M. "Learning to Teach by Uncovering Our Assumptions." *Language Arts* 64 (1987): 727–37.

Newman, K. K., and R. F. Abrahamson. "The Classroom and the Writing Desk: Countering the Negative Teacher Image." *Language Arts* 58 (1981): 58–62.

O'Donnell, R.; W. Griffin; and R. Norris. "Syntax of Kindergarten and Elementary School Children: A Transformational Analysis." *NCTE Research Report no. 8.* Urbana, IL: National Council of Teachers of English, 1967.

Okech, J. G. "Self-Concepts and Attitudes towards Teaching as Predictors of Effective Teaching." *Journal of Instructional Psychology* 14 (1987): 27–35.

Postman, N., and C. Weingartner. *How to Recognize a Good School.* Bloomington, IN: Phi Delta Kappan Educational Foundation, 1973.

Powers, S.; P. Douglas; M. Choroszy; and B. A. Cool. "Attributions for Success and Failure in Algebra of Samoan Community College Students: A Profile Analysis." *Journal of Instructional Psychology* 13 (1986): 3–9.

Read, C. "Pre-School Children's Knowledge of English Phonology." *Harvard Educational Review* 41 (1971): 1–34.

———. *Children's Categorizations of Speech Sounds in English.* Urbana, IL: National Council of Teachers of English, 1975.

Rice, J. M. "The Futility of the Spelling Grind." *The Forum* (1897): 409–19.

Rich, S. "On Becoming Teacher Experts: Teacher Researchers." *Language Arts* 60 (1983): 892–94.

Rosenblatt, L. M. "The Literacy Transaction: Evocation and Response." *Theory into Practice* 21 (1982): 268–77.

Rosenthal, R. "The Pygmalion Effect Lives." *Psychology Today* 7 (1973): 56–63.

Rosenthal, R., and L. Jacobson. *Pygmalion in the Classroom.* New York: Holt, Rinehart, and Winston, 1968.

Rye, J. "The Importance of Attitude: Some Implications." *Reading* 17 (1983): 13–22.

Smith, F. "Demonstrations, Engagement, and Sensitivity: The Choice Between People and Programs." *Language Arts* 58 (1981): 634–42.

———. "Twelve Easy Ways to Make Learning to Read Difficult." In *Essays into Literacy.* Portsmouth, NH: Heinemann, 1983.

———. *Insult to Intelligence.* New York: Arbor House, 1986.

Smith, P. T. "Linguistic Information in Spelling." In *Cognitive Processes in Spelling.* Ed. by U. Frith. London: Academic Press, 1980.

Spradley, J. *Participant Observation.* New York: Holt, Rinehart, and Winston, 1980.

Stephenson, M. "Using Principles of Miscue Analysis as Remediation for High School Students." Unpublished manuscript. Tucson: University of Arizona, 1980.

Teberosky, A. "Construccion de Esctitura Atraves de la Interaccion Grupal." In *Nuevas Perspectivas sobre los Procesos de Lectura y Escritura.* Ed. by E. Ferreiro and M. Gomez Palacio. Mexico City: Siglo Veintiuno Editores, 1982.

Tompkins, G., and D. Yaden. *Answering Students' Questions about Words.* Urbana, IL: National Council of Teachers of English, 1986.

Torbe, M. "Language across the Curriculum: Policies and Practice." In *Language, the Learner, and the School.* Ed. by D. Barnes, J. Britton, and M. Torbe. Middlesex, England: Penguin Books, 1986.

Underleider, D. F. *Reading, Writing and Rage.* Rolling Hills, CA: Jalmar Press, 1985.

Vallins, G. H. *Spelling.* Ed. by D. G. Scragg. London: Andre Deutsch, 1965.

Vygotsky, L. *Mind in Society.* Ed. by M. Cole; S. Scribner; V. J. Steiner; and E. Souberman. Cambridge, MA: Harvard University Press, 1978.
———. *Thought and Language.* Ed. by A. Kozulin. Cambridge, MA: MIT Press, 1987.

Watson, D. J., and P. Crowley. "How Can We Implement the Whole-Language Approach?" In Constance Weaver, *Reading Process and Practice: From Socio-Psycholinguistics to Whole Language.* Portsmouth, NH: Heinemann, 1988.

Webb, E. J.; D. T. Campbell; R. D. Schwartz; and L. Sechrest. *Unobtrusive Measures: Nonreactive Research in the Social Sciences.* Chicago: Rand McNally, 1986.

Wells, G. *The Meaning Makers: Children Learning Language and Using Language to Learn.* Portsmouth, NH: Heinemann, 1986.

Wilde, S. "An Analysis of the Development of Spelling and Punctuation in Selected Third and Fourth Grade Children." In *Dissertation Abstracts International* 47 (1986).

Woodley, J. W., and L. D. Miller. "Retrospective Miscue Analysis: Procedures for Research and Instruction." In *Research on Reading in Secondary Schools.* Vols. 10–11. Ed. by P. Anders. Tucson: University of Arizona, 1983.

Woods, P. *Inside Schools: Ethnography in Eductional Research.* London: Routledge and Kegan Paul, 1986.

Worsnop, C. M. *A Procedure for Remedial Reading Instruction Based on Miscue Analysis Research and Techniques.* Toronto: Canadian Education Department, n.d.

Zumwalt, K. K., ed. *Improving Teaching.* 1986. ASCD Yearbook. Alexandria, VA: Association for Supervision and Curriculum Development, 1986.

STUDENT MATERIALS

Alexander, L. *The Chronicles of Prydain.* New York: Dell, 1964.

Armstrong, W. *Sounder.* New York: Harper and Row, 1969.

Avi. *A Place Called Ugly.* New York: Pantheon, 1981.

Babbitt, N. *Tuck Everlasting.* New York: Farrar, Strauss and Giroux, 1975.

Cleary, B. *Dear Mr. Henshaw.* New York: Dell, 1983.

Cole, J. *Bonylegs.* New York: Four Winds Press, 1983.

Cowley, J. *The Biggest Cake in the World.* Wellington, NZ: Ready to Read, 1983.

———. *The Hungry Giant.* In THE STORY BOX®. Auckland: Shorthand Publications, 1986. Distributed in the U.S. by The Wright Group Publishers, San Diego, CA.

Eager, E. *Half Magic.* New York: Harcourt, Brace, and World, 1954.

Eliot, T. S. "The Love Song of J. Alfred Prufrock." In *The Wasteland and Other Poems.* New York: Harcourt, Brace and World, 1930.

The Gingerbread Man. New York: Scholastic, 1987.

Krauss, R. *Leo, the Late Bloomer.* New York: Windmill Books, 1971.

L'Engle, M. *A Wrinkle in Time.* New York: Dell, 1962.

Lee, H. *To Kill a Mockingbird.* Philadelphia: JP Lippincott, 1960.

Lewis, C. S. *The Lion, the Witch, and the Wardrobe.* New York: Macmillan, 1950.

The Lion's Tail. In Scott, Foresman Reading Unlimited. Glenview, IL: Scott, Foresman, 1971.

MacLachlan, P. *Sarah, Plain and Tall.* New York: Dell, 1986.

Mazer, H. *Island Keeper.* New York: Dell, 1986.

———. *Snowbound.* New York: Dell, 1986.

Myers, W. D. *Sweet Illusions.* New York: Teachers and Writers Collaborative, 1986.

Orwell, G. *Animal Farm.* New York: Harcourt, Brace, Jovanovich, 1946.

Park, B. *Operation: Dump the Chump.* New York: Avon, 1983.

Paterson, K. *Bridge to Terabithia.* New York: Crowell, 1977.

———. *Great Gilly Hopkins.* New York: Crowell, 1979.

Peck, R. N. *A Day No Pigs Would Die.* New York: Knopf, 1972.

Rudy's New Red Wagon. In Scott, Foresman Reading Unlimited. Glenview, IL: Scott, Foresman, 1971.

Sleator, W. *The Green Futures of Tycho.* New York: Dutton, 1981.

———. *Into the Dream.* New York: Scholastic, 1984.

Smith, R. K. *Jelly Belly.* New York: Dell/Delacorte Press, 1981.

Taylor, M. D. *Roll of Thunder, Hear My Cry.* New York: Bantam, 1976.

The Three Billy Goats Gruff. New York: Scholastic, 1987.